POLICE and POLICING
Contemporary Issues

Edited by
Dennis Jay Kenney

PRAEGER

New York
Westport, Connecticut
London

Library of Congress Cataloging-in-Publication Data

Police and policing : contemporary issues / edited by Dennis Jay
  Kenney.
        p.   cm.
    Includes index.
    ISBN 0-275-93086-6 (alk. paper). — ISBN 0-275-93087-4 (pbk. :
  alk. paper)
    1. Police professionalization—United States.   2. Police
  administration—United States.   3. Law enforcement—United States.
  4. Criminal investigation.   I. Kenney, Dennis Jay.
  HV8141.P56   1989
  363.2'0973—dc20   89-33958

Library of Congress Catalog Card Number: 89-33958
ISBN: 0-275-93086-6 (hb.)
      0-275-93087-4 (pbk.)

First published in 1989

Praeger Publishers, One Madison Avenue, New York, NY 10010
A division of Greenwood Press, Inc.

Printed in the United States of America

The paper used in this book complies with the
Permanent Paper Standard issued by the National
Information Standards Organization (Z39.48-1984).

10 9 8 7 6 5 4 3 2 1

POLICE and POLICING

Contents

Introduction

Dennis Jay Kenney

Over the past two decades, practitioners, researchers, and students of policing have witnessed considerable change and evolution in their field of choice and interest. Largely gone are the days when those on the "inside" of policing would routinely deny access to those interested in gaining a better understanding of who the police were, how they operated, and what worked and did not work. As a result of this new openness, our knowledge of American policing and law enforcement has advanced significantly in only a relatively short period of time.

While the benefits of these recent information advances are substantial, simple assessments of how far policing has come are still not possible. The numbers of agencies of differing sizes are many, while the legal, social, and political conditions under which each operates vary substantially. As a result, those searching for easy categorizations and answers are almost always frustrated. Still, as the chapters to follow will illustrate, some general observations and conclusions are possible.

In the opening section of this book, the authors deal with important issues concerning the police as individuals. We are reasonably certain, for example, that since 1965 the quality and educational levels of police officers have generally risen around the country. But how, if at all, has that impacted on the performance of officers or the abilities of agencies to achieve the goals they seek? This issue of college and policing, as well as the role of women in policing, the use of psychological testing for the selection of police, and the interactions between the recruitment, selection, and training processes are explored.

In the book's second section, the traditional approaches to policing are considered and what is known about each is reviewed. Chapter 5, for example, reviews the results of the Kansas City Preventive Patrol Experiment—perhaps the most well-known and most controversial of police experiments. Gary Cordner goes further in Chapter 6 where he discusses the range of activities—some official, some personal—that the police actually engage in while on patrol. Finally, Chapters 7 and 8 present the latest research by England's Home Office on how cases are solved by investigators, as well as Jack Kuykendall's insightful observations about the investigative process in general.

Perhaps the most exciting section of the book concerns the experimental methods of policing currently being tried around the country. It is here that we gain the greatest appreciation and see the greatest value in the works from the previous two decades. In this section, John Eck, Tony Pate, and Lawrence Sherman each report on actual experiments now under way in progressive communities. Chapter 11, on the other hand, describes a previously tested repeat offender strategy now gaining widespread attention throughout the country. In each case, the results are promising. As we consider these efforts we should note that each experimental approach is derived logically from the research that preceded it.

The chapters concerned with policing the police give us the opportunity to think about ethical issues and the problems of controlling police power in a free society. Robert Blecker asks us to consider the social implications of covert police actions, a timely question given the proliferation of STING undercover tactics. Robert Leuci, on the other hand, gives us a personal account of the individual impacts of such efforts. Many readers (especially frequent moviegoers) will remember Detective Leuci, a retired member of New York City's Special Investigations Unit, as the *Prince of the City*.

Accompanying the current focus toward greater citizen involvement in the law enforcement process are important questions about citizen effectiveness and control. Is active citizen involvement directed at crime fighting, or is a more passive role preferable where citizens act as the "eyes and ears" of their local police in a crime prevention role? Does either approach work and what of constitutional protections for persons these citizen activists confront? In Chapter 16, Dennis Rosenbaum reviews what is known today, while Chapters 17 and 18 present differing views on perhaps the best known of citizen groups: the Guardian Angels.

Finally, the last section of this book takes a look at the major issues of police management. While it is still simply too early to reach a clear verdict about the effects of unionization and accreditation on the police evolutionary process, both issues are here and require a manager's attention. Additionally, the police, more than almost any other segment of our society, are awash in information. Obviously, no efforts at improvement—either organizational or operational—can have much future unless we learn to manage that information better. If this point remains in doubt after reading Robert Taylor's chapter, we should return to the section on experimental methods for review. Concluding this section is Samuel Walker's chapter on police reform. As a historian, Walker's insights on where we have been, what we have tried, and how each of the previous sections relates to where we want to go are outstanding. His thoughts are so clear that no other conclusion to the book is necessary.

I

The Characteristics of the Police and Policing

1

Women in Policing: The Eighties and Beyond

Susan E. Martin

For more than half a century after acceptance of the first female sworn officer in 1910, women in policing were selected according to separate criteria from men, employed as "policewomen," and limited to working with "women, children and typewriters" (Milton, 1972). With the passage of the 1972 Amendments to the Civil Rights Act of 1964, however, women officers obtained the legal right to an equal opportunity in a law enforcement career. Since that date, many departments, often under the threat of a court order, have eliminated discriminatory personnel policies.

Just how far these changes have gone, however, is uncertain. Several evaluations of the first generation of women on patrol found that female officers performed patrol work adequately (Bloch and Anderson, 1974; Sherman, 1975; Sichel et al., 1978) but there have been few follow-up examinations of women officers in the 1980s. Even accurate statistical information often is unavailable. The FBI's Uniform Crime Report annually provides statistics on the number of female officers in various agencies, but data on officer sex *and* race, rank, and assignments are "shockingly limited" (Walker, 1985). This chapter examines: (1) changes that have occurred in the status of women in policing in the past decade; (2) male resistance to women and the resulting barriers to full acceptance of women as officers; and (3) the impact of departmental policies on the integration of women officers and supervisors.

Table 1.1
Mean Percentage of Female Police in Municipal Departments by City Size,
Ethnicity, and Year

| City | 1978 | | | 1986 | | |
Size	White	Minority	Total	White	Minority	Total
Millic.1 +	2.5%	3.3%	5.8%	5.7%	4.7%	10.4%
500–1M	2.2	2.1	4.3	4.5	4.8	9.3
250–500	3.0	1.3	4.3	6.1	3.0	9.1
100–250	2.9	0.9	3.8	5.3	1.5	6.8
50–100	2.2	0.4	2.6	4.0	0.9	4.9
TOTAL	2.6 (N=290)	1.6 (290)	4.2 (290)	5.3 (316)	3.5 (316)	8.8 (316)

CHANGES IN THE STATUS OF WOMEN IN POLICING

The Growing Number of Women Officers

The proportion of women among sworn police personnel has grown steadily since 1972. In that year a survey of cities serving populations of 250,000 or more found that women comprised only 2 percent of uniformed law enforcement personnel (ICMA, 1972) and, in virtually all of the agencies surveyed, women were excluded from patrol duties. By 1978, women made up 4.2 percent of sworn personnel in municipal departments serving populations over 50,000 (2.6 percent white and 1.6 percent minorities) and, by 1986, they made up 8.8 percent of the sworn personnel in these departments.

Table 1.1 shows the percentage of women officers in municipal police departments in 1978 and 1986 by size of jurisdiction served and officer ethnicity. It indicates that (1) in both 1978 and 1986, the proportion of officers that were female was directly related to city size and (2) that although there has been growth in the proportion of women across all city size categories, the increases are larger in the departments in larger cities. In cities of over a million, for example, women made up 5.8 percent of the sworn personnel in 1978 and 10.4 percent in 1986; in cities of 50,000 to 100,000, they made up only 2.6 percent of the total in 1978 and 4.9 percent in 1986.

The table also shows that in both years the proportion of minority women—but not white women—was closely related to city size and that minority women make up a disproportionately large share of all women in policing (38 percent of all the women in 1978 and 40 percent in 1986).

In 1978, minority women constituted 3.3 percent of the sworn personnel in the cities with populations over one million but only 0.4 percent in cities serving populations between 50,000 and 100,000. In 1986, the figures in these two size categories were 4.7 and 0.9 respectively.

The large proportion of female officers that are minorities (and mostly black) may be related to several factors. First, black women may view policing as an attractive occupational alternative because they have a narrower range of occupational options due to racial differences in education and job discrimination. Second, black women historically have worked in occupations involving physical labor so may be less put off by this aspect of the work than white women. Third, municipal police agencies may be disproportionately recruiting and selecting minority women to enable them simultaneously to meet affirmative action goals related to racial and sexual integration.

The percentage of women in state police departments lags behind that of municipal agencies. In 1978 women made up only 0.9 percent of all state troopers; by 1986 they had grown to 3.7 percent, of which 3.1 percent were white and 0.6 percent were minority females.

Among federal law enforcement agencies, 8 percent of the FBI's special agents were female in 1987 (and 13 percent of the 769 women agents were minority women) in contrast to the total of 94 women agents in 1978. The Drug Enforcement Agency's 199 women special agents made up 7 percent of the agency's agents in 1987. And the Secret Service's 75 special agents made up 4 percent of the agency's special agents, while the 62 women in the Secret Service uniformed division accounted for 6 percent of that division's work force (McGuinnis and Donahue, 1988:255).

Women in Supervisory Positions

Table 1.2 shows the proportion of women in policing in 1978 and 1986 by rank and city size. It indicates that: (1) women make up a smaller percentage of supervisors than officers; (2) the increase in the proportion of women in supervisory ranks over the eight-year study period is smaller than the overall increase in women's presence in policing; and (3) the higher the rank, the lower its proportion of females. More specifically, in 1978 women made up 5 percent of municipal police officers but only one percent of the sergeants and less than one percent of the lieutenants and higher ranking officials. By 1986 women made up 10 percent of the officers and 3.3 percent of all supervisors, including 3.7 percent of the sergeants and 2.5 percent of the lieutenants, but only 1.4 percent of persons at the command staff level above lieutenant.

The size of the jurisdiction made little difference in female representation in supervisory ranks in 1978 because women's representation was

Table 1.2
Mean Percentage of Female Police in Municipal Departments by City Size, Rank, and Year

City Size	OFFICER*		SERGEANT		LIEUTENANT		ABOVE LT	
	1978	1986	1978	1986	1978	1986	1978	1986
Million +	6.6	11.6	1.7	4.2	3.1	2.9	1.6	1.4
500-1M	5.1	10.5	0.7	3.7	0.5	3.8	0.4	2.5
250-500	5.3	10.3	1.4	5.0	1.8	3.3	0.5	2.8
100-250	5.0	8.1	0.8	3.2	0.3	1.6	0.2	0.4
50-100	3.3	6.0	0.6	1.6	0.3	0.6	0.3	0.5
TOTAL	5.0 (N=290)	10.0 (315)	1.0 (284)	3.7 (301)	0.7 (278)	2.5 (302)	0.5 (245)	1.4 (315)

*Includes officers, detectives, and corporals.

so uniformly negligible. In 1986, a higher proportion of women supervisors was found in agencies serving populations over 250,000 than those in the smaller cities at all three supervisory levels in the table.

The picture is even more discouraging for women as supervisors in state police departments. By 1986, women still made up less than one percent of all state police supervisors.

In sum, one may optimistically note that the proportion of women supervisors more than tripled from 1978 to 1986; or more pessimistically note that the increase from one to 3.3 percent of all police supervisors is simply a change from the minuscule to the minute; and that women are virtually excluded from upper level management in police departments just as they are in corporate board rooms and law partnerships.

Data on the proportion of male and female officers eligible for promotion that actually were promoted or were likely to be in 1986, however, are somewhat more encouraging. Although 6.8 percent of all persons eligible for promotion to the rank of sergeant in municipal departments in our survey were female, 8.8 percent of those actually promoted were female; similarly, at the rank of lieutenant, women made up 2.7 percent of those eligible, but 3.5 percent of those actually promoted or likely to have become lieutenants in 1986. Thus women "beat the odds" and were promoted in proportions greater than would be expected on the basis of their representation in the eligible pool for sergeant and lieutenant. Nevertheless, at their current rate, it will be the 21st century before significant numbers of women actually move into policy-making positions.

Women's Assignments

Prior to 1972 women were limited to clerical and juvenile division assignments. Even after the change in the law, departments were slow in integrating them into other assignments. Sulton and Townsey (1981) found that by 1979, 87 percent of the municipal departments serving populations over 50,000 assigned women to patrol and that the proportions of male and female officers assigned to patrol, technical, and administrative functions were quite similar. However, female officers, particularly minority women, were overrepresented in juvenile functions and underrepresented in investigative assignments.

The Police Foundation survey data suggest that the integration of women into all assignments has continued but is not yet complete. By 1986, 98 percent of the responding agencies stated that women are assigned to patrol, and data collected on assignments indicated that women now are assigned to the field operations units (including patrol, special operations, and traffic assignments) in slightly greater proportion than their overall representation in policing. Women make up 8.4 percent of all officers but represented 9.2 percent of the persons assigned to field operations. Women generally were underrepresented in criminal investigations and vice units, except in the small cities categories, and overrepresented in administrative and other support staff units, particularly in cities of more than 250,000.

Sex differences in assignment patterns are probably attributable to several factors. In virtually all agencies rookies of either sex now begin their careers on patrol. Thus the overrepresentation of women in field operations units to some extent may reflect their newness in policing.

Women appear to have moved into staff support assignments in disproportionately large numbers as a result of both pushes out of patrol and pulls toward staff assignments. The pushes result from the persistence of the attitude held by many policemen that most women officers are unsuited for the danger of the street and cannot provide adequate backup for street officers. The pulls are due to the desire of women to escape from patrolmen's harassment, to use the clerical or administrative skills that many possess, and to obtain daytime hours more compatible with family life than the rotating shifts of patrol assignments.

Investigative and vice units tend to be more "elite" and, therefore, more difficult for women to enter; in addition, vice assignments tend to involve extensive overtime and evening working hours difficult to mesh with family life. For these reasons they may be less attractive to many women officers.

Changing Eligibility and Selection Criteria

The rate at which women enter policing is shaped by the eligibility and selection criteria used by various departments. For many years minimum height and weight standards as well as educational standards that were higher for women than men served greatly to limit the pool of female applications (Milton, 1972; Sulton and Townsey, 1981). Both legislation (the Equal Employment Opportunity Act of 1972, the Crime Control Act of 1973, the State and Local Government Fiscal Assistance Act of 1976, and numerous state equal rights and fair employment practices laws) and evolving case law resulting from litigation have dramatically altered police agencies' eligibility and selection criteria. As a result, the pool of eligible candidates for policing has greatly expanded. By 1981, only 13 percent of municipal agencies retained height requirements and, by 1986, fewer than 4 percent of municipal departments had minimum height (mean = 5′ 4″) and weight (mean = 135.3) standards (Fyfe, 1987). Most had replaced them by requiring candidates' weight be in proportion to their height (Fyfe, 1987:5).

Selection criteria also have changed. The vast majority of departments require applicants to pass written, oral, and medical exams, a psychological screening test, and a pretraining physical agility test. In the past, women were eliminated by the physical agility test and oral interview that screened out persons who did not possess "the mark of affinity" that was demonstrated by the candidate's conception of masculinity (Gray, 1975).

Because of numerous legal challenges to the lack of job-relatedness of earlier physical agility tests, the courts have ruled that departments may continue to use such tests but may not use a physical fitness standard that eliminates a disproportionate number of females, unless it is shown to be reasonably job-related and to have a valid purpose. Tests to meet Title VII challenges must be based on job analyses that define the amount of physical strength required and must be validated. Currently, preemployment physical performance tests to assess fitness are used in 76 percent of responding municipal agencies in 1986 (Fyfe, 1987:7) but in many agencies they are now job-related (e.g., the candidate must pull a dummy a certain distance in a limited amount of time) and passing grades are based on age and sex-specific standards. Nevertheless, the survey found that significantly more women completed job applications in departments that did not have preemployment physical tests than those that did.

Interviews in which questions and answers are predetermined and panels of interviewers that include minorities and females leave far less room for subjective and arbitrary decisions. Increasingly, departments are moving toward structuring and standardizing the interview process as lawsuits have challenged arbitrary practices.

Our survey found that 76 percent of the municipal agencies and 88 percent of the state agencies that use oral interviews have standardized questions; and 60 percent of those municipal departments and 44 percent of those state departments using interviews have pre-identified acceptable responses. Only about a quarter of departments using panels, however, mandate that they include a female or minority representative. These are significantly more frequently found in agencies in cities of more than 100,000 (31 percent) than those of between 50,000 and 100,000 (12 percent), which may contribute to the higher proportion of women officers in the former.

To permit examination of the selection process, departments provided data on the number of male and female officers of each ethnic group that: (1) filed an application in 1986; (2) were offered employment by the department; (3) entered the training academy; and (4) completed training. We found that 20 percent of the applicants were women; virtually the same proportion as those accepted (20.6 percent) and completing training (19.2 percent). Because the actual qualifications of the male and female applicants is unknown, it is impossible to determine whether there is discrimination in the selection process. The data suggest, however, that there is wide variation in the recruitment and selection process among departments but that there currently does not appear to be a systematic bias against selection of women applicants.

BARRIERS TO THE INTEGRATION OF WOMEN INTO POLICING

Barriers to the integration of women into policing stem from both the *structural* characteristics of the occupation and the work organization, and the ways that cultural mandates and behavioral norms related to gender shape interpersonal interaction in specific occupational contexts.

Structural and Cultural Limitations on Sex Integration

In a study of men and women employed in corporations Kanter (1977) suggested that occupational behavior is shaped by three key features of the organization and the individuals' position in it: the opportunity structure, the power structure, and relative numbers. These variables shape possibilities for action and press people to adapt to their situations.

Kanter observed that men and women behave differently in work organizations because men have more real power and greater opportunities for mobility. When either a man or a women is placed in a powerless and low mobility situation the response is different from a person with greater power and opportunities. Blocked mobility leads to limited motivation which, in turn, sets in motion a downward cycle of deprivation and discouragement. Conversely, people with power and opportunities use these resources to gain allies and supporters and prove themselves, triggering an upward cycle of success. Although both cycles appear to be related to individual motivation, in fact they arise in response to organizational factors.

Kanter also noted that *numbers* affect occupational behavior because minority individuals or "tokens" are treated differently from others in three ways. First, tokens face performance pressures due to their high visibility. Second, tokens face heightened in-group boundaries and social isolation because they polarize differences between themselves and dominants. Third, they are focused into stereotypic roles as a result of dominants' distortion of their characteristics.

Occupational behavior also is shaped by culturally prescribed norms guiding sex-role enactment. Cultural definitions prescribe appropriate "masculine" behavior for men and "feminine" behavior for women. Norms of sex-appropriate behavior, however, may conflict with occupationally prescribed behaviors. For women in male-dominated occupations, dilemmas arise when occupational norms call for "masculine" behavior and interaction with other workers as peers but gender-related norms prescribe "feminine" behavior and interaction with men guided by asymmetrical norms (Goffman, 1956 and 1976). Thus, women officers must decide when and how to "act like a cop" and still "act like a lady" on the job.

Sexism also affects women workers. Even when female tokens have job skills and commitment, they are harassed on the job and excluded from the informal social life of their fellow workers, while male tokens are not subject to the same amount or type of harassment or job discrimination (Schreiber, 1979; Fottler, 1976; Kadushin, 1976).

The Police Culture and Male Opposition to Female Officers

Certain aspects of police work lead to unique problems for female officers. Police officers have enormous discretionary decision-making authority. Across the diverse policing tasks there is always the potential for violence and the authority to use force to ensure the officer's definition of the situation. Because the police act as the representatives of the coercive power of the state and legitimate users of force in everyday life, certain attitudes and behavioral characteristics have emerged as part of the police work culture.

The presence of danger and the potential for violence lead to suspiciousness, isolation from the community, and a cohesive, informal occupational group with its own stratification system and norms. These, in turn, heighten the barriers to informal acceptance for anyone who is perceived as an "outsider" and, therefore, cannot be counted on to conform to group norms.

The policemen's opposition to female officers has been amply documented (Bloch and Anderson, 1974; Sherman, 1975; California Highway Patrol, 1976; Martin, 1980; Charles, 1981; Linden, 1984). Linden, for example, points to three reasons that men object to women on patrol: fear that the image of the police will suffer; concern that women are not committed to policing as a career; and fear that women will not be able to cope with physical violence. Nevertheless, a variety of other, less "acceptable" concerns underlie their opposition. As Martin (1980) noted, women threaten to disrupt the division of labor, the work norms, the work group's solidarity, their insecure occupational image, and the sexist ideology that undergirds the men's definition of the work as "men's work" and their identity as masculine men.

The use of women on patrol implies either that the men's unique asset, their physical superiority, is irrelevant (as it is, on most assignments) or that the man with a female partner will be at a disadvantage in a physical conformation that he would not face with a male partner. The possibility that women officers may reduce the likelihood of a physical confrontation or act appropriately in protecting a male partner is no comfort because it undermines both the male and female sex role stereotypes that permeate the officers' perceptual world. Women are not "supposed" to fight or control other male citizens. Moreover, being "defended" by a woman is regarded as an affront to a policeman's manhood.

Women also pose a threat to work group solidarity by exposing the men's emotional masks, inhibiting their use of "raunchy" language, posing the threat of sexual intimacy between partners, fostering competition among male officers and thus a competing set of loyalties, and making public the fact that routine policing does not revolve around crime-fighting but involves emotional labor and requires interpersonal skills. Thus policemen's sexism is a crucial element in their occupational identity.

Structural Barriers: Equality versus Equity

Women enter police work at a disadvantage. Few went through a long period of anticipatory socialization in which they vicariously rehearsed police roles. Unlike many of the men, most women have not served in the military, used firearms, or played team sports that involve physical contact and imbue the spirit of the team player.

Inequality may be fostered in the training academy in several ways. An emphasis on meeting physical fitness standards that do not have to be maintained beyond the academy magnifies the importance of the physical differences between the sexes. Informal coddling of women by some physical education instructors also negatively affects the women. It permits some to move to the next stage of recruit training not fully prepared, fosters the expectation of those women that they can get along by being "different" rather than learning the lessons of group loyalty, undermines the confidence of male officers in all female officers, and divides the women.

Academy training also often fails to focus on or develop the inter-personal skills essential to effective police work. Such skills usually are more highly developed in women than men, and their omission from the curriculum deprives the women of a job-relevant training oppor-tunity in which they are likely to excel. As a consequence, new women officers enter male turf on male terms with little recognition of their own problems or strengths.

The early months on the street are very important because the rep-utation that follows an officer through a career is formed at that time. Opportunities for learning and gaining self-confidence have a multiplier effect because once established, habits and reputations are difficult to change. Self-confidence grows with mastery of policing skills and pos-itive feedback on performance. An officer who does not have or take opportunities to develop street patrol skills because of limited assign-ments, instruction, or overprotection is likely to act hesitantly, be re-garded as a threat to the safety of others, and be deprived of subsequent opportunities to handle situations.

Women rookies face several disadvantages on the street. Most had little previous exposure to street life and are not as physically strong as the male rookies. They must overcome the hostile attitudes of some supervisors and partners, the dual standard of evaluation for men and women, and the performance pressures they face as tokens.

Unless the timidity of some female rookies and the protectiveness of many male officers are not consciously reversed, many women do not get opportunities to learn to act with decisiveness and confidence. The result is that a self-fulfilling prophecy becomes a reality as the women seek to manipulate others' *expectations* of them, rather than altering their *own* behavior.

Cultural Norms and Interactional Obstacles

Female officers also face dilemmas in interacting with fellow officers. As police officers they are expected to act according to the norms governing relations among equals; as women they are expected to adhere to asymmetric norms governing male-female relationships that make females subordinates of males. Thus, in addition to dilemmas as "tokens," women officers must cope with norms that put them at a disadvantage in dealing with male officers.

Men use language to keep women officers "in their place" by constantly referring to them as "ladies" or "girls" (suggesting that women should be protected), or calling those that do not conform to sex-role stereotypes, "lesbians," "broads," "bitches," or "whores." Their cursing also creates dilemmas. Many men are uncomfortable cursing in front of women officers but resent the inhibition on their expressiveness. Similarly, when women swear men become offended and withdraw the deference they give to "ladies." Avoiding curse words, however, makes what they say less emphatic.

Frequent sexual jokes and sexual harassment remind women officers that they are desired sexual objects, visible outsiders, and feared competitors. Joking and harassment make many of the women, concerned about even the appearance of impropriety, avoid interactions that might be viewed as having a sexual connotation. To maintain their moral reputation they sacrifice the opportunity to build close interpersonal relationships necessary for gaining sponsors and mentors.

Sex-role stereotyping allows men to put women in roles that reflect in men's linguistic categories, limit women's behavioral options, and have a negative impact on their work. Women either get cast into the "seductress," "maiden," "mother," or "pet" roles or get labeled "lesbians" or "bitches" (Kanter, 1977). The former are protected from occupational demands, excluded from opportunities to develop occupational skills, and criticized for failing to fulfill their responsibilities as officers. The latter are permitted to remain in the policeman's informal world but their dangerous qualities are *neutralized by defeminization*.

In short, women are not permitted to be "just officers." They are visible but excluded from career-promoting networks, vulnerable to harassment but held responsible for the outcomes of such interactions. Not only on the street but in the stationhouse, their interpersonal world often is hostile and their work environment more stressful than that faced by male officers (Johnson et al, 1985; Wexler and Logan, 1983). They face barriers and handicaps that are built into both the formal and informal work structures and culturally mandated patterns governing male-female interaction that force women officers to "think like a man, work like a dog and act like a lady" (Martin, 1980: 219).

IMPACT OF DEPARTMENTAL POLICIES

Departmental policies have a substantial impact on the recruitment and retention of female officers as well as on their effectiveness on the

Table 1.3
Impact of Affirmative Action Policy on Representation of Women Officers
and Supervisors by Policy Type

Policy Type	WHITE OFFICERS	MINORITY OFFICERS	TOTAL OFFICERS	TOTAL SUPERVISORS
Court ordered (N=45)	5.7%	4.4%	10.1%	3.5%
Voluntary (N=126)	5.5	2.8	8.3	2.4
None (N=126)	4.1	2.0	6.1	2.2
TOTAL	5.3	3.5	8.8	3.5

job. In our survey we sought to determine the presence and effect of three policies of particular concern to women: sexual harassment, pregnancy and/or maternity leave, and affirmative action. We found that only 49 percent of the municipal agencies that responded have their own sexual harassment policies (although a number stated that they follow citywide policies that are in effect), and only 25 percent have policies explicitly related to pregnancy.

Because of the nature of police work, most police agencies permit or require pregnant officers to leave patrol assignments. Yet only 74 percent of the agencies state that their actual practice is to reassign a pregnant officer to a "light duty" assignment until delivery; 14 percent force the woman to go on leave when she can no longer continue in her "normal" assignment (and 12 percent have not yet had to deal with a pregnancy). It is likely that the absence of sexual harassment and pregnancy-leave policies as well as actual departmental practices related to them contribute to the finding that in 1986 women voluntarily left policing at a rate slightly higher than that of men (4.3 versus 3.0 percent).

Affirmative action policies also have had a major impact on both the representation of women in policing and the rate at which they are entering policing. In 1986, 15 percent of the municipal agencies that responded to our survey had court-ordered affirmative action for both hiring and promotion; 42 percent had voluntary affirmative action plans in effect; and 43 percent had none. As indicated in Table 1.3, in agencies under court order to increase the representation of women and minorities, women made up 10.1 percent of the sworn personnel in 1986; in those with voluntary affirmative action plans, women made up 8.3 percent of the personnel; and in those without affirmative action plans women comprised only 6.1 percent of the personnel. The effect of affirmative action is even greater for minority women than white women.

In addition, affirmative action has an impact on the proportion of women in supervisory positions; in departments with court-ordered affirmative action, women make up 3.5 percent of the supervisors; in those with voluntary affirmative action, 2.4 percent; and those without affirmative action, 2.2 percent of the supervisory personnel. Even after statistically controlling for the effects of city size and region (which are both associated with the presence of affirmative action policies), both court-ordered and voluntary affirmative action remained significantly associated with the proportion of women in a department and with the increase in the proportion of women from 1978 to 1986.

CONCLUSION: THE CHANGING STATUS OF WOMEN AND FURTHER POLICY NEEDS

This chapter has shown that there is good news and bad news regarding the changing status of women in policing. The good news is that the representation of women in police departments found in each population category and geographic region has increased steadily in the past 15 years and that women are now assigned to patrol and other line units in proportion to their representation in policing. This has occurred despite federal efforts to eliminate affirmative action programs which are found in more than half the municipal agencies that responded to the survey.

The bad news is that the pace of change is slow and women are present in policing, particularly at supervisory ranks, in only token numbers (i.e., between 1 and 15 percent of the workers in the occupation). Although more women are being promoted than might be expected based on their proportion among the eligibles, at the current rate of change, women are not likely to assume departmental leadership and policy-making positions for many years in any but a handful of agencies.

In addition, although women now are proportionately represented in the patrol or field operations divisions, their career paths seem to diverge from those of the men in the patterns of "special" assignments they obtain. While men are more likely to be in investigative assignments, women tend to transfer into administrative and other staff units. Such differential career paths may have longer-term negative impacts on women's upward mobility in policing.

In conclusion, women have surmounted the highest hurdle, gaining the right to enter and have equal opportunities for a career in policing. But they still face subtle barriers to integration that limit their options and opportunities for advancement. The challenge is to continue and accelerate the slow pace of change so that women officers achieve *actual* as well as *legal* status in policing.

REFERENCES

Bloch, P. and D. Anderson (1974). *Policewomen on Patrol: Final Report.* Washington, D.C.: Urban Institute.

California Highway Patrol (1976). *Women Traffic Officer Project.* Sacramento, CA: Author.

Charles, M. (1981). "Performance and Socialization of Female Recruits in the Michigan State Police Training Academy." *Journal of Police Science and Administration,* 9:209–223.

Fottler, M. (1976). "Attitudes of Female Nurses toward the Male Nurse: A Study of Occupational Segregation." *Journal of Health and Social Behavior,* 17:98–110.

Fyfe, J. (1987). *Police Personnel Practices, 1986.* (Baseline Data Report, Volume 18, Number 6). Washington, D.C.: International City Management Association.

Goffman, E. (1956) "The Nature of Deference and Demeanor." *American Anthropologist,* 58:473–502.

———. (1976). "Gender Displays." *Studies in the Anthropology of Visual Communication,* 3.

Gray, T. (1975). "Selecting for a Police Subculture." Pp. 46–56 in Jerome Skolnick and Thomas Gray (eds.). *Police in America.* Boston, MA: Little, Brown.

International City Management Association (1972). "Personnel Practices in Municipal Police Departments." Urban Data Service, 5.

Johnson, L., V. Nieva, and M. J. Wilson (1985). *Police, Work Home Stress Study: Interim Report.* Unpublished manuscript. Rockville, MD: Westat.

Kadushin, D. (1976). "Men in a Women's Profession." *Social Work,* 21: 440–47.

Kanter, R. (1977). *Men and Women of the Corporation.* New York: Basic Books.

Linden, R. (1984). *Women in Policing: A Study of Lower Mainland R.C.M.P. Detachments.* Ottawa, Canada: Solicitor General of Canada.

McGuinness, K. and T. Donahue (1988). "Women in Law Enforcement" Pp. 252–257 in S. Rix (ed.). *The American Woman 1988–89: A Status Report.* New York: W. W. Norton & Co.

Martin, S. (1980). *Breaking and Entering: Policewomen on Patrol.* Berkeley: University of California Press.

Milton, C. (1972). *Women in Policing.* Washington: Police Foundation.

Powell, G. (1988). *Women and Men in Management.* Beverly Hills, CA: Sage.

Schreiber, C. (1979). *Men and Women in Transitional Occupations.* Cambridge, MA: MIT Press.

Sherman, L. (1975). "Evaluation of policewomen on patrol in a suburban police department." *Journal of Police Science and Administration,* 3:434–438.

Sichel, J.; L. Friedman; J. Quint; and M. Smith (1978). *Women on Patrol: A Pilot Study of Police Performance in New York City.* Washington, D.C.: National Institute of Law Enforcement and Criminal Justice.

Sulton, C. and R. Townsey (1981). *A Progress Report on Women in Policing.* Washington, D.C.: Police Foundation.

Walker, S. (1985). "Racial minority and female employment in policing: The implications of 'glacial' change." *Crime and Delinquency,* 31:555–572.

Wexler, J. and D. Logan (1983). "Sources of Stress among Women Police Officers." *Journal of Police Science and Administration,* 11:46–53.

College and the Police: A Review of the Issues

Chris Eskridge

Law enforcement education has had a rather brief but stormy history. Although Sir Robert Peele made reference to the need for a professionally trained police force as long ago as 1829, perhaps the first real emphasis on professional training and education for American police had to await the appointment of August Vollmer as Chief of Police of Berkeley, California. Started by Vollmer in 1908, the coursework in what became the Berkeley Police School covered not only vocational training topics but also general social science matters as well. Vollmer felt the need for police officers to have not only specific skills obtained through training, but also felt that officers needed to have a general broad-based, social science background so that they might better understand and be better prepared to deal with the human aspects of their work. Higher education, he noted, was "indispensable to the future of the police profession" (Carte and Carte, 1975:95).

Years ahead of his time, Vollmer formally proposed as early as 1916 that police officers have college degrees. Largely due to his efforts, the University of California-Berkeley began offering law enforcement related courses in 1916. At about the same time, but at the other end of the country, Columbia University got involved in training activities for the New York City Police Department. A number of other schools also offered police related courses for a short time in this same era, but few survived for more than a year or two. Some of the early programs that did survive and have continued to this day are the University of California-Berkeley, University of Southern California, San Jose State, Michigan State, University of Indiana, Washington State and Wichita State (Mathias, 1976:378-380). Despite these early efforts, however, the movement to educate our police did not begin in earnest in this country until the mid–1960s.

LEEP ERA

Following the publication in 1967 of the Presidential Crime Commission's recommendation that by 1984 all police officers be required to have at least a bachelor's degree, the Law Enforcement Education Program (LEEP) was created and funded by Congress. Suddenly, dollars were literally poured into police education. The LEEP program provided grants to in-service justice system personnel and offered forgivable loans to prospective justice system employees. Where perhaps 200 police science degree programs existed before the advent of LEEP, after its creation and the resulting influx of dollars, literally hundreds of police programs sprang up almost overnight at colleges and universities all across the country. By the mid–1970s, more than 1,000 academic institutions were offering police-related courses to tens of thousands of students backed with federal LEEP money (Kobetz, 1975:3). By the end of the decade, however, significant concern regarding the rapid and relatively unregulated growth of police science programs began to be raised from varied sources, and a call went out for increased caution and restraint.

In response to these concerns, the National Advisory Commission on Higher Education for Police Officers was created. This commission conducted an evaluation of police education and filed its report in December 1978. Critical in its focus, the Commission concluded that the overall quality of police science education was rather poor from many perspectives. The reality of police education, noted the report, was a far cry from Vollmer's original intent (Sherman et al., 1978:38). Among its many recommendations, the Commission went on to propose that:

1. Academic credit not be granted for in-service training or police academy course work.

2. The general academic quality of faculty be stressed and prior employment in a criminal justice agency should not be considered as a prime selection criterion.

and A. S. Blumberg (eds.), *The Ambivalent Force*. Hinsdale, Illinois: Dryden Press.

Meadows, R. (1987). "Beliefs of Law Enforcement Administrators and Criminal Justice Educators Towards the Needed Skill Competencies in Entry-Level Police Training Curriculum." *Journal of Police Science and Administration*, March:1–9.

Mills, C. and W. Bohannon (1980). "Personality Characteristics of Effective State Police Officers." *Journal of Applied Psychology*, 65:680–684.

Sherman, L. et al. (1978). *The Quality of Police Education*. San Francisco, CA: Jossey-Bass.

Smith, A., B. Locke, and A. Fenster (1970). "Authoritarianism in Policemen Who Are College Graduates and Noncollege Police." *Journal of Criminal Law, Criminology, and Police Science*, 313–315.

Sparling, C. (1975). "The Use of Educational Standards as Selection Criteria in Police Agencies." *Journal of Police Science and Administration*, September: 332–334.

Topp, B. and C. Kardash (1986). "Personality, Achievement, and Attrition." *Journal of Police Science and Administration*, September:234–241.

Trojanowicz, R. and T. Nicholson (1976). "A Comparison of Behavioral Styles of College Graduate Police Officers vs. Non-College Going Police Officers." *Police Chief*, August:56–58.

Weiner, N. (1976). "The Educated Policeman." *Journal of Police Science and Administration*. December:450–457.

Selection, Training, and Discipline of Police Officers

Vance McLaughlin and Robert Bing

Selection, training, and discipline are primarily classified as "personnel matters" and thus become the domain of administrators. For most police departments, salaries represent the agency's largest operating expense. In addition, the quality of personnel is essential to the long-term success of the law enforcement agency. And while selection, training, and discipline are issues largely controlled by each agency, departmental policies are almost always influenced by elements on the periphery of the police organization. Legislative bodies, the media, public interest groups, and the Constitution limit the power of managers and compete for influence over agency actions. As a result, police control of key personnel decisions may vary and at times appear muddled. With this in mind, the purpose of this chapter is to discuss issues based upon two fundamental premises:

1. Politics is and will always be pervasive in police personnel matters.
2. Selection, training, and discipline are inextricably tied together, yet may result in conflicting goals.

THE HISTORICAL ROOTS OF POLITICS IN POLICING

From the beginning, politics has been at the cornerstone of police selection. During the mid–1800s, the impact of the Sir Robert Peel revolution was being felt in the United States. The growth of cities created pressures to modernized police departments. Social problems in the highly urban areas during this period were quite different from those in rural areas. In fact, between 1830 and 1870, there was unprecedented civil disorder in many major cities (Cole, 1986). Ethnic conflict as a consequence of massive immigration, hostility toward non-slave blacks and abolitionists, bank robberies, and violence involved with questions of morality created fears that democratic institutions could not survive (Cole, 1986). These troubled times marked the formation of organized police departments which soon would be besieged with problems of autonomy and political control. For example, Smith (1960:105) states:

Rotation in office enjoyed so much popular favor that police posts of both high and low degree constantly changed hands, with political fixers determining the price and condition of each change.... The whole police question simply churned about in the public mind and eventually became identified with the corruption and degradation of the city politics and local governments of the period.

In another illustration of the extent of politics and policing, McLaughlin (1984) offers an example, originally cited by Fosdick, of how two different departments reacted to partisan politics; he states:

In Indianapolis, a law existed in 1916 that the police force be equally divided politically between Democrats and Republicans. Vacancies were to be filled according to the political affiliation of the men who left.... In Louisville, three wholesale changes of personnel took place between 1907 and 1917. Whenever the Republicans or Democrats regained control of the city, most members of the police force were dismissed. In the 1917 victory, 300 policemen in a force of 429 were replaced.

To respond to the problems created by politics and policing, several strategies were recommended, if not adopted. Appointed and elected commissions were, for example, suggested as a reform strategy to neutralize the political influence that so frequently resulted in corruption and graft. In some cities these commissions were vulnerable and governance at the state level became the alternative. Thus, the point to be made here is that political pressure is not a new phenomenon—it has always been a part of law enforcement and police policy. There was never a "golden era" when politics and policing functioned independently. Today, the difference is that political influence is likely to manifest itself in more complex ways.

THE POLITICAL INFLUENCES TODAY

When the term politics is used to discuss police personnel matters, it takes on an elastic meaning. It may refer to partisan politics or may be grounded in a type of intrigue with certain groups. These groups may be comprised of the nine justices who sit on the U.S. Supreme Court, elected individuals serving in the legislative branches of government, or even local officials (i.e., law enforcement administrators, etc.). Politics, then, takes on different dimensions and different meanings because different factions are continually competing for influence. At a lower, but significant level, individuals within the police organization may have a hidden agenda that can effectively subvert the written dictums of the more formal groups. Therefore, at the formal and informal level, there is the possibility that police policy may be improved, or hamstrung. This perpetual uncertainty creates a void that is filled by political grandstanding. Politics and the struggle for influence that accompanies it become part of the turmoil in which police departments must operate on a day-to-day basis.

THE SELECTION OF POLICE OFFICERS

The history of policing can be divided into three eras: spoils, civil service, and job-related testing. The spoils system existed to reward others for party affiliation and political involvement. The civil service system, which includes testing, qualifications, and numerical rankings based upon test scores, represents an attempt to correct the abuses of the spoils era by interjecting a "scientific" approach to employee selection. This system of selection has a clear advantage over the spoils system but is not without its own problems. For example, politicians in some areas continue to select those charged with the responsibility of running civil service boards. As a result, these appointed officials are able to use various strategies to manipulate applicant rankings so as to accomplish their own, often unrelated, objectives. Broad standards and large applicant pools, for example, facilitate manipulation and create the impression that applicants are being selected solely upon merit.

Moreover, there is the feeling that instead of raising standards, civil service boards may also be responsible for erecting barriers to impede the change process. As for job-related testing, this era emerged from court cases (introduced by minorities and women). These court cases challenged the predictive validity of tests used under the civil service system. Given the success of these challenges, job requirements that adversely impact upon protected classes (minorities and women who have traditionally been excluded from police employment) may be invalidated in a court of law.

Issues

A number of current issues involving police selection have been raised. First, the courts have ruled that a legally defensible job-related test *may* be used, even if it has an adverse impact on minorities and women. Ironically, a police department does *not* have to use this job-related test if it is pursuing affirmative-action goals. This adds a new dimension to the debate over scientific selection versus political hiring. Second, if qualifications are not used in the selection process, should salaries be adjusted to reflect the marketplace? Can we justify paying a recruit a police salary in excess of what his or her marketable skills would otherwise command? And third, the issue of testing and predictability of performance has not been resolved. Psychological testing of applicants is in vogue and recommended by most national studies and commissions. However, most psychological tests have not been comprehensively evaluated for their validity (Nislow, 1988).

In summary, a sound selection process is vital to the long-term health of a law enforcement agency. While politics and political goals have always been the cornerstone of police selection, a broader focus must be established. The selection process should be robust, open, and based upon qualifications.

THE TRAINING OF POLICE OFFICERS

Upon joining a police department, the new recruit immediately faces the reality of the organization. He or she may have a citizen's understanding of the *work*, but little knowledge of the *procedures* (Cole, 1986). In most cities, new officers must attend a police training academy with classes ranging from the handling of weapons to the handling of people. Once completed, a probationary period follows before the recruit is fully accepted as a police officer.

The training of police took place originally only in the large urban areas like Boston and New York. While some departments have conducted training programs for years, it was not until recently that jurisdictions throughout the country moved toward mandatory training programs. These programs, usually directed at the state level, have various names, but most are known generically as P.O.S.T. (Police Officer Standards and Training) Councils. New York and California established the first Councils in 1959; Tennessee, West Virginia, Hawaii, and Mississippi were the last states to establish Councils in 1981.

Strangely enough, police training continues to vary throughout the United States. There is considerable disagreement with regard to the rigor of these programs and time allocation for them. The state of Missouri, for example, requires 150 hours of training in smaller departments, while Hawaii requires 790 hours (plus four months of field training). Moreover, the focus of mandatory training has regrettably been on the number of hours at the expense of quality and skill retention. As a result, many P.O.S.T. Councils have less than rigorous standards. In many programs, for example, the curriculum for recruits is written at the sixth grade level.

Issues

Some current issues in training are directly related to time and rigor. Michigan conducted a comprehensive and far-reaching needs assessment for two law enforcement categories: patrol and investigations. Moreover, the state established job-related physical agility standards in 1981 for its police officers. The establishment of these standards adversely affected female recruits and shortly thereafter changes in the standards were designed to accommodate the female officers. There were only marginal changes in the pass rate and dissension on this policy, coupled with continued high female failure rates, resulted in the test's termination. The test was seen as politically unpalatable. Thus, as with selection, training standards are also secondary to what is politically expedient.

In the same vein, Minnesota established a program whereby police applicants were required to have a two-year degree and to have passed the training academy before they could become patrol officers. While this could be perceived by some as a positive development, the "real" world is inundated with college graduates with reading and writing deficiencies. Therefore, it should never be assumed that academic credentials are sufficient because they may not reflect meaningful standards. With several two-year colleges offering the approved P.O.S.T. educational program, it is possible that competition for tuition and other resources could result in schools compromising their academic integrity. Far from an attack on the Minnesota program, which was certainly an innovative step, from this example the reader should see that hidden agendas (in this case the college's) can hamstring progressive efforts at training as well. A final issue pertains to requalification. In many states, a minimum level of competency is obtained at the academy, but it may not be maintained during the officer's career. Which competencies are vital and to what extent they should be maintained are important, yet unanswered questions.

In sum, law enforcement standards and training should coincide with job expectations. To achieve this goal, standards should emerge from empirical research and analysis. This may reduce the wide diversity in the levels of competency police officers bring to their jobs.

THE DISCIPLINE OF POLICE OFFICERS

Discipline is often thought of in a strictly negative sense because in practice and common parlance, it is usually punishment. Discipline, however, has the potential to instruct, teach, and train.

Historically, discipline problems have been placed in two categories: officer misconduct that harms the public, and officer misconduct that violates organizational policy. Officer misconduct that harms the public can include corruption, harassment, and brutality, as well as the violation of guaranteed civil rights. On the other hand, officer misconduct that violates organizational policy can include serious problems such as substance abuse and insubordination, or even minor problems associated with dress and tardiness.

In many cases, the same political reasons used to select police officers are the ones used to retain them and, ironically, the justification for discipline may be linked to the selection and training process as well. Discipline is used with great variation depending upon the masked agendas. Many agencies in the past, particularly during the mid–1800s, were visibly corrupt to the extent that they accepted money to overlook or enforce certain criminal acts. Individuals who were personal friends or political allies with high-ranking police officials were allowed to violate the law.

A more recent investigation has revealed that a large state police agency disciplined minority officers very strictly when compared to whites (Deal, 1986). This revelation points to the existence of double standards within some police departments. The question of double standards can manifest itself in other ways as well. Older personnel, for example, who are well connected with their supervisors are more likely to have their behavior interpreted positively. Meanwhile, newer employees, who may be younger and from different backgrounds, may be negatively evaluated for minor transgressions. Thus, the favorable treatment of older employees is explained by the supervisor's perception and job experiences. Having felt the stress of the job, these supervisors hope that if they should ever "act out," they will be treated with similar leniency.

Issues

A relatively new disciplinary action, drug testing, has become a major concern. Consider the following: In most public employment settings, if an individual should test positive for illegal drugs, the person is likely to be offered counseling and medical assistance and returned to his or her job-setting upon rehabilitation. Law enforcement officers, on the other hand, may face dismissal. While the courts are evaluating the legality of different tests, the likelihood that police officers will be sanctioned in more negative ways than other public employees seems an absolute certainty.

Another issue, civil litigation, casts a specter over current disciplinary actions against police officers. Officers know that they can be civilly liable for violating departmental *policy* (in many states), even though they may not have violated any particular *law*. As a result, some officers will be less likely to cooperate with their departments when disciplinary matters are involved. For example, in Los Angeles, before an officer who is involved in a shooting talks with investigators, he or she makes sure that the record indicates that any conversation being held is under duress. The rationale here is to reduce the chances of any incriminating statements being used in a court of law.

In sum, discipline must be consistent, visible, and fairly applied. Doing so may eliminate the negative traits so frequently associated with this concept. Additionally, while often the organizational concerns of the department overshadow the officer's rights, fairness and impartiality are mandatory if the disciplinary action is to have the desired effect.

A CONCLUDING COMMENT

As already suggested, the politics of police personnel selection offers no clear voice of direction. The resulting dilemma is that politically active groups and their goals dominate each of the three facets: selection, training, and discipline. With this in mind, there must be coordination among these three facets if progress is to be realized. As it now stands, those who enter into litigation against police agencies hold an advantage due to conflicting personnel practices.

Consider the following: It is possible for one court to rule that police selection should be based on very specific variables (i.e., race, gender, and testing) while other courts may require police departments to adhere to specific standards (i.e., training and strategies). The real conflict is that unless police departments have respectable and integrated guidelines, selection and recruitment may compromise training, while poorly selected officers may result in a disproportionate number of disciplinary actions. For this, we offer no specific solutions—the goal is to alert the reader to a few of the potential problems that plague police administrators. As it is now, the right of the individual citizen to have the best possible officer protecting his or her community is rarely an issue.

REFERENCES

Charles, M. (1983). "Contemporary Police Training." *Journal of Police Science and Administration*, 11(3).

Cole, G. (1986). *The American System of Justice*. Monterey, California: Brooks/Cole Publishers.

Deal, A. (1986). *The Pennsylvania State Police: Findings and Recommendations*. A report the the Special Committee to Investigate the Pennsylvania State Police. Harrisburg, PA: Pennsylvania House of Representatives.

McLaughlin, V. (1984). *Police Selection Practices in Large Pennsylvania Municipal Police Departments*. Unpublished Ph.D. dissertation, The Pennsylvania State University.

McLaughlin, V. and R. Bing (1987). "Law Enforcement Selection: A Commentary." *Journal of Police Science and Administration*, 15(4).

Nislow, J. (1988). "How to Find Psychologically Sound Recruits." *Law Enforcement News*, 14.

Smith, B. (1960). *Police Systems in the United States*. New York: Harper and Row.

4

Psychological Testing of Police Candidates

Robin Inwald and
Dennis Jay Kenney

In the stressful, unpredictable world of policing, officers must have the emotional resources to perform a variety of often difficult and taxing duties. They need a certain amount of dominance and assertiveness to enforce the law while, at the same time, restraint and self-control are essential in maintaining the peace. They must be able to tolerate high levels of provocation, ambiguity, boredom, and the ever-present possibility of physical harm. Individual attributes or behaviors such as chronic anxiety, misperception, impulsivity, low assertiveness, and withdrawal can be highly detrimental to both the officer and the police organization's mission.

Despite a widespread awareness of the importance of psychologically fit officers, law enforcement agencies and managers have only recently begun to recognize the usefulness of psychological screening for their officer candidates. In response, during the past decade, many agencies have chosen to go beyond the more traditional methods of officer selection to institute comprehensive programs of psychological testing. Such programs are an effort to better identify those candidates most likely to succeed at police work and most able to cope with the physical and emotional pressures that officers confront. This chapter will describe the current practice and issues surrounding the uses of these psychological tests for law enforcement officers. It will conclude with suggestions regarding their use.

PSYCHOLOGICAL TESTS

Written psychological tests can be cost-effective and are able to provide objective data that can aid in identifying personality characteristics and/ or disorders of applicants. Test results can also be used to generate normative data (information that demonstrates how individuals responded in comparison to other test takers), predictive validity coefficients (indicators of how scores are related to future job performance), and leads for follow-up investigations (such as subsequent interviews and background investigations).

Among the disadvantages of psychological tests are the fact that they are impersonal and may miss critical behaviors by not asking the right questions of the candidates. On the other hand, they are more objective than interviews and can ask more questions of applicants than can be asked in a one- or two-hour interview. Tests can also be "faked good" by candidates who deliberately attempt to conceal characteristics believed to be undesirable. In some instances, psychological tests may erroneously suggest the presence of adjustment disorders in applicants who are unusually candid about their shortcomings. Poor language skills can also adversely affect the validity of written test results. Nonetheless, written tests—both aptitude and personality—are currently being used as the initial step in the evaluation of a candidate's job suitability.

The MMPI

The most commonly used personality test in law enforcement screening is the MMPI (Minnesota Multiphasic Personality Inventory). This test, which consists of 566 true–false items, was developed in the 1930s to measure psychopathology and to aid in the diagnosis of mentally disturbed hospital patients. Since then, it has been widely used with many different populations. Thousands of studies have been completed concerning this test's validity for identifying psychological disturbances and character disorders.

Still, the MMPI is not without its critics. For example, some have questioned why items appear to have little to do with the scales in which they appear, while others are concerned that the test discriminates against racial minorities (Gynther, Lachar, and Dahlstrom, 1978; Hargrave and Berner, 1984). Still, while the research with the police suggests that the MMPI is not sufficiently predictive to warrant using it alone to reject candidates as unsuitable, it continues to be a useful screening tool for identifying applicant psychopathology (Inwald, 1984; Inwald and Shusman, 1984).

The CPI

The CPI (California Psychological Inventory) was developed in the 1950s to measure characteristics of "normal" individuals. Although this widely used test contains many of the same items that appear on the MMPI (there are 178 common items), it is geared less towards identifying psychopathology and more towards identifying social interaction skills and reaction styles. Some experimental scales have been developed that have been demonstrated to be related to police performance (Hogan, 1975; Spielberger, Spaulding, and Vaag, 1981) and the CPI has been shown to be useful in identifying desirable and undesirable characteristics of normal behavior (Hargrave and Berner, 1984).

The IPI

In response to the dissatisfaction and concern expressed by some psychologists about the use of general psychological inventories (such as the MMPI and CPI) in screening police candidates, the Inwald Personality Inventory (IPI) was developed specifically for law enforcement agencies in 1980. The IPI is a 310 true-false item instrument which yields 26 separate scales intended to measure candor, "acting out" behaviors, internalized conflicts and stress symptoms, and interpersonal conflicts. Recent research suggests that the IPI is, in fact, somewhat more accurate than the MMPI in predicting police and correctional officer performance such as subsequent absence, lateness, disciplinary infractions, supervisory ratings, and termination rates. These findings are most likely due to the behavioral nature of the IPI items which include questions relating to past behaviors such as drug and alcohol use, job difficulties, trouble with the law and society, as well as symptoms suggestive of serious psychopathology or emotional adjustment difficulties. One study by Ostrov (1985) found a significant correlation between high scores on the IPI drugs scale and medical tests showing the presence of drugs in the urine of police applicants. Another independent study found differences on IPI scales for officers who stayed on the job versus those who did not (Los Angeles Police Department, 1986). Used in over 500 police agencies, the IPI does appear to be gaining popularity among police psychology practitioners.

Vocational Preference Tests

Much like the personality measures, the vocational preference tests are also objective, cost-effective, and easy to administer. These tests, which focus on an individual's motivation for specific types of work, are also used by some agencies for officer selection, although to a lesser degree. Included among the vocational preference tests are the Strong-Campbell and Guilford-Zimmerman Interest Inventories.

The primary disadvantage of vocational preference tests is that they relate primarily to expressed interest in a particular type of job rather than to a candidate's ability or overall personality "fit" for that job. As such, they may indicate an applicant's *desire* to perform a job, while overlooking his or her *ability* to do so. Nonetheless, it has been suggested that the inclusion of measures designed to assess a candidate's motivation for police work may be valuable in predicting later employment tenure (Pendergrass, 1984).

Projective Tests

Finally, some projective tests, such as the Rorschach, the Draw-A-Person, the House-Tree-Person, and the sentence completion tests, have been used in police selection programs. However, they are difficult to score, their interpretations rely upon the largely subjective judgments of clinicians, and they have not been demonstrated to be either reliable or valid in the research literature.

While useful to clinicians in some contexts, these tests are very difficult to evaluate regarding their ability to predict police officer performance. As such, their use has not been recommended by reviewers of tests for law enforcement screening programs (Hargrave and Berner, 1984; Inwald, 1984; Pendergrass, 1984).

New Test Instruments and Future Research Trends

While most psychological screening programs are geared to identifying "unfit" candidates, few have focused on "positive" qualities in police applicants. This is partially due to the fact that professionals have never been able to agree on the definitions of a "good officer." Yet, some minimum levels of intelligence, social skills, initiative, and self-confidence are most often cited as necessary in order to "get the job done." Standard IQ tests to measure intelligence have not commonly been used in police screening due to the controversy regarding possible racial biases in these tests.

However, a new test of "positive" qualities has recently been introduced that has not shown significant overall differences among law enforcement candidate racial groups in preliminary studies. This test, the Hilson Personnel Profile/Success Quotient (HPP/SQ), is a 150-item behavioral questionnaire that yields an overall "Success Quotient" score by focusing on past actions and experiences (Inwald, 1987).

Five major scales evaluate a history of achievement in school (Achievement History Scale), the presence of social skills (Social Abilities Scale), self-confidence ("Winner's" Image Scale), demonstrated willingness to work diligently at tasks and meet responsibilities (Initiative Scale), and candid responding on the test (Candor Scale). Use of this instrument in the law enforcement field is currently being tested with different officer groups including hostage negotiating teams and officers assigned to specialized units. Profiles of individuals rated by their supervisors as "successful" in various police assignments will be used as guides in the future development of this "positive" test for police screening.

THE PSYCHOLOGICAL INTERVIEW

Clinical interviews generally follow test-scoring procedures and the review of applicant tests by psychologists. Unfortunately, preemployment interviews as they are presently conducted have not been extensively validated or demonstrated to be predictive of police performance (Bartol, 1983). In fact, there is evidence to suggest that interviews conducted by mental health professionals are less valid than written test results and may be useful primarily to build rapport with the candidate. Still, there is significant justification for the inclusion of interviews for all candidates.

Perhaps foremost is the standard ethical practice in the mental health professions that no decisions that may adversely affect an individual's life may be made without a personal interview involving that individual. Indeed, candidates showing elevated scores on the paper-and-pencil instruments may have observable personality disorders. It may also be, however, that some of these candidates—who often come from diverse linguistic and cultural backgrounds—may have tested in the abnormal ranges due to difficulties in understanding the essence of the written questions. On interview, they are found only to have language difficulties and not psychological disturbances.

Additionally, there are occasionally individuals who, at the time of their testing, are undergoing severe and unusual personal problems such as a parent dying, a divorce, or some other external trauma. On the testing day, these candidates may admit to emotional states or attributes that are not characteristic of their general emotional adjustment and are unrelated to their future abilities to handle and cope with the responsibilities of law enforcement. These factors may surface and be more fully understood during an interview and may counter strong negative, and essentially incorrect, evaluations based on test results.

At the other extreme are the "test-wise," yet disturbed individuals who are able successfully to conceal psychological difficulties on virtually any written test battery. These individuals show no elevated test scores, yet may exhibit evidence of psychological disturbances and adjustment difficulties when given a personal interview by a qualified professional.

Therefore, while interviews cannot be expected to identify each case where there may be evidence of a clear hiring risk, the failure to conduct interviews—even with candidates showing no elevated test results—may place a police agency in an unnecessary, potentially costly, and vulnerable position. It is also realistic to expect that most psychologists engaged in clinical practice would testify to the professional need for an interview before evaluating a candidate regarding his or her psychological stability.

ISSUES WITH PSYCHOLOGICAL TESTING

Although the actual number remains unclear, recent estimates suggest that at least 50 percent of the major police agencies in this country now make use of some psychological screening process (Wyatt and Lavorn, 1987). Still, the use of such testing in an effort to ensure that "unsuitable" applicants will not be hired continues to be the subject of much debate. Since psychological testing is an intrusive procedure that must, by definition, look into the private lives and emotional adjustment of job applicants, some have challenged it as an infringement upon the rights and privacy of an applicant. In one such case, where the use of psychological testing of firefighters was questioned, the court ruled that although "a psychological evaluation may intrude on an applicant's privacy," the security of the community, as well as the lives at stake, provide a need for such evaluations (McKenna v. Fargo, 1978). In another challenge, it was ruled that a chief of police could order a psychological evaluation of an officer whose conduct was questionable, because "it is the duty of the police chief to maintain a capable and efficient force" (Conte v. Horcher, 1977). This should not, however, suggest that all psychological screening will automatically be deemed acceptable.

Perhaps the most pressing difficulty arises in trying to define the exact nature of an "unsuitable" applicant in a way that is both legally and professionally defensible. The EEOC's *Uniform Guidelines* attempt to aid employers in making such definitions by adding specifications for selection practices. For example, the guidelines specify that if hiring practices (or definitions of "unsuitable" candidates) affect different sex or ethnic groups differently, then all selection instruments or methods must be validated. In general, judges can be expected to rule in favor of agencies charged with having discriminatory hiring procedures only when those agencies have demonstrated that their screening exams meet professional validity standards and are directly related to job performance. This translates into a practical need to demonstrate that low or poor scores on selection devices that lead to a candidate's being disqualified for a job are actually predictive or poor performance on that job.

This leads to catch–22 number one. Departments may be held responsible (negligent) for hiring individuals they suspect are unsuitable or unstable. However, in order adequately to validate selection devices, administrators must hire candidates whom they know have done poorly on preemployment tests—including psychological tests and interviews. Unfortunately, if research is done only on candidates who were hired because they did well on selection devices, it will do little to help to prove that those who do poorly on tests will also do poorly on the job.

Next comes the difficulty of identifying and defining poor performers on the job. This is catch–22 number two. The process of determining which candidates have performed poorly on the job must be based upon a performance evaluation system developed from a job analysis which, though desired by most administrators and required by governmental guidelines, is nonexistent in many police departments.

Departments have recently been required to do complete job analyses in order to justify the adequacy and thoroughness of performance evaluations of officers. If the criteria used to measure performance are not shown by the department to tap the most relevant aspects of the job, officers may protest formal evaluations of their work as unfair and, perhaps, as discriminatory. However, most departments do not have the funding or personnel that would allow them to do a job analysis that would satisfy professional and government standards. The end result is that there are few departments who have completed job analyses for their officers and even fewer who have developed performance evaluations based on these job analyses.

In addition, the job analyses that have been done usually do not include the psychological characteristics judged necessary for the performance of the various tasks of law enforcement officers. Rather, they focus upon the knowledge, skills, and abilities necessary to perform specific job tasks. And finally, though some departments have attempted to develop job analyses, it is unknown whether data from one department would be appropriate for use in another agency. Thus, much time and money must be spent in order professionally to evaluate on-the-job performance, not to mention the time required for researching the ties between formal evaluations and preemployment psychological screening results.

The last hurdle to be considered here involves the psychological test and procedures themselves. Professional test-usage standards require that before any tests are used for employee selection purposes, they must be validated and normed on the appropriate populations. Yet, since the field of psychological testing in law enforcement is relatively new, there are few tests that have been researched extensively for use in screening officers. Thus, the psychologist in law enforcement agencies runs into catch–22 number three. Psychological tests cannot be made operational in formal psychological screening programs until they are validated and normed. Yet, tests cannot be validated and normed until they are used with law enforcement officers. Of course, one solution might be to test officers already on the job, obtain performance data on them, and examine how the tests relate to their relative level of performance. Unfortunately, however, most agencies and officers are reluctant to participate in such research due to fears that any negative results might end up being used against them. Even if this type of research was to be sanctioned by the courts, it would take many years and much funding before results would become available.

RECOMMENDATIONS FOR THE FUTURE

While the standards calling for fully validated tests, complete job analyses, and defensible performance evaluations may be impossible to meet at the present time, adopting the spirit in which these guidelines were intended may be a more accessible goal. Following are a few suggestions for the development of psychological testing in law enforcement agencies that may be of assistance in reaching this goal.

1. Use psychological screening as only one component of the overall selection process. Avoid using psychological results as the sole reason for rejecting a candidate. Instead, find evidence in the candidate's background that supports a negative psychological recommendation.
2. Provide psychological interviews for all candidates who are given written psychological tests.
3. Build in a validation project where psychological test results and ratings can be evaluated in-house to determine their usefulness to the agency. Include staff or advisors qualified to evaluate the research design for its appropriateness and ease of implementation in the department.
4. Select as many tests, evaluations, and procedures as possible, so that different measures can verify significant findings. Use tests where there is at least some research suggesting they may be validly used for screening law enforcement officers. Also, avoid subjective psychological instruments and nonspecific evaluation ratings.
5. Steer clear of adopting arbitrary cutoff scores on psychological tests or scales unless there is clear evidence that such cutoff scores are valid and have been cross-validated in documented research studies in the agency where they will be used.
6. Document all procedures and selection practices.

REFERENCES

Bartol, C. (1983). *Psychology and American Law*. Belmont: Wadsworth.
Equal Employment Opportunity Commission (1979). *Standards For Educational*

and Psychological Tests. Washington, D.C.: American Psychological Association.

Gynther, M.; D. Lachar; and G. Dahlstrom (1978). "Are Special Norms for Minorities Needed? Development of an MMPI F Scale for Blacks." *Journal of Consulting and Clinical Psychology*, 46:1403.

Hargrave, G. and J. Berner (1984). *POST Psychological Screening Manual*. Sacramento: California Commission on Peace Officer Standards and Training.

Hogan, R. (1975). "Personality Characteristics of Highly Rated Policemen." *Personnel Psychology*, 24.

Inwald, R. (1984). "Law Enforcement Officers Screening: A Description of One Pre-Employment Psychological Testing Program." Proceedings of the National Symposium on Police Psychological Services, FBI Academy, Quantico.

Inwald, R. (1985). "Administrative, Legal, and Ethical Practices in the Psychological Testing of Law Enforcement Officers." *Journal of Criminal Justice*, 13:367–372.

————. (1987). "Use of Psychologists for Selecting and Training Police." *Police Managerial Use of Psychology and Psychologists*, H. More and P. Unsinger, ed. Springfield, IL: Charles Thomas Publishers.

Inwald, R. and E. Shusman (1984). "The IPI and MMPI as Predictors of Academy Performance for Police Recruits." *Journal of Police Science and Administration*, 12:1.

Ostrov, E. (1985). "The IPI 'Drug' Scale and the Prediction of Drug Use in Police Applicants." Paper presented at the American Psychological Association meeting.

Pendergrass, V. (1984). *Psychological Assessment of Police for Entry-Level Selection*. Washington, D.C.: American Federation of Police.

Solotoff, L. (1983). "Merit Selection Procedures: Strategy and the Law." Paper presented at State Personnel Director's Conferences.

Spielberger, C.; H. Spaulding; and P. Vagg (1981). *Professional Manual for the Florida Police Standards Psychological Test Battery*. Tampa: Human Resources Institute.

Wyatt, B. and C. Lavorn (1987). "A National Survey of the Extent and Nature of Psychological Services in Police Departments." Paper presented at the 1987 Annual Meeting of the Academy of Criminal Justice Sciences.

II

The Traditional Methods of Policing

5

The Kansas City Preventive Patrol Experiment

George L. Kelling, Antony Michael Pate,
Duane Dieckman, and
Charles E. Brown

Ever since the creation of a patrolling force in 13th-century Hangchow, preventive patrol by uniformed personnel has been a primary function of policing. In 20th-century America, about $2 billion is spent each year for the maintenance and operation of uniformed and often superbly equipped patrol forces. Police themselves, the general public, and elected officials have always believed that the presence or potential presence of police officers on patrol severely inhibits criminal activity.

One of the principal police spokesmen for this view was the late O. W. Wilson, former chief of the Chicago Police Department and a prominent academic theorist on police issues. As Wilson once put it, "Patrol is an indispensable service that plays a leading role in the accomplishment of the police purpose. It is the only form of police service that directly attempts to eliminate opportunity for misconduct. . . . " Wilson believed that by creating the impression of police omnipresence, patrol convinced most potential offenders that opportunities for successful misconduct did not exist. To the present day, Wilson's has been the prevailing view. While modern technology, through the creation of new methods of transportation, surveillance, and communications, has added vastly to the tools of patrol, and while there have been refinements in patrol strategies based upon advanced probability formulas and other computerized methods, the general principle has remained the same. To-

From "The Kansas City Preventive Patrol Experiment—A Technical Report," (1974). Reprinted with permission of the Police Foundation.

day's police recruits, like virtually all those before them, learn from both teacher and textbook that patrol is the "backbone" of police work.

No less than the police themselves, the general public has been convinced that routine preventive patrol is an essential element of effective policing. As the International City Management Association has pointed out, "for the greatest number of persons, deterrence through ever-present police patrol, coupled with the prospect of speedy police action once a report is received, appears important to crime control." Thus, in the face of spiraling crime rates, the most common answer urged by public officials and citizens alike has been to increase patrol forces and get more police officers "on the street." The assumption is that increased displays of police presence are vitally necessary in the face on increased criminal activity. Recently, citizens in troubled neighborhoods have themselves resorted to civilian versions of patrol.

Challenges to preconceptions about the value of preventive police patrol were exceedingly rare until recent years. When researcher Bruce Smith, writing about patrol in 1930, noted that its effectiveness "lacks scientific demonstration," few paid serious attention.

Beginning in 1962, however, challenges to commonly held ideas about patrol began to proliferate. As reported crime began to increase dramatically, as awareness of unreported crime became more common, and as spending for police activities grew substantially, criminologists and others began questioning the relationship between patrol and crime. From this questioning a body of literature has emerged.

Much of this literature is necessarily exploratory. Earlier researchers were faced with the problem of obtaining sufficient and correct data, and then devising methodologies to interpret the data. The problems were considerable, and remain so.

Another problem facing earlier investigators was the natural reluctance of most police departments to create the necessary experimental conditions through which definitive answers concerning the worth of patrol could be obtained. Assigned the jobs of protecting society from crime, of apprehending criminals, and of carrying out numerous other services such as traffic control, emergency help in accidents and disasters, and supervision of public gatherings, police departments have been apprehensive about interrupting their customary duties to experiment with strategies or to assist in the task of evaluation.

It was in this context that the Kansas City, Missouri Police Department, under a grant from the Police Foundation, undertook in 1972 the most comprehensive experiment ever conducted to analyze the effectiveness of routine preventive patrol.

From the outset the department and the Police Foundation evaluation team agreed that the project design would be as rigorously experimental as possible, and that while Kansas City Police Department data would be used, as wide a data base as possible, including data from external measurements, would be generated. It was further agreed that the experiment would be monitored by both department and foundation representatives to insure maintenance of experimental conditions. Under the agreement between the department and the foundation, the department committed itself to an eight-month experiment provided that reported crime did not reach "unacceptable" limits within the experimental area. If no major problems developed, the experiment would continue an additional four months.

The experiment is described in detail later in this summary. Briefly, it involved variations in the level of routine preventive patrol within 15 Kansas City police beats. These beats were randomly divided into three groups. In five "reactive" beats, routine preventive patrol was eliminated and officers were instructed to respond only to calls for service. In five "control" beats, routine preventive patrol was maintained at its usual level of one car per beat. In the remaining five "proactive" beats, routine preventive patrol was intensified by two to three times its usual level through the assignment of additional patrol cars and through the frequent presence of cars from the "reactive" beats.

For the purpose of measurement, a number of hypotheses were developed, of which the following were ultimately addressed:

1. Crime, as reflected by victimization surveys and reported crime data, would not vary by type of patrol;

2. Citizen perception of police service would not vary by type of patrol;

3. Citizen fear and behavior as a result of fear would not vary by type of patrol;

4. Police response time and citizen satisfaction with response time would vary by experimental area; and

5. Traffic accidents would increase in reactive beats.

The immediate issue under analysis in the preventive patrol experiment was routine preventive patrol and its impact on crime and the community. But a much larger policy issue was implied: whether urban police departments can establish and maintain experimental conditions, and whether such departments can, for such experimentation, infringe upon that segment of time usually committed to routine preventive patrol. Both questions were answered in the affirmative, and in this respect the preventive patrol experiment represents a crucial first step, but just one in a series of such steps toward defining and clarifying the police function in modern society.

DESCRIPTION OF THE PREVENTIVE PATROL EXPERIMENT

The impetus for an experiment in preventive patrol came from within the Kansas City Police Department in 1971. While this may be surprising to some, the fact is that by that year the Kansas City department had already experienced more than a decade of innovation and improvement in its operations and working climate and had gained a reputation as one of the nation's more progressive police departments.

Under Chief Clarence M. Kelley, the department had achieved a high degree of technological sophistication, was receptive to experimentation and change, and was peppered with young, progressive, and professional officers. Short- and long-range planning had become institutionalized, and constructive debates over methods, procedures, and approaches to police work were commonplace. By 1972, this department of approximately 1,300 officers in a city of just over half a million—part of a metropolitan complex of 1.3 million—was open to new ideas and recommendations, and enjoyed the confidence of the people it served.

As part of its continuing internal discussions of policing, the department in October of 1971 established a task force of patrol officers and supervisors in each of its three patrol divisions (South, Central, and Northeast), as well as in its special operations division (helicopter, traffic, tactical, etc.). The decision to establish these task forces was based on the beliefs that the ability to make competent planning decisions existed at all levels within the department and that if institutional change was to gain acceptance, those affected by it should have a voice in planning and implementation.

The job of each task force was to isolate the critical problems facing its division and propose methods to attack those problems. All four task forces did so. The South Patrol Division Task Force identified five problem areas where greater police attention was deemed vital: burglaries, juvenile offenders, citizen fear, public education about the police role, and police-community relations.

Like the other task forces, the South task force was confronted next with developing workable remedial strategies. And here the task force met with what at first seemed an insurmountable barrier. It was evident that concentration by the South Patrol Division on the five problem areas would cut deeply into the time spent by its officers on preventive patrol. At this point a significant thing happened. Some of the members of the South task force questioned whether routine preventive patrol was effective, what police officers did while on preventive patrol duty, and what effect police visibility had on the community's feelings of security.

Out of these discussions came the proposal to conduct an experiment that would test the true impact of routine preventive patrol. The Police Foundation agreed to fund the experiment's evaluation.

As would be expected, considerable controversy surrounded the experiment, the central question being whether long-range benefits outweighed short-term risks. The principal short-term risk was seen as the possibility that crime would increase drastically in the reactive beats; some officers felt the experiment would be tampering with citizens' lives and property.

The police officers expressing such reservations were no different from their counterparts in other departments. They tended to view patrol as one of the most important functions of policing, and in terms of time allocated, they felt that preventive patrol ranked on a par with investigating crimes and rendering assistance in emergencies. While some admitted that preventive patrol was probably less effective in preventing crime and more productive in enhancing citizen feelings of security, others insisted that the activities involved in preventive patrol (car, pedestrian, and building checks) were instrumental in the capture of criminals and, through the police visibility associated with such activities, in the deterrence of crime. While there were ambiguities in these attitudes toward patrol and its effectiveness, all agreed it was primary police function.

Within the South Patrol Division's 24-beat area, nine beats were eliminated from consideration and unrepresentative of the city's socioeconomic composition. The remaining 15-beat, 32-square mile experimental area encompassed a commercial–residential mixture, with a 1970 resident population of 148,395 persons and a density of 4,542 persons per square mile (significantly greater than that for Kansas City as a whole). Racially, the beats within this area ranged from 78 percent black to 99 percent white. Median family income of residents ranged from a low of $7,320 for one beat to a high of $15,964 for another. On the average, residents of the experimental area tended to have been in their homes from 6.6 to 10.9 years.

Police officers assigned to the experimental area were those who had been patrolling it prior to the experiment, and tended to be white, relatively young, and somewhat new to the police department. In a sample of 101 officers in the experimental area taken across all three shifts, 9.9 percent of the officers were black, the average age of the officers was 27 years, and average time on the force was 3.2 years.

The 15 beats in the experimental area were computer-matched on the basis of crime data, number of calls for service, ethnic composition, median income, and transiency of population into five groups of three each. Within each group, one beat was designated reactive, one control, and one proactive. In the five reactive beats, there was no preventive patrol as such. Police vehicles assigned these beats entered them only in response to calls for service. Their noncommitted time (when not answering calls) was spent patrolling the boundaries of the reactive beats or patrolling in adjacent proactive beats. While police availability was closely maintained, police visibility was, in effect, withdrawn (except when police vehicles were seen while answering calls for service).

In the five control beats, the usual level of patrol was maintained at one car per beat. In the five proactive beats, the department increased police patrol visibility by two to three times its usual level both by the assignment of marked police vehicles to these beats and the presence of units from adjacent reactive beats.

Other than the restrictions placed upon officers in reactive beats (respond only to calls for service and patrol only the perimeter of the beat or in an adjacent proactive beat), no special instructions were given to police officers in the experimental areas. Officers in control and proactive beats were to conduct preventive patrol as they normally would.

It should be noted, however, that the geographical distribution of beats avoided clustering reactive beats together or at an unacceptable distance from proactive beats. Such clustering could have resulted in lowered response time in the reactive beats.

It should also be noted that patrol modification in the reactive and proactive beats involved only routine preventive patrol. Specialized units, such as tactical, helicopter, and K–9, operated as usual in these beats but at a level consistent with the activity level established the preceding year. This level was chosen to prevent infringement of these specialized units upon experimental results.

Finally it should be noted that to minimize any possible risk through the elimination of routine preventive patrol in the reactive beats, crime rate data were monitored on a weekly basis. It was agreed that if a noticeable increase in crime occurred within a reactive beat, the experiment would be suspended. This situation, however, never materialized.

While the Kansas City experiment began on July 19, 1972, both department and Police Foundation monitors recognized by mid-August that experimental conditions were not being maintained, and that several problems had arisen. Chief Kelley then saw to it that these problems were rectified during a suspension of the experiment.

One problem was manpower, which in the South Patrol Division had fallen to a dangerously low level for experimental purposes. To correct this problem additional police officers were assigned to the division and an adequate manpower level restored. A second problem involved violations of the project guidelines. Additional training sessions were held, and administrative emphasis brought to bear to ensure adherence to the guidelines. A third problem was boredom among officers assigned to reactive beats. To counter this, the guidelines were modified to allow an increased level of activity by reactive assigned officers in proactive beats. The revisions emphasized that an officer could take whatever action was deemed necessary, regardless of location, should a criminal incident be observed. The revised guidelines also stressed adherence to the spirit of the project rather than to unalterable rules.

On October 1, 1972, the experiment resumed. It continued successfully for 12 months, ending on September 30, 1973. Findings were produced in terms of the effect of experimental conditions on five categories of crimes traditionally considered to be deterrable through preventive patrol (burglary, auto theft, larceny—theft of auto accessories, robbery, and vandalism) and on five other crime categories (including rape, assault, and other larcenies). Additional findings concerned the effect of experimental conditions on citizen feelings of security and satisfaction with police service, on the amount and types of anticrime protective measures taken by citizens and businessmen, on police response time and citizen satisfaction with response time, and on injury/fatality and non-injury traffic accidents. The experiment also produced data concerning police activities during tours of duty, and police officer attitudes toward preventive patrol.

DATA SOURCES

In measuring the effects of routine preventive patrol, it was decided to collect as wide a variety of data from as many diverse sources as possible. By so doing, it was felt that overwhelming evidence could be presented to prove or disprove the experimental hypotheses.

To measure the effects of the experimental conditions on crime, a victimization survey, departmental reported crime, departmental arrest data, and a survey of businesses were used. While reported crime has traditionally been considered the most important indicator of police effectiveness, the accuracy of both reported crime and arrest data as indicators of crime and police effectiveness has come under scrutiny in recent years. Both types of data are subject to wide degrees of conscious and unconscious manipulation, and to distortion and misrepresentation. Because of these, a criminal victimization survey was used as an additional source of data.

To measure the impact of experimental conditions on community attitudes and fear, attitudinal surveys of both households and businesses (in conjunction with the victimization surveys) and a survey of those citizens experiencing direct encounters with the police were administered. Estimates of citizen satisfaction with police services were also recorded by participant observers.

Because many of these sources were used to monitor the degree to which experimental conditions were maintained or to identify unanticipated consequences of the experiment, only findings derived from the following data sources are presented in this report.

Community Survey

The community survey, which measured community victimization, attitudes, and fear, was taken on a before-and-after basis. A sample of 1,200 households in the experimental area (approximately 80 per beat) was randomly selected and interviewed in September of 1972. In September of 1973, 1,200 households were again surveyed, approximately 600 chosen from the same population as the 1972 survey (for a repeated sample) and 600 chosen randomly from the experimental area (for a non-repeated sample). Since 11 cases had to be excluded because of missing data, the 1973 sample totalled 1,189.

Commercial Survey

The commercial survey involved interviews conducted both in 1972 and 1973 with a random sample of 110 businesses in the experimental area to measure victimization rates and businessmen's perceptions of and satisfaction with police services.

Encounter Survey (Both Citizen and Participant Observers)

Because household surveys tend to interview relatively few citizens who have experienced actual contact with the police, citizens in the three experimental areas who experienced direct encounters with police officers were interviewed. Although three survey instruments were developed (one to elicit the response of the citizens, a second for the police officers, and a third for the observers riding with the officers) only the observer and citizen responses were analyzed. Identical questions were used as often as possible. The survey was conducted over a four-month period (July through October, 1973). Interviewed were 331 citizens who were involved in either an officer-initiated incident (car check, pedestrian check, or a traffic violation) or citizen-initiated incident (one in which the citizen called for police service: burglary, robbery, larceny, assault, etc.).

Participant Observer Transaction Recordings

While the community encounter survey focused on the location of the police-citizen contact, the observer transaction recordings focused on police-citizen interactions in terms of the assignment of the officer involved (reactive, control, or proactive beats). These data were obtained by observers while riding with officers assigned to the experimental area, and involved observer estimates of citizen satisfaction as a result of direct contact with the police. Observations covered all three watches in all 15 beats. As a result, 997 incidents of police-citizen transactions were systematically recorded.

Reported Crime

Monthly totals for reported crime by beat over the October 1968 through September 1972 (preexperimental) period and over the October 1972 through September 1973 (experimental) period were retrieved from departmental records. Time-series analyses were then performed on these data to produce the findings.

Traffic Data

Two categories of traffic accidents were monitored: non-injury and injury/fatality. Monitoring was maintained over two time periods, October 1970 through September 1972 for the preexperimental period, and October 1972 through September 1973 for the experimental period.

Arrest Data

Arrest data by month and beat for the experimental year and the three preceding years were obtained from department records.

Response Time Survey

Police response time in the experimental area was recorded between May and September 1973 through the use of a response-time survey completed by the participant observers and those citizens who had called the police for service. In measuring the time taken by the police in responding to calls, emphasis was placed on field response time (i.e., the amount of time occurring between the time a police unit on the street received a call from the dispatcher and the time when that unit contacted the citizen involved). In measuring citizen satisfaction with response time, the entire range of time required for the police to answer a call was considered (i.e., including time spent talking with the police department operator, police dispatcher, plus field response time).

Spillover Effect

One major concern in an experiment of this type is the so-called spillover or displacement theory: that as crime decreases in one area due to increased police presence, it will increase in other, usually contiguous, areas. This would mean that the effect of the experiment within the experimental area would be offset by countereffects in other areas. To test this, various correlations between contiguous beats were calculated and analyzed. Except for auto theft, there were no noticeable alterations in the correlations of crime levels. These results, combined with an examination of the actual monthly crime figures, tend to indicate that, in general, there was *no* spillover effect.

EXPERIMENTAL FINDINGS

The essential finding of the preventive patrol experiment is that decreasing or increasing routing preventive patrol within the range tested in this experiment had *no* effect on crime, citizen fear of crime, community attitudes toward the police on the delivery of police service, police response time, or traffic accidents. Given the large amount of data collected and the extremely diverse sources used, the evidence is overwhelming. Of the 648 comparisons made to produce the 13 major findings that follow, statistical significance occurred only 40 times between pairs, or in approximately 6 percent of the total. Of these 40, the change was greater 15 times in reactive beats, 19 times in control beats, and 6 times in proactive beats.

Finding 1: Victimization

The Victimization Survey found no statistically significant differences in crime in any of the 69 comparisons made between reactive, control, and proactive beats.

This finding would be expected for such categories as rape, homicide, and common or aggravated assault. For one thing, these are typically impulsive crimes, usually taking place between persons known to each other. Furthermore, they most often take place inside a building, out of sight of an officer on routine preventive patrol. The spontaneity and lack of high visibility of these crimes therefore make it unlikely that they would be much affected by variations in the level of preventive patrol.

Given traditional beliefs about patrol, however, it is surprising that statistically significant differences did not occur in such crimes as commercial burglaries, auto theft, and robberies.

Nonetheless, as measured by the victimization survey, these crimes were not significantly affected by changes in the level of routine preventive patrol.

Finding 2: Departmental Reported Crime

Departmental reported crimes showed only one statistically significant difference among 51 comparisons drawn between reactive, control, and proactive beats.

Statistical significance occurred only in the category of "Other Sex Crimes." This category, separate from "Rape," includes such offenses as molestation and exhibitionism. Since this category is not traditionally considered to be responsive to routine preventive patrol, however, it appears likely that this instance of significance was a statistically random occurrence.

Finding 3: Rates of Reporting Crime

Crimes citizens and businessmen said they reported to the police showed statistically significant differences between reactive, control, and proactive beats in only five of 48 comparisons, and these differences showed no consistent pattern.

Of the five instances of statistical significance, three involved vandalism and two residence burglary. But where statistical significance was found, no consistent pattern emerged. On two occasions the change was greater in the control beats, on two occasions greater in the proactive beats, and once it was greater in the reactive beats. Given the low number of statistically significant findings combined with a lack of consistent direction, the conclusion is that rates of reporting crimes by businessmen and citizens were unaffected by the experimental changes in levels of patrol.

Finding 4: Arrest Patterns

Police arrests showed no statistically significant differences in the 27 comparisons made between reactive, control and proactive beats.

While arrest totals for 16 categories of crime were determined, it will be noted that in seven categories—common assault, larceny-purse snatch, homicide, non-residence burglary, auto theft, larceny-auto accessory, and larceny-bicycle—either the number of arrests was too small to allow for statistical analysis, or the preexperimental pattern of arrests was so distorted that statistical significance could not be determined. On the basis of the comparisons that could be made, however, the conclusion is that arrest rates were not significantly affected by changes in the level of patrol.

Finding 5: Citizen Fear of Crime

Citizen fear of crime was not significantly affected by changes in the level of routing preventive patrol.

In the Community Survey, citizen estimates of neighborhood safety and perceptions of violent crime were obtained. Citizens were then asked what they thought the probability was that they might be involved in various types of crime, including robbery, assault, rape, burglary, and auto theft.

Of the 60 comparisons made between experimental areas, statistical significance was found in only five cases. Three involved the probability of being raped, one the probability of being robbed, and one the probability of being assaulted. The change in the level of fear was greater in reactive beats four times and greater in proactive beats once.

Yet when statistical significance is found, the patterns are inconsistent. For example, all cases in which the change in the reactive beats are significantly higher than in other beats are found in the repeated sample. These findings are not confirmed by the non-repeated sample, however, The one area in which control registered the higher change occurs in the non-repeated sample; but this is not confirmed by the repeated sample.

The findings thus lead to the conclusion that citizen fear is *not* affected by differences in level of routine patrol.

Finding 6: Protective Measures (Citizens)

Protective and security measures taken by citizens against the possibility of being involved in crime were not significantly affected by variations in the level of routine preventive patrol.

The questions asked of citizens in the Community Survey on this subject dealt with the installation of such devices as bars, alarms, locks, and lighting, the keeping of various types of weapons or dogs for protection, and the taking of certain actions, such as staying inside, as preventive measures.

Here, 84 comparisons were made between experimental areas, with statistical significance occurring 11 times. The significance occurred most often (6 times) in those beats where preventive patrol had not changed, that is, in control beats. The change in the reactive beats showed significance three times, and in the proactive beats twice. There is no apparent explanation for the fact that the use of protective measures supposedly increased in the control beats relative to the other two conditions. For the most part, the findings are inconsistent and occur either in the non-repeated sample or the repeated sample but never uniformly in both.

Thus, as measured by the use of protective and security measures, experimental preventive patrol conditions did not significantly affect citizen fear of crime.

Finding 7: Protective Measures (Businesses)

Protective and security measures taken by businesses in the experimental area to protect offices or other places of business did not show significant differences due to changes in the level of routine preventive patrol.

In the Commercial Survey, businessmen were asked such questions as whether they had installed alarm systems or reinforcing devices such as bars over windows, whether they had hired guards, or whether they kept watchdogs or firearms in their places of business.

All told, 21 comparisons were made and statistical significance was found once, where the change in the control beats was the greater as compared with the reactive beats.

Because this was a telephone survey, however, some problems with the findings were evident. Briefly, some businessmen were reluctant to talk about protective measures over the phone to persons unknown to them.

The conclusion remains, however, that preventive patrol variations seem to have little effect on fear of crime as indicated by protective measures taken by commercial establishments.

Finding 8: Citizen Attitudes Toward Police

Citizen attitudes toward police were not significantly affected by alterations in the level of preventive patrol.

A large number of questions in the Community Survey were designed to measure citizen attitudes toward the police. As a result, more comparisons were made here than in other cases and more instances of statistical significance were found. Altogether, 111 comparisons were made and statistical significance occurred 16 times. Items with significant differences included the need for more police officers in the city, the reputation of police officers, citizen's respect for police, police effectiveness, harassment, and change in neighborhood police officers.

Of the 16 instances of significance, the change in reactive beats was greater five times, in control beats ten times, and in proactive beats once, demonstrating no consistent pattern of statistical significance. The indication is that there was little correlation between level of patrol and citizen attitudes.

Finding 9: Businessmen's Attitudes Toward Police

Businessmen's attitudes toward police were not significantly affected by changes in the level of routine preventive patrol.

Like citizens in the Community Survey, businessmen in the Commercial Survey were asked about their attitudes toward police. Some of the questions in the Commercial Survey were similar to those in the Community Survey and some specifically selected with regard to businessmen's interests.

In all, 48 comparisons were made to measure differences in businessmen's attitudes, but no statistically significant differences were found or even approached. The clear indication here is that variations in the level of preventive patrol have no effect on businessmen's attitudes.

Finding 10: Police–Citizen Encounters

Citizen attitudes toward police officers encountered through the initiative of either the citizen or the officer were not significantly affected by changes in patrol level.

Citizen attitudes were measured by both questions asked of citizens themselves and observations of trained observers. Citizens and observers alike were asked about such items as response time, characteristics of the encounter, the attitude and demeanor of the officers in the encounter, and citizen satisfaction. Observers in officer initiated encounters also recorded things not likely to be noted by citizens, including the number of officers and police vehicles present.

Including both citizen-initiated and officer-initiated encounters, a total of 63 comparisons were made and statistically significant differences were found.

Finding 11: Police–Citizen Transactions

The behavior of police officers toward citizens was not significantly affected by the officers' assignment to a reactive, control, or proactive beat.

The finding is distinct from the previous finding in that the focus here is upon the police-citizen interaction in terms of the beat assignment of the officers rather than on the location of the contact. (Many police contacts with citizens take place outside of the officer's beat.) Data were recorded by participant observers riding with the officers.

In all, 18 comparisons were made between experimental areas, and no statistically significant differences were found.

Finding 12: Response Time

The amount of time taken by police in answering calls for service was not significantly affected by variations in the level of routine preventive patrol.

To obtain this finding, data were gathered on such matters as distance from police car to scene of incident, mean time from receipt of calls to start of call, mean time from receipt of call to arrival at scene, and observer's estimate of patrol car speed. Citizens estimates of time and satisfaction were also measured.

In the area of response time, a total of 42 comparisons were made between patrol conditions. Statistical significance occurred only twice: in the number of officers present at the scene of incidents in the reactive beats. The reason for this is unclear, but it can be theorized that police officers were exhibiting their concern for the safety of fellow officers and citizens in reactive beats.

While variations in the level of patrol did not significantly affect police response time, the Kansas City findings suggest that more research is necessary. It appears that response time is not only the result of rate of speed and distance, but also reflects the attitude of the officers involved and possibly other variables not investigated in this study.

Finding 13: Traffic Accidents

Variations in the level of routine preventive patrol had no significant effect upon traffic accidents.

A total of six comparisons were made in this area, with statistical significance not occurring in any.

SUMMARY AND CONCLUSIONS: EXPERIMENTAL FINDINGS

Of the 648 comparisons used to produce the major findings of the preventive patrol experiment, statistical significance between pairs occurred 40 times, representing approximately 6 percent of the total. Of these 40 findings, the change in the reactive beats was greater 15 times, in the control beats 19 times, and in the proactive beats 6 times. Given the large amount of data collected and the extremely diverse sources used, the overwhelming evidence is that decreasing or increasing routine preventive patrol within the range tested in this experiment had no effect on crime, citizen fear of crime, community attitudes toward the police on the delivery of police service, police response time or traffic accidents.

6 ———————————————————————

The Police on Patrol

Gary W. Cordner

Today, ordinary routine patrol continues to serve, as it seemingly always has, as the backbone of policing, despite the discouraging findings of the Kansas City patrol experiment (Kelling et al., 1974) and the PERF study of rapid police response to reported crimes (Spelman and Brown, 1981); despite the development of such new strategies as directed patrol (Cawley and Miron, 1977) and differential responses to calls for service (Farmer, 1981); and despite such radical innovations as community-oriented (Goldstein, 1987) and problem-oriented (Eck and Spelman, 1987) policing. Most citizen requests for police service continue to be handled, at least initially, by patrol officers. Most arrests are made by patrol officers. In nearly all police departments, more personnel are assigned to the patrol function than to any other function.

What is patrol work? What kinds of incidents are handled by patrol officers? How do patrol officers spend their time? The aim of this chapter is to answer these questions, but the reader must first be made aware of some very serious limitations on any such attempt. There are approximately 15,000 police departments in the United States alone, and *every one* is to some extent unique. Not only are the police departments of New York City (with well over 30,000 employees) and Goldsboro, Maryland (with one employee) different—agencies of similar size in the same state, such as the Lexington/Fayette County and Jefferson County departments in Kentucky, are likely to differ in workload, personnel, style, and philosophy. Thus, generalizations about the nature of patrol work derived from studies in a few jurisdictions may or may not accurately portray patrol work elsewhere. Moreover, no national averages can be cited, since there is no systematic national collection of any police administrative statistics other than reported crime.

A second fundamental problem impedes any effort to validly describe patrol work. In addition to variations among police departments, *every patrol officer* behaves differently. Neither police training nor police supervision succeeds in creating uniformity in police behavior. In fact, the autonomy and discretion granted patrol officers, together with the low visibility of most patrol work, create a situation closer to anarchy than to uniformity in most police departments. Within the same department it is common to find some patrol officers who write no traffic tickets while others do little else; some officers who drive their patrol cars continuously while others remain parked for hours on end; and some officers who nearly always make arrests in public disturbance situations while others never make such arrests. Regardless of whether this individual variation in police behavior results in good or bad police service, it stands in the way of developing an authoritative description of patrol work.

In spite of these severe problems, it is possible to make some cautious generalizations about police patrol work, thanks to a number of studies of incoming calls to police departments, calls assigned to patrol officers, police time utilization, and police encounters with citizens. As will be shown, the image of patrol work provided by these studies has changed over the past 20 years, with more recent studies reaffirming the crime-related and law enforcement aspects of police patrol work.

INCOMING CALLS TO POLICE DEPARTMENTS

Calls coming in to police departments are among the readiest indicators of patrol workload. The nature of these calls reveals the kinds of problems for which citizens request police assistance. Data on these calls can usually be retrieved from telephone logs or from recordings of conversations between citizen callers and police operators.

Several of the most important early studies of patrol work relied on incoming calls data. Cumming et al. (1965) studied 801 calls to a metropolitan police department over an 82-hour period; Bercal (1970) examined over one million calls to the Detroit and St. Louis police departments; Reiss (1971) reviewed all calls to the Chicago Police Department over a 28-day period; and Lilly (1978) analyzed 18,000 calls to the police in Newport, Kentucky. The findings of these studies naturally varied, in part because they used different categories and definitions to classify calls. In general, though, the most consistent finding was that the portion of all calls coming into the police that pertained directly to law enforcement or crime was small. In Detroit, for example, Bercal found that only 16 percent of calls pertained to Part I or Part II crimes; in Chicago, Reiss classified 17 percent of calls as crime-related.

These studies found that many of the calls to police departments were requests for information, requests for services, and reports of disputes and disturbances. Lilly found that 60 percent of all calls were information requests; Bercal found that 36 percent of calls in Detroit and 21 percent in St. Louis were handled over the telephone without dispatching a patrol unit; Cumming et al. found 25 percent handled without sending a patrol car. Citizen demand for police services was discouraged to encompass a much wider range of problems than just crime.

The primary difficulty with these studies is that they reveal something about police telephone operator workload, but not necessarily much about *patrol officer* workload. It is useful to know that only 16 percent of incoming calls to the Detroit Police Department pertained to Part I or Part II crimes, but it does not directly follow that only 16 percent of patrol officer workload is crime-related, as so many have mistakenly concluded. A sizeable portion of calls coming into a police department are information requests that are handled without dispatching a patrol unit. When these calls are deleted, the remaining calls actually assigned to patrol units provide a better indication of the nature of patrol work-load.

CALLS RADIOED TO PATROL OFFICERS

Wilson's (1968) analysis of a sample of 312 calls radioed to patrol units in Syracuse, New York during one week in 1966 is unfortunately the most commonly cited study of this type (see *Report to the Nation on Crime and Justice*, 2nd Edition, 1988 for an example of the continuing impact of Wilson's study). Only 10 percent of the calls were classified as law enforcement, while 38 percent were service, 30 percent were order maintenance, and 22 percent were information gathering.

This study, which has repeatedly been cited to demonstrate that police work is mainly a matter of providing services and maintaining order, illustrates the dramatic effect of definitions and classifications schemes on the description of patrol work that results. In the analysis, taking crime reports was categorized as information gathering; investigating traffic accidents was considered a service task; and assaults were labelled order maintenance. Another researcher could just as legitimately have placed crime reports, traffic accidents, and assaults within the law enforcement category, greatly altering the final distribution of calls. So much of police work is ambiguous and multifaceted that it is extremely difficult to devise clear and reliable classification schemes.

Matters of definition aside, Bercal's (1970) analysis of a sample of 200,000 + calls dispatched to patrol in Detroit and St. Louis is more persuasive than Wilson's analysis of 312 calls in Syracuse. Bercal found the following distributions among his categories:

	Detroit	St. Louis
Predatory and Illegal Service Crimes (crimes, prowlers, alarms, recovery of property)	38.7%	51.0%
Public Disorder (family trouble, parking, missing person)	34.8%	27.2%
Crimes of Negligence (accidents, vehicles)	12.0%	9.6%
Service (health, safety)	14.5%	12.2%

More recent studies have yielded figures similar to these. In San Diego (Boydstun et al., 1977) 43 percent of calls radioed to patrol pertained to crime, 30 percent to peacekeeping, 10 percent each to traffic and to medical emergencies, and 7 percent to miscellaneous problems. In Wilmington, Delaware (Tien et al., 1978) 57 percent of dispatched calls dealt with crime, 14 percent with traffic, 8 percent with alarms, 3 percent with medical problems, and 18 percent with miscellaneous matters. In Minneapolis (Sherman, 1987) 32 percent of calls were classified as conflict management, 28 percent as property crime, 19 percent as traffic problems, 13 percent as service, 5 percent as miscellaneous, and 2 percent as stranger-to-stranger violent crime. The author of this 1987 Minneapolis study of 321,000 calls concluded that the majority of citizen requests handled by patrol pertained either to crime or to potential violence.

These studies demonstrate two points very clearly: that a much greater portion of calls handled by patrol officers are crime-related than the earlier studies suggested; and that sizeable portions of patrol workload are also accounted for by order maintenance, traffic, and service responsibilities. It is important to realize, however, that to this point we have only considered one aspect of patrol workload, namely, calls dispatched. Patrol officers also perform self-initiated activities that must be incorporated into any analysis of the nature of patrol work.

TOTAL PATROL ACTIVITY

Determining total patrol activity is much more difficult than analyzing calls radioed to patrol. The least satisfactory approach to gathering data on total activity is to rely on dispatch records; these data include only the self-initiated activity about which patrol officers *choose* to notify dispatchers. Considerable nonpolice-related activity (taking breaks, meeting friends, conducting personal business) as well as police-related activity (parking and traffic enforcement, field interrogations, business security checks) is routinely undertaken by patrol officers in many departments without any notification being given to dispatchers. Consequently, reliance on dispatch records can be expected to considerably underestimate the total amount of patrol activity.

Another approach is to utilize activity reports completed daily by patrol officers. In principle, these reports should provide comprehensive information concerning patrol activity, but in practice they are often incomplete and are sometimes referred to as "cheat sheets." Depending upon customs and pressures prevailing in a police department, officer activity sheets could either over- or underestimate the real amount of patrol activity.

Because of the limitations of dispatch records and activity sheets, the best approach to gathering data on total patrol activity is to utilize observers who "ride along" with officers and record their workload. While it is true that the presence of observers may influence patrol officers to change their behavior, the experience of many researchers has been that following an initial ice-breaking period, most officers adhere to their habits and respond to the demands of their jobs with little concern for the observers.

Studies of total patrol activity have identified two major categories of workload over and above calls dispatched. One category, usually labelled administration, includes such things as going to court, going to the police station, meeting with supervisors, and patrol car maintenance. Webster's (1970) dispatch records study and Cordner's (1978) observation study each found that this category accounted for about 40 percent of all patrol activities. The other major category includes on-view or proactive patrol activities such as traffic enforcement, parking enforcement, and checking into suspicious circumstances. Webster and Cordner both found that police-initiated on-view activities accounted for about 20 percent of all patrol workload; if administrative activities were deleted from consideration, on-view activity represented one-third of patrol workload.

Patrol activity can also be examined in terms of time expended rather than numbers of activities. This avenue of inquiry is important because it focuses attention on the periods of time during which patrol officers are not performing discrete, identifiable tasks. This period of time is substantial: O'Neill and Bloom (1972) found that patrolling and non-duty activities accounted for 45–50 percent of patrol time in 18 California cities; Kelling et al. (1974) reported that 60 percent of patrol time in Kansas City was uncommitted; Arkell and Knight (1975) discovered that 56 percent of patrol time was taken up by preventive patrol and abstractions in the Bristol Constabulary; Cordner (1978) observed that 55 percent of patrol time was uncommitted in a midwestern city; and Whitaker (1982), in his observation study of 60 neighborhoods served by 24 police departments, found that 67 percent of patrol time was unassigned.

Patrol officers vary greatly in how they utilize this uncommitted, un-assigned, or free patrol time. Kelling et al. found that officers divided their time about equally among four categories of activity: mobile police-related (such as looking for traffic violations); nonpolice-related (taking breaks and nonchalant driving to relieve boredom); stationary and contact personnel, police-related (writing reports in the car and discussing cases with other personnel); and residual time (such as travel time to and from court). Cordner observed somewhat greater amounts devoted to both mobile police-related and nonpolice-related activity, with less allocated to stationary and residual activity. Whitaker found that mobile police-related activity accounted for two-thirds of all uncommitted patrol time in his study.

The studies cited thus far clearly indicate that the preponderance of patrol work involves not doing anything very specific, but rather taking breaks, meeting with other officers, and engaging in preventive patrolling. When only specific activities are considered, it appears that administrative duties are the most common. The remaining patrol time (perhaps 25 percent of the total amount of time available to patrol officers) is composed of about one-third police-initiated activities and about two-thirds dispatched calls. The police-initiated activities are probably inordinately law enforcement-related, especially traffic enforcement. The dispatched calls are a mix of crimes, disputes, traffic problems, and service requests, with the crimes and disputes most common.

POLICE–CITIZEN ENCOUNTERS

A different slant on determining the nature of patrol work was taken in the Police Services Study (Whitaker, 1982). This study focused on encounters between citizens and patrol officers, whether police- or citizen-initiated, in 60 neighborhoods served by 24 police departments. The primary type of problem in 38 percent of the 5,688 encounters observed was crime, while disorder and traffic problems each accounted for 22 percent of encounters and service accounted for 18 percent.

Also recorded in this study were the types of actions taken by patrol officers in the encounters. This is especially interesting because it illuminates not only the kinds of problems encountered in patrol work but, additionally, the kinds of actions taken most often by patrol officers to resolve incidents. The percentages of encounters in which each type of action was taken are indicated below. (The figures total more than 100 percent because officers often took more than one action during an encounter.)

Interviewed a witness or person requesting service	57%
Interrogated a suspect	40%
Conducted a search or inspection	29%
Lectured or threatened (other than threat of force)	28%
Gave information	27%
Gave reassurance	23%
Used force or threat of force	14%
Gave assistance	11%
Gave a ticket	9%
Used persuasion	8%
Made an arrest	5%
Gave medical help	2%

These figures indicate the great importance of *verbal* communication in patrol work. They also indicate that patrol work involves the frequent utilization of *police* powers and techniques—interrogating, searching, lecturing, threatening, using force. Patrol work is more than simply a social service function of providing information, reassurance, and support as some (Cumming et al., 1965; Shane, 1980) have argued.

VARIATIONS AND PECULIARITIES

In the introduction the extent of individual and organizational variation in police work was emphasized. Considerable individual officer variation in patrol activity was observed by Cordner (1978) in a midwestern city, where the amount of time spent patrolling during an eight-hour shift ranged from zero minutes to 173 minutes and the number of traffic stops during a shift ranged from zero to fifteen. Similar variation among neighborhoods was discovered in the Police Services Study (Whitaker, 1982). The number of arrests per neighborhood ranged from almost one per shift to only one every fifteen shifts; the average amount of time devoted to meals and other personal business ranged from 19 minutes per shift in one neighborhood to 109 minutes in another.

The Police Services Study also discovered wide differences among neighborhoods in the types of encounters between citizens and patrol officers. While in one neighborhood 54 percent of all encounters were primarily crime-related, in another only 22 percent pertained to crime. In one neighborhood 43 percent of encounters had primarily to do with disorder, while in another only 8 percent involved such problems. Services accounted for 33 percent of encounters in one neighborhood but only 8 percent in another. Finally, traffic problems generated 46 percent of encounters in one neighborhood but only 5 percent in another. These ranges illustrate that the nature of patrol work varies tremendously from place to place.

Another source of variation in patrol work is time of day. The number and kinds of calls from citizens differ by time of day, as does the amount of traffic on the streets, the number of people on the sidewalks, the number of people likely to be intoxicated, and the number of businesses open and closed. One study found that patrol officers vary their use of free patrol time and the emphasis they give to different tasks by shift (Cordner, 1982). During the daytime officers spend the most free patrol time on mobile patrol; in the evening they spend the most time on self-initiated police work; and on the late night shift they spend the most time taking breaks. During the day shift, the most emphasized work-related tasks are checking and enforcing traffic, checking residential areas, and talking to the general public. The priorities of evening shift officers are checking and enforcing traffic, checking suspicious people, and checking business establishments. During the late night shift the activities of checking businesses and suspicious people predominate.

Further evidence of variability in patrol workload comes from a five-nation study conducted by Shane (1980). While it is not always clear whether his data refer to incoming calls to the police, calls radioed to patrol officers, or total patrol activity, his comparative analysis is unique. He included two sites each from Britain, India, Israel, and the Netherlands in his study, along with one U.S. city. He found that 38.9 percent of patrol activity in Jerusalem pertained to arbitration/mediation, compared to only 9.6 percent in Baltimore. Service activity accounted for 30.4 percent of patrol activity in Baltimore but only 4.9 percent in Julundar, India. Law enforcement tasks represented 61.7 percent of patrol activity in Ludhiana, India but only 7 percent in Gloucestershire, England. Traffic work comprised 34.6 percent of patrol activity in Groningen, Netherlands but only 3.6 percent in Ludhiana. The category of patrol, which included alarms and serving warrants among other tasks, accounted for 26.9 percent of total activity in Gloucestershire but only 8.5 percent in Jerusalem. Although these comparisons of polar examples tend to highlight differences between countries, Shane also found considerable variation within countries. For example, in the two Netherlands sites the traffic portions of patrol activity were 34.6 percent and 13.7 percent.

One other important source of variation in patrol work that needs to be mentioned is size of jurisdiction. Most of the studies have tended to focus on urban departments, although the Police Services Study included small-to-medium size departments within several SMSAs. Not much information is available concerning patrol work in small town and rural settings away from metropolitan areas. In one small town studied by the author, two-thirds of the identifiable patrol activity was parking- or traffic-related. The portion of patrol time spent handling calls from citizens was quite small, leaving a tremendous amount of free patrol time. Inordinate attention tended to be directed toward traffic enforcement and, during the night, business security, largely because of the small number of calls and low incidence of crime and disorder. There are probably many other small town and rural police departments with similar activity patterns.

CHANGING PATTERNS

Several current developments in patrol strategies have the potential to alter the character of patrol workload. Directed patrol, for example, gives patrol officers specific assignments to perform during what would otherwise be their free patrol time. Obviously, this reduces free patrol time, and thus could reduce preventive patrolling, self-initiated police activity, and/or time spent on personal business. The directed patrol assignments generally require officers to proceed to particular locations to perform such activities as directed preventive patrol, field interrogations, selective traffic enforcement, or stakeouts. Although directed patrol assignments can run the whole gamut of police work, most tend to be crime- or traffic-related. Consequently, the utilization of directed patrol generally increases the extent to which patrol activity is concerned with crime and law enforcement.

Many departments are now employing differential responses to calls for service, a strategy that encourages handling as many calls as possible by means other than dispatching a patrol unit. Alternatives such as taking reports over the telephone, mailing report forms to victims, and utilizing nonsworn personnel to respond to some calls are frequently used to reduce the call-handling workload of the patrol force. To the extent that more and more minor and noncriminal matters are siphoned off to alternative responses, the remaining calls dispatched to patrol units are liable to be increasingly crime- and enforcement-related. One study in Garden Grove, California (McEwen et al., 1986) found that over half of all incoming calls could be handled without dispatching a patrol unit. Of the calls that were dispatched, 30 percent pertained to alarms of suspicious circumstances, 23 percent to crimes, 19 percent to disturbances, 15 percent to traffic problems, and 13 percent to services. This distribution of calls, with one-third disturbances and services and two-thirds crimes, potential crimes, or traffic problems, may be an indication of things to come, and gives a far different picture of patrol workload than the celebrated studies from the 1960s and early 1970s.

Two possibly countervailing forces are community-oriented policing and problem-oriented policing. The community-oriented strategy typically utilizes foot patrol, storefront offices, door-to-door surveys, and similar techniques to increase police-citizen contacts and to make officers more familiar with citizens' concerns. Officers may also be expected to take a more active role in enforcing community norms regarding such minor disorders as panhandling, loud radios, and loitering. In order to undertake all these efforts, officers are often relieved of at least some of their call-handling responsibilities. Thus, under community-oriented policing, patrol work may become somewhat more proactive than traditional patrol, and possibly more oriented toward order maintenance and service provision.

Problem-oriented policing emphasizes analyzing the underlying causes of community problems instead of simply responding to symptoms. Traditional patrol work is termed "single-complaint" policing because patrol officers are sent to handle each call as if it is unrelated to any others. Using the problem-oriented approach, by contrast, officers identify patterns of repeat calls and then search for explanations for the calls. When they discover an underlying cause they attempt to treat the problem at that deeper level in order to have a more lasting effect than is typical under single-complaint policing. The utilization of problem-oriented policing increases the amount of time spent by patrol officers in gathering and analyzing information, and decreases the amount of time spent handling calls. The kinds of problems addressed tend to be crimes, traffic hazards, and neighborhood disorder. Thus patrol work under problem-oriented policing would probably become more analytical than traditional patrol, but perhaps no less oriented toward crime and law enforcement.

CONCLUSIONS

The biggest portion of patrol officers' time is uncommitted, and officers vary greatly in how they utilize this time. The next biggest portion of their time is consumed by administrative chores of one kind or another. When the focus is shifted to the kinds of activities they perform and the kinds of encounters they have with citizens, a mix of crime-, traffic-, disorder-, and service-related workload is found. The mix varies from place to place, and also from time to time but, contrary to the popular wisdom of the last two decades, the crime- and enforcement-related aspects of patrol work are substantial and far exceed the service-related portion. Such current trends in patrol programming as directed patrol and differential responses to calls for service may have the effect of further increasing the crime-related and enforcement-related nature of patrol work, although the widespread adoption of community-oriented policing could have the opposite effect.

REFERENCES

Arkell, P. and R. Knight (1975). "The Analysis of a Territorial Division." *Police Research Bulletin*, 25(Summer): 14–26.

Bercal, T. (1970). "Calls for Police Assistance." *American Behavioral Scientist*, 13:267–277.

Boydstun, J.; M. Sherry; and N. Moelter (1977). *Patrol Staffing in San Diego*. Washington, D.C.: Police Foundation.

Cawley, D. and J. Miron (1977). *Managing Patrol Operations: Manual*. Washington, D.C.: U.S. Government Printing Office.

Cordner, G. (1978). "While on Routine Patrol . . . : A Study of Police Use of Uncommitted Patrol Time." Master's thesis, Michigan State University.

———. (1982). "While on Routine Patrol: What the Police Do When They're Not Doing Anything." *American Journal of Police*, 1(2):94–112.

Cumming, E.; I. Cumming; and L. Edell (1965). "Policeman as Philosopher, Guide and Friend." *Social Problems*, 12:276–286.

Eck, J. and W. Spelman (1987). *Problem Solving: Problem-Oriented Policing in Newport News*. Washington, D.C.: Police Executive Research Forum.

Farmer, M., ed. (1981). *Differential Police Response Strategies*. Washington, D.C.: Police Executive Research Forum.

Goldstein, H. (1987). "Toward Community-Oriented Policing: Potential, Basic Requirements, and Threshold Questions." *Crime and Delinquency*, 33(1):6–30.

Kelling, G.; T. Pate; D. Dieckman; and C. Brown (1974). *The Kansas City Preventive Patrol Experiment: A Technical Report*. Washington, D.C.: Police Foundation.

Lilly, R. (1978). "What Are the Police Now Doing?" *Journal of Police Science and Administration*, 6(1):51–60.

McEwen, T.; E. Connors III; and M. Cohen (1986). *Evaluation of the Differential Police Response Field Test*. Washington, D.C.: U.S. Government Printing Office.

O'Neill, M. and C. Bloom (1972). "The Field Officer: Is He Really Fighting Crime?" *The Police Chief*, 39 (February):30–32.

Reiss, A. (1971). *The Police and the Public*. New Haven: Yale University Press.

Report to the Nation on Crime and Justice, 2nd ed. (1988). Washington, D.C.: U.S. Government Printing Office.

Shane, P. (1980). *Police and People: A Comparison of Five Countries*. St. Louis: The C.V. Mosby Company.

Sherman, L. (1987). *Repeat Calls to Police in Minneapolis*. Washington, D.C.: Crime Control Institute.

Spelman, W. and D. Brown (1981). *Calling the Police: Citizen Reporting of Serious Crime*. Washington, D.C.: Police Executive Research Forum.

Tien, J.; J. Simon; and R. Larson (1978). *An Alternative Approach in Police Patrol:*

The Wilmington Split Force Experiment. Washington, D.C.: U.S. Government Printing Office.

Webster, J. (1970). "Police Task and Time Study." *Journal of Criminal Law, Criminology and Police Science*, 61:94–100.

Whitaker, G. (1982). "What Is Patrol Work?" *Police Studies*, 4:13–22.

Wilson, J. (1968). *Varieties of Police Behavior: The Management of Law and Order in Eight Communities*. Cambridge, MA: Harvard University Press.

7

Investigating Burglary: The Measurement of Police Performance

John Burrows

Residential burglaries are a major problem for the police. Although far from being the most common crime reported to them, the police are well aware of the seriousness with which members of the public regard any intrusion into their homes. Indeed, research has established that residential burglary is viewed by the wider public as the most serious aspect of the crime problem (Maxfield, 1984; Hough and Mayhew, 1985), and that the offense can have a devastating emotional impact on some victims (Maguire, 1982).

It is not surprising, therefore, that it has long been a primary police objective to trace those responsible for such crimes. But in doing so the police face particular difficulties. The majority of cases are committed while victims are absent from their homes, and are thus reported to the police only after some time has elapsed. Passersby have long since disappeared and, more often than not, neighbors have seen and heard nothing. Once it is established that there are no witnesses, and that no telltale physical evidence has been left, generally the only option left open to the police is to hope that additional information offered to them, or perhaps the recovery of stolen property, will lead them to the perpetrators. Alternatively, a person apprehended for some other reason may admit earlier offenses.

From *Investigating Burglary: The Measurement of Police Performance*, (1986). Reprinted with the permission of the Controller of Her Britannic Majesty's Stationery Office.

The comparatively low clear-up rate achieved for residential burglary—one in four of the offense recorded in 1984—is a reflection of
these difficulties. It is, however, significant that this national figure con-
ceals very considerable differences between individual police forces,
and—to a lesser extent—between the different divisions and subdivisions of any one. These differences have not gone unnoticed in the
national press, in Parliament or in local council chambers—where they
frequently give rise to conjecture or criticism.

The research reported here aimed to explore such differences in the
clear-up rates for residential burglary. The central purpose in doing so
was to see if it was possible to identify factors that would account for
discrepancies in burglary clear-up rates. In particular, the research
sought to examine whether there was evidence to support the view that
the police in areas with poor clear-up rates were in some respects less
effective than others—or, on the other side of the coin—that those with
high clear-up rates employed "better" practices that others could use-
fully implement.

The research was designed with a view to directly comparing aspects
of burglary investigations in areas that had been broadly "matched"
with one another. That is, each area was paired with another which
experienced a similar level of residential burglary in the same sort of
environment, and had similar numbers of police officers to respond to
these. The critical factor distinguishing the areas matched together was
that they achieved quite different clear-up rates (see Table 7.1).

Table 7.1
Comparison of Clear-up Rate for Burglary with Arrest Rate

AREA (Burglary Rate)	CLEAR-UP RATE	ARREST RATE
LOW CLEAR-UP CITIES:		
Walton (low)	13%	14%
Bitterne (med)	18	23
Clapham (high)	11	11
HIGH CLEAR-UP CITIES:		
Epping (low)	24%	23%
Syston (med)	46	16
Chapeltown (high)	65	18

Six police areas were chosen, each from different police forces. This
produced three matching pairs. Clapham and Chapeltown, both inner
city areas, of course constituted the high-risk pair. The medium risk
areas examined were Bitterne (18 percent clear-up rate in 1983) which
was compared with Syston (46 percent). The pair experiencing a relatively low risk of burglary were Walton-on-Thames in Surrey (13 percent

clear-up rate) and Epping (24 percent). In all six areas the research explored the reasons for these differences in clear-up rates by examining police recording practices, the characteristics of recorded burglary cases, the activities of investigating officers and the methods of detection they employed.

ARRESTING BURGLARS

There are a number of widespread misconceptions about clear-up rates. Some of the most misleading arise from a belief that clear-up rates are able to impart information about the number of *offenders* that are traced by the police and the number that are not caught. To some, low clear-up rates signal that the majority of offenders go unpunished. Even those familiar with the complexities of crime statistics frequently tend to the view that forces with high clear-up rates in all probability owe this to their greater effectiveness in identifying offenders.

Despite the fact that clear-up rates measure the proportion of recorded *offenses* "solved" by the police, and say nothing about numbers of *offenders*, the frequency with which this parallel is drawn is an indication of the importance attached to the issue and the clouds of misapprehension surrounding it. The parallel can be particularly misleading when applied to the case of burglary, for the crime is known to be one where a good many clear-ups can result from a single arrest (Burrows and Tarling, 1982). This being the case, one of the first aims of the research was to assess the extent to which differences in burglary clear-up rates reflect differences in the number of burglars actually arrested.

Recognizing that public interest tends to focus on the number of persons arrested for crime rather than on the number of crimes for which they are subsequently held to be responsible, countries like the USA have long used the "arrest rate" as an alternative measure of investigative productivity (i.e., the ratio of persons arrested for crime to all crimes recorded). While this too has been the subject of criticism in the countries where it has been employed, this measure has the advantage that it gives some indication of the number of offenders arrested for each offense recorded. An equivalent measure was therefore derived for the six areas under review [in this research].

The effects of employing this alternative performance indicator are dramatic. In two of the three comparisons made, the use of the arrest rate as a measure of investigative performance dramatically reduces the differences between areas suggested by the clear-up rate and, in one, actually reverses the situation.

Thus, in the case of the high-risk areas of Chapeltown and Clapham, a 54-percentage point difference in clear-up rates is reduced to a 10-point difference measured by an arrest rate. In the low-risk areas of Epping

Table 7.2
Ratio of Burglary Offenses Cleared-up to Burglary Offenders Dealt With

AREA (Burglary Rate)	TOTAL CRIMES CLEARED	OFFENDERS DEALT WITH	OFFENSES CLEARED PER/OFFENDER
LOW CLEAR-UP CITIES:			
Walton (low)	29	30	1.0
Bitterne (med)	153	200	0.8
Clapham (high)	180	140	1.3
HIGH CLEAR-UP CITIES:			
Epping (low)	46	43	1.1
Syston (med)	588	202	2.9
Chapeltown (high)	967	265	3.7

and Walton, this difference is reduced less dramatically, from 11 to 9 percentage points. In the remaining case (the medium-risk areas), the substantial variation in clear-up rates is turned upside down, so that Bitterne now appears "better" at investigating burglary than Syston.

An explanation for the wide differences between "arrest" and clear-up rates may be found when the ratio between the number of cleared burglaries in each area and the number of burglars "dealt with" by the police is examined. Table 7.2 shows that the police in the areas with the better burglary clear-up rates, while apprehending more burglars, do not arrest as many as the differences in clear-up rates imply. What is striking, however, is that they clear more offenses per offender. This distinction is particularly notable in the areas with high clear-up rates, such as Chapeltown (3.7 burglaries cleared for each offender detained) and Syston (2.9), when compared with their counterparts of Clapham (1.3) and Bitterne (0.8).

Taken at face value, the data suggest that burglary clear-up rates present a misleading view of the police ability to arrest offenders. While this seems to be the case in the areas reviewed, the interpretation of this data should be treated with certain caution. *If* burglaries in the areas with high clear-up rates (particularly Syston and Chapeltown) were primarily the work of those committing numerous offenses each, and those in the low clear-up rates were primarily the work of "one-off opportunists," it would be expected that only the police in the former areas could achieve several clear-ups for each arrest made. Any conclusion that high clear-up rates for burglary derive from the more careful interrogation of known offenders is therefore based on an assumption (which can be neither clearly proved, nor disproved) that the number of burglaries committed per burglar is roughly consistent between areas. On balance, the evidence collected about offenders and burglary offenses in each of the areas gave no reason to suggest this was not the case (see Burrows, 1986); moreover, the evidence reviewed later in this report indicates that it is differences in police practices—rather than in criminal behavior— that account for the disparity between arrest and clear-up rates.

PRIMARY DETECTIONS: REFLECTIONS ON ARREST RATES

An interest in how many offenders the police actually identify underlies much of the public debate on crime. This accounts for the fact that many commentators have not been content to treat the clear-up rate as an offense measure but have sought to use it as something akin to an "arrest" index. Behind the continued attempts to do this is no doubt a belief that any deterrent effect achieved by police actions is the result of the initial arrest of an offender, and not any subsequent admissions he may make in police custody. Researchers, too, have long sought to calculate police effectiveness in achieving arrests and have done so by separating "primary" or "direct" clear-ups from those cleared up through interviewing offenders already in custody about their past offending; traditionally labelled as "secondary" detections or those obtained by "indirect" means.

Means of Detection

Table 7.3 portrays how those held responsible for burglaries initially came to police notice in the six areas studied.

The table shows several consistent patterns in all areas. Above all, it emphasizes the extent of police dependence upon the public—generally in the form of a witness or the victim himself—to provide them with good information, descriptions, or identifications that lead to arrests. Nearly half of the cases cleared up were dependent on this direct assistance. In about a third of all cases (32 percent) the police were called while the burglar was still at or near the scene of the crime and they arrested him there. Alternatively they were called soon after and given an offender's name or even provided with a "citizen arrest" (17 percent). The importance of these two means of detection in all areas serves to emphasize the point that, while the majority of burglaries are reported after "the trail is cold," many primary detections are achieved by the combined efforts of the police and public, each responding quickly to those burglaries where a fast response is appropriate. Clearly it is essential for the police to be able to identify the latter cases in order to stand the greatest likelihood of obtaining "on scene" arrests.

This is not to argue, however, that all investigation is fruitless if a

Table 7.3
Primary Means of Detection

AREA (Burglary Rate)	Inter- rogation	Lengthy Investi- gation	BY POLICE Susp Context	Other Means	W/LEADS FROM PUBLIC	BY PUBLIC ONLY
Clapham (H)	5%	10%	18%	4%	46%	17%
Walton (L)	5	16	5	16	32	26
Syston (M)	15	17	11	9	35	12
Chapeltown (H)	19	19	4	6	32	19
Epping (L)	17	17	39	0	17	11
Bitterne (M)	13	28	3	8	18	28
ALL AREAS	11	18	11	7	32	17

burglary is reported some time after the event and without the burglars having been seen. The questioning of those connected with non-burglary cases or arrested by neighboring police divisions provided a significant number of clear-ups (11 percent and 7 percent). Occasionally arrests were made by patrolling officers interviewing those who appeared to be "acting suspiciously" (11 percent). This left less than one case in five (18 percent) where police traced an offender after "lengthier" enquiries— classified as those lasting more than 24 hours after a report—where generally there were no direct leads for the police at the outset.

In comparative terms, the striking feature of Table 7.3 is the absence of any very significant differences in the means of detection either between areas with high and low clear-up rates or, indeed, between those with different arrest rates. In the main, those with high rates appear no more or less dependent on public support than their counterparts, and no more effective in lengthier investigations. There are, however, exceptions to this rule. One is that Bitterne police appear more successful than other areas on pursuing "lengthier" burglary enquiries. Many of these clear-ups seemed to be the result of a close knowledge of local criminals and their movements: that is, of an effective criminal intelligence network. The other is the case of Epping, where an unusually high proportion of arrests derive from police questioning of those "acting suspiciously." This is probably attributable to its geographical location. A "green belt" of woodland divides the rural town of Epping from London and makes the identification of "outsiders" by the police far easier; it is nonetheless evidence of the benefits that can accrue from police vigilance and the stopping of those acting suspiciously. The police in Epping have clearly been effective in building upon the advantages offered by their particular local circumstances, and there are certainly lessons here that other, similarly placed, police forces should learn from. There is, however, a need for caution. The police in more populated areas may not find such a strategy either so easy to implement, or so effective; moreover, police stops of those acting suspiciously, if pursued indiscriminately, can damage relations with sections of the community (see Scarman, 1981).

Cost of Investigation

Given that the areas studied did not achieve very different numbers of arrests (in relation to the numbers of burglaries each recorded) it might be assumed that the costs of investigation in each—as reflected in the time spent by officers—would not differ markedly either. Two methods were employed in this study to assess the time spent by police officers on the investigation of a typical burglary and the resultant costs. A survey of victims provided one perspective: those interviewed were

Table 7.4
Average Time Spent by Officers on Burglary Investigations (in hours)

Arrest Rates	AREA (Burglary Rate)	UNIFORM OFFICERS	CID	SCENE CRIME OFFICERS	TOTAL
LOW	Clapham (High)	1.0	0.1	0.1	1.2
	Walton (Low)	6.9	4.1	0.6	11.6
	Chapeltown (High)	0.6	1.1	0.9	2.6
HIGH	Epping (Low)	1.6	3.3	0.6	5.5
	ALL AREAS	1.8	1.4	0.5	3.7

asked to assess the amount of time spent at the burglary scene by police officers during each visit (this assessment was, however, only of the police activity "visible" to the victim). In addition, police officers in four of the six areas completed activity logs in respect of all the burglaries investigated in a given period. These covered the activities of uniform officers, CID, and "scenes of crime" officers; all the cases reviewed proved to be "undetected" at the end of the survey period. Table 7.4 gives details of the latter survey's findings.

The findings of these separate surveys provide consistent evidence that, contrary to expectation, the outcomes of investigations are not simply a consequence of the time spent on them (police time is of course the main component of cost). The suburban areas of Walton and Epping consistently spent more time on burglary investigation than the more heavily pressed inner city areas of Clapham and Chapeltown. This picture is supported by the accounts of both victims and police officers.

The principal implication of this finding is that much of the time spent by police officers in less heavily pressed areas produces no tangible benefits (at least in terms of arrest or crime clearance). The introduction of burglary-case screening by a number of metropolitan forces—a procedure designed to distinguish the few burglaries that are likely to repay further investigation from the majority that are not—is witness to this point, and an indication that the message is not lost on the police themselves. Clearly, however, the pressures to adopt such cost-cutting strategies are not experienced so strongly in the more rural forces and many will take the view that victim satisfaction is a dividend of lengthier investigation.

SECONDARY DETECTIONS: REFLECTIONS ON CLEAR-UP RATES

The point has been made that some areas appear to obtain relatively high clear-up rates for burglary, despite achieving comparable numbers of arrests; and the implication that has been drawn is that they go out of their way to extract, from those they arrest, a full record of the previous break-ins they have committed.

Up to this point, this report has dwelt on "primary" detections; that is, crimes cleared directly by the arrest of the burglar responsible: the police in such instances will generally institute charges or issue a summons against the offender or—exercising the discretionary powers vested in the Chief Constable—caution him (if he admits his guilt). The offender charged by the police may however produce "secondary" clear-ups. One way by which these are obtained is when the offender, having been found guilty on a particular charge, asks the court to take additional offenses into consideration (TIC) in sentencing him. Alternatively, the offender serving a custodial sentence may subsequently admit additional offenses which the police can count as "cleared" without recharging him.

These four methods of clearance—charge, caution, TIC, or clearance "without proceedings"—are quite independent of the way in which the police initially identify a suspect. For example, the fact that an offender is caught red-handed carrying out a burglary certainly does not predetermine which method the police will select to deal with him. However, it is well established that the majority of "secondary" clear-ups (i.e., those derived from the questioning of those already in custody) are obtained by utilizing two particular clearance methods: the TIC (if the offender is in police custody before trial) or "otherwise without proceedings" (if he is already in prison).

The information about the clearance methods employed in the six study areas is shown in Table 7.5. It shows that areas with higher clear-up rates are not alone in looking to TICs or even clearances "without proceedings" to maintain their burglary clear-up rates. Around a third of the burglaries cleared in Clapham and Bitterne were cleared by TIC, and the subdivision of Walton-on-Thames relied as heavily on clearances "without proceedings." There is therefore no single clearance method employed by areas with high clear-up rates that is not also used in their apparently less effective counterparts. This said, there were extreme examples of particular areas pursuing one practice to the virtual exclusion of others: in Chapeltown, for example, 85 percent of all burglary clear-ups were attributable to "write-offs" from those already serving prison sentences.

When the proportion of crime cleared by "primary" as opposed to "secondary" means is compared, significant differences in police practices become apparent. What is striking is the very significant dependence on "secondary" detections in areas with high clear-up rates—Chapeltown owes 89 percent of its burglary clearances to "secondary" detections and Syston 75 percent, compared with 32 percent in Clapham

Table 7.5
Method of Clear-up: All Residential Burglaries in 1983

Clear-up Rates	AREA (Burglary Rate)	PRIMARY		SECONDARY		Total Crimes Cleared-up
		Charge/ Summons	Caution	TIC	Without Proceed	
LOW	Walton (Low)	38%	14%	10%	38%	29
	Bitterne (Med)	50	2	39	9	153
	Clapham (High)	68	0	30	2	180
HIGH	Epping (Low)	52	2	26	20	46
	Syston (Med)	24	1	61	14	588
	Chapeltown (High)	11	0	4	85	967

and 48 percent in Bitterne. The exceptions are the two low-risk areas of Walton and Epping, which in fact achieve a broadly equitable breakdown between "primary" and "secondary" clear-ups. However, caution should be exercised in respect of this particular comparison because percentages have been derived from a low number of recorded burglaries.

In general, therefore, areas with high clear-up rates have no monopoly over any particular clearance method. However, an explanation for differences in clear-up rates can be found in the proportion of clear-ups attributable to "secondary" detections, either in the form of TICs or of "prison write-offs." While forces with low clear-up rates obtain some "secondary" detections, they do not rely on them to the same extent as others to sustain clear-up rates.

SUMMARY AND IMPLICATIONS

This analysis of the clear-up rates for residential burglary makes the point that clear-up rates give little or no indication of police effectiveness in arresting burglars. Rather, it suggests that differences in clear-up rates across forces are largely an artifact of police policies pursued in each: particularly that police areas achieving high burglary clear-up rates often owe their success to local procedures designed to ensure that the burglars they arrest give a full account of their past offending.

Viewed in this light, some of the criticism directed at areas with low clear-up rates—or even at declining national clear-up rates—is at least ill-informed. While many of those raising such criticism see poor police performance as their target, in reality it is often police *priorities* they should question. It may be argued that, when responding to such criticism, the police have not always ensured that they have made this point or clarified the complexities of the clear-up rate (although a few senior police officers have become more outspoken on the issue in recent years). Nonetheless, public debate of clear-up rates has tended to follow a depressingly familiar pattern, with participants seldom going beyond the overall clear-up statistic to examine the merits and demerits of specific aspects of police performance. Quite often, the consequence is that some police efforts attract unwarranted criticism and public fears that offenders remain "at large" escalate.

In reality, the police here are on the horns of a dilemma. On the one hand they display an understandable desire to satisfy public expectations by returning high clear-up rates for burglary: but such rates can only be achieved by emphasizing the need to obtain "secondary" detections. On the other hand, many police officers will maintain that focusing on "secondary" detections diverts resources from strategies aimed at increasing the number of burglars arrested by the police. They may view the prospect of fellow officers painstakingly going through crime records and conducting interviews with offenders in search of "secondary" clear-ups as simply wasteful and ultimately pointless.

As a step towards rectifying some of the misconceptions about the clear-up rate, this report suggests that greater attention should be drawn to—and more use made of—the important distinction between "primary" clear-ups (cases where police have successfully identified and arrested an offender), and "secondary" clear-ups (the product of interviews with offenders already in custody). The benefits in adopting this distinction are straightforward. It allows those drawing on burglary clear-up statistics, whether for management purposes and/or for use in public debate, to separate the police ability to identify and arrest offenders from their skill at interrogation. This would represent an important step forward in the attempt to derive useful output indicators for the police.

This [chapter] reviews police policies aimed at maximizing either the arrest of burglars or the admissions made by those in custody. In practice, of course, the senior police officer will pursue a combination of strategies in dealing with household burglaries in his locality. He can aim at the reduction of burglary by persuading the public to protect their homes. He may combine this strategy with one aimed at improved detection, for example, by the encouragement of neighborhood watch schemes, designed to bring the police and communities they serve into closer contact. He can train and deploy his officers with a view to maximizing their ability to arrest active burglars: for example by "grading" the police response to burglary reports according to their urgency or by mounting surveillance operations in target areas. Finally, he may focus police resources on the interrogation of burglary suspects, with a view to extracting from them a full record of their past offending. The weight given to each of these strategies depends on a series of judgments about the appropriate balance of police resources and the acceptability of each to the burglary victim and the wider public. It also reflects the priority attached to prevention or deterrence.

Policies Aimed at Improved Clear-up Rates

Alongside changes in recorded crime, the clear-up rate has tended to be judged as a central indicator of police performance. Given this elevated status, there are undeniable attractions to the police in boosting the number of clear-ups they achieve, whatever the methods used. The benefit of being able to report an improved clear-up rate for burglary to the public, as well as to the Home Office and police authorities, is likely to prove a formidable incentive. In pursuing this goal, the police will have implicitly accepted that the primary aim of their investigative work should be to "solve" the maximum number of recorded burglaries—a judgment certainly some police would contest. The research evidence, however, offers several ways forward on this front.

While previous research has demonstrated that burglary clear-up rates are particularly dependent on admissions (secondary detections), the present research has illustrated that forces can obtain these by different methods: either by "TIC" procedures before sentence or by "write-offs" from those already serving custodial sentences. While most of the areas made some use of the latter procedure, national statistics suggest that it has been employed with liberality in some forces but great restraint elsewhere. The benefits of such a policy are—sometimes reluctantly— coming to be realized; for example, in the light of in-house research comparing its own clear-up figures with those of other forces, the Metropolitan Police has recently decided—on an experimental basis—to adopt the practice of visiting prisons to elicit more admissions from inmates.

The signs are that any policy aimed at increasing the number of "secondary" clear-ups can be pursued with relatively little investment of police time. While research has not specifically explored the question of how much such detections cost in terms of police time, there are strong grounds for believing that they require considerably less expenditure of effort than "primary" clear-ups. No "secondary" clearance, for example, requires the police to collect the same degree of evidence as would be necessary to justify arrest and support a prosecution. Equally, while it may require a good deal of perseverance to extract confessions to past offenses, it is frequently the case that the police extract quite a few admissions from the offender willing to talk freely with them.

Set against the presentational value of "secondary" clearances and the probability that they can be obtained at low "unit" costs, it is important to consider the argument that informing the victims of burglary that the police have obtained an admission to their burglary gives them peace of mind and promotes satisfaction with the police service. The views of burglary victims were explored in the course of this research by engaging a survey research company to conduct interviews with victims in each area. While the aim was to explore victim response to both successful and unsuccessful police enquiries, and was not focused on "secondary" detections as such, it provided some means of assessing their impact on victims generally.

The survey revealed that victim satisfaction with the police investigation is certainly not determined solely by the outcome of burglary cases. Overall, two-thirds (64 percent) of the 738 respondents described themselves as "very" or "fairly" satisfied, 17 percent were dissatisfied, and the remainder "neutral." In general terms, there was no indication that victim satisfaction with burglary investigations was significantly higher in areas where the local police achieved better clear-up rates.

Other findings from the survey of burglary victims go some way towards explaining why victims do not react differently. First, it is clear that few victims are well informed about clear-up rates in the first place, and that considerable numbers are disappointed by the lack of information they received from the police about their case. Second, it is apparent that victims expect various "services" from the police and that their views will not automatically be transformed by knowledge of an arrest (even where victims had been informed that an arrest had been made, a substantial minority—20 percent—still did not declare themselves "satisfied" with the police investigation).

From this evidence, it seems unlikely that—without specific instruction that the victims of crime should be informed of any admissions—the police will do this extensively. If this is not done, the satisfaction of victims of "secondary" clear-ups can hardly be expected to improve, and there is no reason at all to believe that the overall views of victims will change in any marked way. So although the number of "secondary" detections can probably be boosted in many forces, at a relatively low cost, it should not be assumed that victim satisfaction will increase as a direct result.

Policies Aimed at Improved Arrest Rates

The question of how the police can achieve more arrests of burglars was one of the more insurmountable questions posed by this research. Given that the major differences in the clear-up rates of the six areas studied—ranging from 11 to 65 percent—were not matched by similar differences in arrest rates (these only ranged from 8 to 23 percent: certainly a substantial difference, but not so extreme), it is now easy to escape the pessimistic conclusion that there are few pointers to positive action that offer guaranteed payoffs.

An obvious question this prompts—though it is one frequently overlooked despite this—is what constitutes a *good* arrest rate? Such rates, of course, represent the *number of offenders* dealt with proportionate to the total number of *recorded offenses*. Evidence from a wide range of sources suggest that typically burglary is not a "one-off" crime, and that a limited number of persistent burglars may in fact account for a large proportion of recorded offenses. In recent public debate there has been a tendency to overlook this simple fact: some take it for granted that if a hundred crimes are committed, a hundred offenders are at large and that the arrest of ten represents poor "value for money." However, in the case of burglary it is more than likely that a much smaller number

Table 7.6
Target Areas and Their Characteristics

AREA	Burglary Clear-up Rate (1982)	Popu- lation	Burglary Rate (per 1000)
Walton on Thames, Surrey	7.4	49,817	4.7
Epping, Essex	30.1	34,159	4.9
Bitterne, Hampshire	16.9	121,580	6.0
Syston, Leicestershire	60.4	207,300	6.1
Clapham, Metropolitan Police District	7.0	65,000	27.2
Chapeltown, West Yorkshire	55.0	70,900	23.5

of offenders were responsible—perhaps only the ten arrested. No one of course knows how many active burglars there are in any given area. The more widespread distinction between "primary" and "secondary" detections should serve better to inform some about the complexities of this question. It may also allay fears, founded on occasional ill-informed criticism of clear-up rates, that the majority of burglars are never apprehended.

Turning from this central question, the evidence from the present study does suggest that one superficially attractive course of action in fact appears to have little payoff. This is the practice, perhaps only restricted to rural areas experiencing less pressure on police resources, of devoting a great many hours to each and every burglary enquiry. The data suggest that this is not a valuable use of police resources either in terms of achieving improved arrest or clear-up rates; nor is it a certain means of promoting victim satisfaction.

A lesson that may be drawn here is that of the need for selectivity in responding to burglary incidents: for example, separating those victims who might require concentrated police attention from those who do not. The same message is also conveyed by the evidence that the police rely heavily on public assistance in apprehending offenders. The majority of burglaries do not warrant rapid police response, having been committed some time before any report is made. Others, however, do—offenders may still be at the scene of an offense or in the close vicinity—and a system of graded response operated by the police radio controller should serve to identify these cases and give them the attention they clearly warrant.

Finally, the research points to the fact that particular police strategies can be employed to good effect in the right circumstances: the case of Epping and its reliance on arrests of those "acting suspiciously" is a prime example. Here local circumstances—the geographical separation of Epping from London, the fact that it seems to suffer particularly from the predations of burglars form London—make this police policy an effective one in achieving arrests. This certainly may not be true in less auspicious circumstances. Nonetheless, this sort of example underlines the need for police forces to engage in careful scrutiny of their particular burglary problems, informed by comprehensive and detailed analysis of the data available to them.

REFERENCES

Burrows, J. (1986). *Burglary: Police Actions and Victim Views.* Home Office Research and Planning Unit Paper No. 37. London: HMSO.

Burrows, J. and R. Tarling (1982). *Clearing-up Crime.* Home Office Research Study No. 73. London: HMSO.

Hough, M. and P. Mayhew (1985). *Taking Account of Crime: Key Findings from the 1984 British Crime Survey.* Home Office Research Study No. 85. London: HMSO.

Maguire, E. M. W. (1982). *Burglary in a Dwelling: The Offense, the Offender, and the Victim.* London: Heinemann Educational Books.

Maxfield, M. (1984). *Fear of Crime in England and Wales.* Home Office Research Study No. 75. London: HMSO.

Scarman (1981). *The Brixton Disorders, 10–12 April 1981.* Report of an inquiry by the Rt Hon The Lord Scarman, OBE. Cmnd 8427. London: HMSO.

8

The Municipal Police Detective

Jack Kuykendall

A crime is a continuum with three or four phases: a concept or plan, the act itself, escape and fugitive status, and, in some instances, disposal of the fruits of the crime. Municipal police primarily respond to two types of crimes: those involving a victim and a criminal and those with, in effect, two criminals. The latter type of crime usually involves the buying and/or selling of illegal goods or services.

A proactive response to a crime occurs when the police attempt to intervene in the planning phase, during its commission, or even during the disposal phase (for example, a "sting" operation). A reactive intervention occurs after the crime has been committed and the escape and fugitive phase begins. The police response tends to be covert when the intervention is in the planning, act, or disposal phases, because the police are required to play the role of a criminal or victim, or to observe a specific location or person in anticipation of a crime. Other interventions tend to be overt. When the police respond in a proactive and covert mode, the focus is usually on the criminal. When the response is reactive and overt, the emphasis tends to be on the case or investigation of a crime after the act.

The responsibility of reactive detectives is to establish a case, identify a suspect, locate the suspect, obtain a confession if possible, and dispose of the case (Sanders, 1977). Proactive detectives tend to function in the

From *Criminology* 24(1), 1986. Reprinted with permission of The American Society of Criminology.

same way, except that instead of obtaining a confession they attempt clandestinely to develop knowledge about and/or a relationship with a criminal. This often involves playing the role of a criminal in the commission of a crime. For both the reactive and proactive detective, the disposal phase of the investigation often includes case development, processing, and coordinating with other criminal justice agencies in order to obtain a prosecution and conviction.

The primary purpose of any investigation is to produce information. Information is most easily obtained from victims and witnesses because of a desire to redress a grievance and/or to meet the civic responsibility of citizenship. Other information acquiring techniques available to police include bargaining, manipulation or deceit, coercion, and purchase. Some detectives are also capable of deriving information through perceptive observation and analysis (Reppetto, 1978). All of these approaches are utilized to obtain information from informers, while all but purchase are employed with suspects.

The types of cases that detectives investigate can be grouped into one of three categories: "walk-throughs," "where are they's," and "whodunits" (Sanders, 1977; McNerney, 1980). "Walk-throughs" are cases in which a suspect is easily determined and located and detectives must only observe legal guidelines to reach a solution. A substantial majority of all cases "solved" fall into this category. In "where are they" cases a suspect has been tentatively identified but has not been located. These cases may have simple solutions or be complex mysteries. "Whodunits" are those cases in which there are initially no suspects. A substantial majority of crimes reported to police fall into this category, and they are rarely solved.

Klockars (1985) suggests that detectives can be divided into those who are primarily concerned with either means or ends. Classical detectives or deontologists live by the morality of means; they believe that "the creative, disciplined and determined application of morally exemplary mental means can triumph over even the most skilled and sinister of evils" (Klockars, 1985:88). While the classical detective tends to be a myth of fiction writers, the character embodies a perspective that has helped to shape public perceptions about the detective.

Consequentialists are the "hard-boiled" detectives who are more concerned with ends than means. As fictional characters they are intended to represent the reality of investigative work. For these types of detectives the means used to apprehend suspects can only be judged in terms of consequence. Dirty or immoral means become acceptable, even desirable, if the ends are compelling enough.

To this classification should be added the clerical detective. Detectives of this type spend most of their time coordinating with and providing expertise to criminal justice agencies and recording and processing information that may prove useful to their department, other agencies, and such organizations as insurance companies for which detectives function as external auditors. Only a minimal amount of effort is invested in producing information about the identity or location of suspects. Clerks are "snappy bureaucrats" who do what they are told; bureaucratic performance replaces a concern for either the means or ends of the investigation (Klockars, 1983: 428–438).

Secretive rogues are consequentialists. They were proactive, covert, and primarily bargained, manipulated, and coerced informers and suspects to produce information. They essentially tried to prevent crimes by focusing on criminals and intervening in the planning phases or during the commission of the crime. In responding to crimes after they occurred they utilized "stool pigeons." Police reformers hoped that the secretive rogue would be replaced by a morally superior scientific criminal investigator, or classicist, who would rely primarily on perceptive observation and analysis. However, this was more the rhetoric of reform than what was to emerge as a reality. Instead, another type of consequentialist, the inquisitor, appeared. This type of detective was essentially reactive and overt but still tended to rely primarily on bargaining, coercion, and manipulation to produce information. The inquisitor tended to emphasize the most expeditious means of solving cases: obtaining a confession.

With the influence of the bureaucratization of police and the increasingly demanding due process requirements, the role of detective gradually changed to that of clerk. This detective tends to be reactive and overt with the primary responsibility to process "walk-throughs." To the degree that they produce information not already in the possession of the organization, they do so by some bargaining but tend to solicit cooperation by appeals to civic responsibility and through purchase. The detective as clerk is a principal actor in one stage of the complex organization and legal process that has become more concerned with internal requirements than external problems.

While there are some contemporary detectives who tend to be proactive, covert, and more likely to focus on criminals than crimes, they constitute only a small percentage of those engaged in detective duties. These detectives tend to be successful only in the most obvious cases, and they must also invest considerable time to satisfy the information requirements of the organization. However, with the emergence of the drug problem and with the innovation emphasis prevalent among some police departments since the 1960s, the detective may be breaking out of the bureaucratic box. Unfortunately, the results of innovation have tended only to revive past practices and probably false hopes. Computerized fingerprint systems and psychological profiles of criminals stress the importance of science, historically of little value in identifying suspects. Sting operations, decoy programs, and other clandestine police pursuits in which officers play the role of criminal or victim, while more structured and closely supervised, are approaches to detection that are controversial and corruption-prone.

From the perspective of apprehension, the detective function has probably never been an efficient or effective activity. Although a speculative observation, it is unlikely that secretive rogues, inquisitors, or clerks are more or less effective, in general, or in solving "whodunits" or complex "where are they's" (Murphy and Plate, 1977:183). Police effectiveness and efficiency is determined more by the *complexity* of the problem than the methods, techniques, and skills of those attempting a solution. Police concentrate on the problems with easy solutions, because the alternative is problems of such difficulty that only a substantial investment of resources provides a reasonable possibility of success. Since police departments can rarely do this, the range of possible efficiency and effectiveness has been and continues to be constrained.

Are there alternatives to the role presently played by detectives? Since police departments and the court system have become so dependent upon them to process information, changes in the role will be difficult to make. Police organizations are not inclined to ask basic questions about their strategies and organizational design. However, to the degree that they are so inclined, the following questions need to be addressed. Can part or all of detective resources be more productively invested in other strategies, such as education? Should the persons called detectives concentrate on the easiest crimes to solve, or only on the most serious and difficult? When police play the role of criminal or victim, do the costs in the damaged moral capital of society, corruption, human suffering, and mistrust justify the benefits derived? Are crimes in which government uses the deceit and treachery of a few equally as amenable to solution by the skills and tactics of the many?

REFERENCES

Klockars, C. (1983). "The Dirty Harry Problem." In C. Klockars (ed.), *Thinking About Police*. New York: McGraw-Hill.
———. (1985). *The Idea of Police*. Beverly Hills: Sage.
McNerney, T. (1980). A personal interview. Unfinished Doctoral Dissertation.
Murphy, P. and T. Plate (1977). *Commissioner*. New York: Simon and Schuster.
Reppetto, T. (1978). "The Detective Task: State of the Art, Science, or Craft." *Police Studies*, 1:5–10.
Sanders, W. (1977). *Detective Work*. New York: Free Press.

III

*Experimental Methods
of Policing*

9

A Problem-Oriented Approach to Police Service Delivery

John Eck and William Spelman

INCIDENTS AND PROBLEMS

During a six-month period, detectives investigate a string of seemingly related hotel robberies in one area of a city.

Young men sell crack cocaine in front of a house. Their neighbors complain to the police about the noise, traffic, and gunshots created by the drug market. And patrol officers make periodic sweeps and arrests along the block.

Every Friday and Saturday night, residents of a suburban neighborhood complain to the police about teenagers who come in from another part of town. The youths make noise, drink, and commit minor acts of vandalism.

The parking lots around a large manufacturing plant are a haven for thieves. Thefts from autos parked in these lots account for 10 percent of all crimes reported in the city.

An apartment complex is notorious for its high burglary rates. One of every four residents are burglarized each year; follow-up investigations—and occasional arrests—seem to do no good at all.

Patrol officers and detectives spend millions of hours each year responding to incidents like these. Despite their efforts—and despite the arrests, convictions, and incarcerations that sometimes result—the incidents persist. Police agencies are organized to handle such incidents. So their recurring nature calls into question the effectiveness of this style of policing. Should the police do more than respond to events after they have occurred? Shouldn't the police do more to prevent future incidents?

Results of research spanning two decades have converged on a new approach for delivering police services—problem-oriented policing. Problem-oriented policing is a departmentwide orientation to the police mission: the services a police department provides the public and the means by which it delivers these services. At its core, a problem-oriented approach is about *effectiveness*. Using this approach, police officers do more than handle individual crimes and calls for service. Police officers and detectives take on the underlying problems that give rise to these incidents. To understand problems, police collect facts from a wide variety of sources, from outside as well as from inside police agencies. To develop and implement solutions, police enlist the support of other public and private agencies and individuals. The objective of all these efforts is to reduce and eliminate problems, or to provide better means for handling them.

Problem-oriented policing is not a means of improving police-community relations. Nor is problem-oriented policing a means to decentralize decision-making authority in police departments. Though close police-community relations and decentralized decision making are instrumental to a problem-oriented approach, it is the successful resolution of problems that is being sought.

Problem solving is not new to police work—some officers have always engaged in this mode of policing, with or without their departments' consent. Three things distinguish a problem-oriented approach from the ad hoc problem solving that may have always been a part of policing. First, problem solving is a central element of a problem-oriented approach, not a peripheral activity. Second, everyone in the department contributes to this mission, not just a few innovative officers or a special unit or function. And third, a problem-oriented approach places special emphasis on careful analysis of problems before officers develop solutions, and seeks to avoid instant answers that are unsupported by good information.

Problem-oriented policing is so new that only a few departments have begun experimenting with this strategy. Most of the research to date has been done in the Newport News Police Department; so this description will rely heavily on descriptions of the problem-solving efforts in that department. Before we look at problem-oriented policing in Newport News, we will review the research that led to this approach.

THE EVOLUTION OF A PROBLEM-ORIENTED
APPROACH TO POLICING

People create organizations to carry out missions. Entrepreneurs create businesses to deliver services and products to customers at a profit.

Public officials create agencies to deliver social services businesses do not or cannot market. Measures of effectiveness describe how well organizations are achieving their missions.

In the United States, the police have adopted the notion that their principal mission is to control crime and maintain order. And they believe they should carry out this mission through legal systems such as traffic courts, the criminal justice system, the juvenile justice system, and other legal processes (Fogelson, 1977). Police administrators, elected officials, and the press assess effectiveness by looking at how the police perform at various stages of legal processes. They ask, for example, how fast officers get to victims, how many arrests are made, and what percentage of cases are cleared.

Throughout the 1950s and 1960s scholars and researchers questioned this view of police work. They noted that police officers do not apply the law in all cases to which they could apply it (Goldstein, 1960). In short, scholars discovered "police discretion." These findings led to a debate over the nature, role, and control of police discretion.

Some scholars proposed that police administrators should develop policies to guide officers' actions (Davis, 1975; Goldstein, 1977). This idea stimulated managers' interest in policies. And this led to the establishment of the Commission for Accreditation of Law Enforcement Agencies (Mastrofski, 1986).

To help officials clarify the actions their officers should take in various circumstances, Herman Goldstein looked at the meaning of police effectiveness. He proposed that the nature of the police mission is to handle problems of concern to the public. Many of these problems are crime related, but many others are not.

Police officials, Goldstein argued, define effectiveness by the means they use to address crime problems. They measure effectiveness by response time, arrests, clearance rates, and other statistics that describe activities. In doing so, police managers lost track of the *ends* these means were to achieve. Because of a "means over ends syndrome," police officials did not use alternatives to the legal systems that might help them resolve problems.

To find the most appropriate methods for handling problems, police managers needed to conduct thorough studies of problems. Managers would have to look at the behavioral characteristics of problems instead of relying on the legal definitions. Further, they would need to gather information from a variety of sources. Goldstein specifically advocated tapping the knowledge of street officers and community members. This would assure that managers understood the perspectives of the people with a stake in the problem. Goldstein called this a "problem-oriented approach to policing." As a means for developing useful policies for structuring discretion, he described it as a management function (Goldstein, 1979).

Goldstein and Susmilch conducted the first test of this theory in Madison, Wisconsin (1982). Members of the police department, with assistance from the study team, addressed two citywide problems—drunk driving and sexual assaults. Their study showed that police managers could learn much from problem analysis, and this knowledge was useful for policy formation. It also revealed that a problem-oriented approach may be difficult to achieve.

Only two years later, a London Metropolitan Police study reached similar conclusions (Hoare et al., 1984). London police officials wanted to "evaluate the feasibility of adopting the 'Problem-Oriented Approach.' " They decided to pilot-test the approach on four neighborhood problems: Asian gangs, auto thefts, thefts from shoppers, and prostitution. Police managers assigned one or more low-ranking members of the force to carry out the analysis of these problems. Additionally, headquarters created a team to study the problem-solving process and make recommendations to the commissioner. Although its report was issued before solutions to these problems became apparent, the study team nonetheless felt that problem-oriented policing was a strategy the agency should pursue.

London police moved problem analysis closer to the street by placing it in division stations; in Madison, this was a staff function. Still, we should not make too much of this, since at the time of the London pilot tests, a division had roughly as many constables as Madison had officers.

In 1982, the Baltimore County Police Department created three units of 15 officers each. Called Citizen-Oriented Patrol Enforcement (COPE) units, these units worked with communities to solve fear of crime problems. As in London, the department designed COPE to carry out a problem-oriented approach to its work. Also as in London, the department consulted regularly with Goldstein.

Gary W. Cordner carried out an evaluation of COPE. He found that community members were less fearful after COPE officers had addressed their problems than they were before COPE had intervened. Furthermore, reported crime in problem neighborhoods dropped after most of these efforts (1985).

Cordner also looked at the way COPE officers addressed problems and the impact on problems. At first, COPE officers relied on saturation motorcycle patrols and citizen surveys. Cordner found that this was frustrating for the officers and their problem-solving efforts were only slightly effective. When COPE added more emphasis on providing crime prevention information to citizens, the effectiveness of the problem-solving efforts increased. Finally, the department tried a problem-oriented approach. COPE officers tailored solutions to neighborhoods' problems by seeking the assistance of other county agencies as well as citizens. Cordner reported that operating in this manner COPE became still more effective (1985).

COPE changed the nature of problem-oriented policing. Baltimore County was the first police agency to make this approach routine. It also continued the trend, begun with the London tests, of making problem-oriented policing a part of line operations. Still, the COPE units operated separately from patrol, which means that the bulk of police operations were not problem-oriented. For problem-oriented policing to become a replacement for current methods of policing, police administrators need to view current methods as being less effective.

QUESTIONING THE EFFECTIVENESS OF INCIDENT-DRIVEN POLICING

In fact, in a series of studies conducted during the 1970s, researchers showed that current policing methods are not very effective. These studies caused police officials to search for alternative ways of conducting police business. Several of these alternatives complement a problem-oriented approach by helping to manage workload and organize information.

Current police practice is primarily incident-driven. That is, most police aim most of their activities at resolving discrete incidents. The incident-driven police department has four characteristics.

First, it is *reactive*. Most of the workload of patrol officers and detectives consists of handling crimes that have already been committed—disturbances in progress, traffic violations, and the like. The exceptions—crime prevention and narcotics investigations, for example—make up but a small portion of police work. As a consequence, the harm stemming from the incidents has often already occurred, and there is little that can be done to prevent similar incidents from happening again.

Incident-driven police work relies on limited information, gathered mostly from victims, witnesses, and suspects. Only limited information is needed because the police have limited objectives: patrol officers and detectives are only trying to resolve the incident at hand. As a consequence, policy know relatively little about the circumstances that gave rise to the incidents.

The primary means of resolving incidents is to invoke the criminal justice process. Even when an officer manages to resolve an incident without arresting or citing anyone, it is often the threat of enforcing the law that is the key to resolution. Alternative means of resolution are seldom invoked. This limited the police search for more effective ways of handling problems that lay outside criminal justice processes.

Finally, incident-driven police departments use aggregate statistics to measure performance. The department is doing a good job when the citywide crime rate is low, or the citywide arrest rate is high. The best officers are those who make many arrests, or service many calls. So the police cannot assess the well-being of particular neighborhoods, or population groups.

No department is purely incident-driven, but almost all agencies are incident-driven almost all of the time. Appropriately responding to incidents can be effective: police aid victims, they bring serious offenders to justice, and they help citizens with a myriad of difficulties every day. But handling calls for service is time-consuming, and rarely produces tangible results. The constant repetition of similar calls shows that the incident-driven police department has been unable to do anything about the underlying conditions. Further, many citizen concerns are never reported to the police or, when reported, do not accurately describe the reasons for the distress (complaints about noise that are really the result of a drug-dealing operation, for example).

These conclusions about incident-driven policing were only reached after much research that showed that the basic assumptions of incident-driven policing were probably wrong.

The presumed effectiveness of incident-driven policing rests on three assumptions: that marked patrol cars deter crooks; that rapid response catches them; and that when uniformed officers do not catch them, detectives will. The Kansas City preventive patrol experiment (Kelling, et al., 1974) questioned the first assumption. The study also showed that the public was unaware of the level of patrol coverage. Though some people have questioned the methods used in this study (Larson, 1976; Fienberg et al., 1980), other studies came to the same conclusions (Dahman, 1975; Schnelle et al., 1975; Schnelle et al., 1977; Lewis et al., 1977; and Wagner, 1978).

Researchers also attacked the response time assumption. The first research supported the widespread use of rapid response (Isaacs, 1967). But biased data formed the basis for the findings (Spelman and Brown, 1984). In 1980, the Kansas City Police Department conducted the first research on the entire response-time continuum—from the moment a citizen could report a crime, until a patrol car arrived and contacted the complainant. The results showed that rapid response made little or no difference in catching offenders (Kansas City Police Department, 1980). Spelman and Brown (1984) confirmed these conclusions in four other cities. Finally, Pate (1976) demonstrated that response time, in and of itself, does not affect citizen satisfaction. Instead, the difference between the response time and the caller's expectation of how soon an officer will arrive affects satisfaction.

Finally, researchers questioned the effectiveness of follow-up investigations by detectives. A series of studies (Isaacs, 1967; Greenwood,

1970; Greenberg et al., 1973; Greenwood et al., 1975; and Eck, 1979) demonstrated that follow-up investigations of property crimes, the largest group of crimes investigated, were largely unproductive. If the information that leads to the identification of suspects is not available at the crime scene and collected by patrol officer, detectives are very unlikely to solve the case. A later study by Eck (1982) suggested that these conclusions were too pessimistic, in part because they were derived from incomplete data. Nevertheless, there are severe limits to the effectiveness of follow-up investigations.

These studies led some police managers to look for ways of improving effectiveness. They found three complementary methods.

If random patrol produced few benefits, maybe directing patrol efforts could produce more. So police managers tried directed patrol programs. Supervisors would tell their officers to pay close attention to areas where they could deter offenders or catch them.

To give these directions, managers needed information. So police managers formed crime analysis units to look for patterns of criminal behavior. These units would locate areas with many crimes in a short span of time. They would also spot patterns that could finger offenders. Managers could then tell officers and detectives whom to look for. Officers then might catch more criminals in the act of committing offenses, and detectives could focus their investigations on the most likely suspects.

Officers needed time to carry out directed patrol assignments. And delaying responses could provide more time. Managers, therefore, had to wrest control of patrol workloads from dispatchers and the 911 system. The response time research helped them. It implied that rapid responses were not needed for most calls. Furthermore, call-takers could set citizens' expectations of when an officer would arrive. Slower police responses to nonemergency calls would satisfy citizens if call-takers told citizens an officer would not arrive right away. Managers could free up even more time by having nonsworn employees handle noncrime incidents. So police officials created differential response policies to carry out these and other time-capturing notions.

Investigations managers developed case-screening policies for detectives. These policies were to do for detectives what differential response policies were to do for patrol. Cases with few or no clues were "screened out," that is, not assigned to detectives for further investigative work. Instead, detectives would focus their attention on cases that were potentially solvable or involved repeat offenders (Eck, 1982).

These reforms—differential response and case screening, crime analysis, and directed patrol—had three failings. First, they focused only on crime. Though crime reduction was the implicit objective of these problems, there is little evidence that these programs reduced it. The tactics used to address crime problems were almost always arrest-oriented.

Though several programs showed improved arrest statistics, none showed what increases in arrests achieved. And the studies reported no systematic efforts to look for other ways to handle problems.

Second, though these reforms increased police use of information, the information was from a small number of sources. Crime analysis units only studied police reports to determine the appropriate tactics. Managers seldom built the public and other agencies into the system. This meant that police did not handle community problems unless they fit the police definition of a problem.

Finally, managers, supported by office-bound analysts, told street supervisors, detectives, and officers what to work on. Managers seldom built systems to tap street knowledge. So management's attempts to impose crime analysis and directed patrol on street supervisors often met with failures.

To deal with these difficulties, police managers needed a different approach to the police function. Specifically, they needed to reconsider effectiveness. This, in turn, motivated interest in applying a problem-oriented approach to an entire police department.

DESIGNING PROBLEM-ORIENTED POLICING

This was the research background when in 1984 the Newport News Police Department and the Police Executive Research Forum began the Problem-Oriented Policing Project with a grant from the National Institute of Justice (NIJ). Other departments had implemented problem-solving approaches as part of special units or projects. No department had implemented a problem-oriented approach agency wide. So an operational system that captured the elements of this strategy had to be designed and tested. NIJ required that the problem-solving system follow five basic principles:

- Officers of all ranks and from all units should be able to use the system as part of their daily routine.
- The system must encourage the use of a broad range of information, including but not limited to conventional police data.
- The system should encourage a broad range of solutions, including but not limited to the criminal justice process.
- The system should require no additional resources and no special units.
- Finally, any large police agency must be able to apply it.

Newport News was chosen to design and implement a problem-oriented approach for several reasons. It is a moderate-sized agency, with 280 employees serving a population of 155,000. It was small enough

Figure 9.1
The Problem-Solving Process

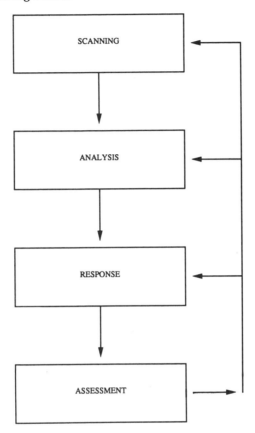

Source: Eck and Spelman, 1987.

that changes could be made in a reasonably short time, but served an urban population with many of the crime problems of big cities.

To design a system to operationalize problem-oriented policing, the Newport News Police Department assembled a task force of 12 department members, representing all ranks and units. As this group had no experience at solving problems, they decided to test the system they were designing on two persistent problems: burglaries from an apartment complex, and thefts from vehicles parked adjacent to a major factory. All subsequent problems were handled by officers in their normal assignments.

As shown in Figure 9.1, the task force designed a four-stage problem-solving process. During the scanning stage, an officer identifies an issue and determines whether it is really a problem. In the analysis stage, officers collect information from sources inside and outside their agency. The goal is to understand the scope, nature, and causes of the problem. In the response stage, officers use this information to develop and implement solutions. Officers seek the assistance of other police units, other public and private organizations, and anyone else who can help. Finally, in the assessment stage, officers evaluate the effectiveness of the response. Officers may use the results to revise the response, collect more data, or even to redefine the problem.

The heart of this process is the analysis stage. To help officers analyze problems, the task force designed a problem analysis guide. This guide breaks the events that make up a problem into three components:

- *Actors*—victims, offenders, and others involved in the events;
- *Incidents*—the social context, physical settings, and actions taken before, during, and after the events; and
- *Responses*—the perceptions and responses of citizens and private and public institutions to the problem.

The guide is a checklist of factors that officers should consider when they study a problem. When addressing problems, officers and their supervisors use the guide to identify elements of the problem they should investigate.

All officers of the rank of sergeant and above were trained in the use of the process and the guide. The training also emphasized the need to encourage officer initiative in finding problems, collecting information, and developing responses. Officers throughout the department then began to apply the process and the guide.

PROBLEM-ORIENTED POLICING AT WORK

Though the process and guide seemed good in theory, it was unclear whether they would be useful in practice. There were two basic questions that needed to be answered:

- Can officers use it routinely to solve problems?
- Are these problem-solving efforts effective?

To answer them, the Forum staff undertook an evaluation of problem-oriented policing in Newport News.

By June 1986, department personnel had identified two dozen problems, and were in various stages of analysis, response, and assessment. As Figure 9.2 shows, officers considered a wide range of problems. Some problems affected citizens throughout the city; others were confined to neighborhoods. Some problems were criminal; others were related to

Figure 9.2
Problems Addressed by Newport News Officers

CRIME PROBLEMS

Citywide	Neighborhood
Domestic Homicides	Personal Robberies (Central Business Dist)
Gas Station Drive-offs	Commercial Burglaries (Jefferson Avenue Business District)
Assaults on Police Officers	Vacant Buildings (Central Business District)
	Residential Burglaries (New Briarfield Apts)
	Residential Burglaries (Glenn Gardens Apts)
	Larcenies (Beechmont Gardens Apts)
	Thefts from Autos (Newport News Shipbuilding)
	Drug Dealing (32nd and Chestnut)

DISORDER PROBLEMS

Citywide	Neighborhood
Runaway Youths	Rowdy Youths (Peninsula Skating Rink)
Driving Under the Influence	Shot Houses (Aqua Vista Apts)
Disturbances at Convenience Stores	Disturbances (Marshall Avenue 7-Eleven)
	Dirt Bikes (Newmarket Creek)
	Disturbances (Village Square Shopping Ctr)

the order maintenance, regulatory, or service roles of police. Officers and their supervisors identified, analyzed, and responded to these problems during their normal work by applying the process and guide. The number and diversity of problems tackled by department members showed that police officers can solve problems routinely.

The second test of the problem-solving process was the effectiveness of the responses. Three efforts were systematically evaluated. The results were encouraging:

- Burglaries in the New Briarfield Apartment complex were reduced by 35 percent and the tenants were relocated to better dwellings and the complex torn down (see below);

- Addressing a prostitution problem in the central business district reduced robberies in this area by 40 percent; and

- Thefts from vehicles parked outside Newport News Shipbuilding were reduced by 55 percent when this problem was addressed.

These results show that problem-solving efforts can be effective. To illustrate how problem solving works, let us examine the first of these efforts.

Burglaries in the New Briarfield Apartments

Briarfield Apartments, a complex of 450 wood-frame units, were built in 1942 as temporary housing for shipyard workers. After World War II the postwar housing shortage was acute, so the apartments remained standing. By 1984, Briarfield was the worst housing and had the highest crime rate in the city: 23 percent of the occupied units were broken into each year.

Detective Tony Duke was assigned to study the problem. To find out how residents felt, he arranged for patrol and auxiliary officers to survey a random sample of one-third of the households in January 1985. The residents confirmed that burglary was a serious problem. But they were equally concerned about the deterioration of the complex.

Indeed, as Duke interviewed employees of city departments, he found that the burglary problem and the deterioration of the complex were part of a much larger problem. The fire department considered New Briarfield to be a firetrap. Public works and the codes and compliance departments were concerned because repeated flooding (the complex had no storm sewers) rotted the floors. Cracks around the door and window frames let in the cold and rain, and made break-ins easy. And many units were vacant, providing hiding places for burglars and drug users.

Immediately after the survey, the patrol officer responsible for the area around New Briarfield, Barry Haddix, decided to clean up the grounds of the complex. By working with the apartment manager and city agencies he was able to fix a variety of unsanitary and unsafe conditions. Trash and abandoned appliances were removed, abandoned cars were towed, the potholes were filled, and the streets were swept.

Meanwhile, Duke found that the owners of the complex were in default on a loan from the U.S. Department of Housing and Urban Development and that HUD was about to foreclose. These circumstances presented the city with a possible solution. Duke wrote a report on New Briarfield, describing the crime problems, the views of the tenants, and the concerns of other city agencies. Police Chief Darrel Stephens used this report to mobilize other city agencies to make a joint recommendation to the city manager: help the tenants find better housing and demolish New Briarfield. The city manager accepted the recommendation. In June 1986, the city proposed that Briarfield be replaced with a new 220-unit apartment complex, a middle school, and a small shopping center. In 1988, HUD agreed to the city's proposal. By that time, fewer than 40 households called New Briarfield home.

This long-run solution had taken many months to implement. To keep crime under control in the interim, the police department assigned Officer Vernon Lyons to the full-time job of organizing residents of Briarfield and the surrounding neighborhoods. Since January 1986, the New Briarfield Community Association has influenced residents to take better care of their neighborhood, lobbied the resident manager and city agencies to ensure that the complex was properly maintained, and helped facilitate the movement of families to better housing.

New Information, New Responses

Police managers have used the problem-solving process and guide to encourage officers to gather more information from a wider variety of sources than before. The survey of New Briarfield residents, and the discussions with the apartment manager and public officials are examples of the breadth of their search for information. While studying other problems, officers in Newport News have conducted literature reviews, interviewed prostitutes and thieves, surveyed businesses, held conferences with public and private officials, photographed problem sites, and searched title and tax records.

As a result, the responses these officers initiated are more comprehensive than standard incident-driven tactics. Some of the responses are improvements on standard tactics. For example, the department responded to the problems of downtown robberies and parking-lot thefts by identifying, arresting, and incarcerating the most frequent offenders.

Even in these examples, the involvement of people outside the criminal justice system was important. Other responses, such as the actions taken in New Briarfield, hardly involved the criminal justice process at all. While responding to other problems, officers have worked with businesses, the military, citizens' groups, state and federal agencies, and nonprofit organizations. So the resources used are as diverse as the problems.

IMPLEMENTING PROBLEM-ORIENTED POLICING

Problem-oriented policing involves a substantial change from current practice. The agency in which problem-oriented policing is fully implemented will be different from present agencies in several ways.

- Problem-solving will be the standard strategy of policing, not just an occasionally useful tactic.
- Problem-solving efforts will focus on problems of the public, not police administration.
- When problems are addressed, police will establish precise, measurable objectives.
- Police managers will constantly look for ways to get all members of the department involved in solving problems.

These characteristics will be true of all agencies that have committed themselves to a problem-oriented approach. As these agencies gain experience with problem-oriented policing, they should develop three additional characteristics:

- Officers will consistently undertake thorough analyses, using data from many sources.
- Officers will engage in an uninhibited search for solutions to all problems they take on.
- All members of the department will be involved in problem solving.

Developing these characteristics will take time; police executives should plan to implement problem-oriented policing over many years, rather than weeks or months.

As a result, there are no police departments with all seven of these characteristics as yet. Newport News has the first four characteristics; several other departments are moving in this direction. Nevertheless, problem-oriented policing represents an enormous change in the way officers think about their jobs, and in the way the entire department does business. While it will take a long time to develop, the Newport News experience has demonstrated that police executives interested in pursuing the problem-oriented approach can make their agencies more effective.

Problem solving will be easier to implement if police departments change practices that pose barriers to problem solving. For example, many Newport News officers reported that lack of time was a major constraint to their problem-solving activities. So the police manager should consider such tactics as differential police response and case screening. Use of crime analysis and proactive patrol and investigation tactics can also help the department get ready for less conventional activities. Constantly changing assignments and rotating shifts can make problem-solving activities inconvenient and difficult; police executives should consider stable assignments and shift schedules to remove these obstacles. Changes in promotion and reward procedures, implementation of management-by-objectives, and explicit training in effective problem-solving techniques can both motivate officers to solve problems and show them that the administration is serious about its efforts.

Getting support from institutions outside the police department is critical, since they provide information about problems and assistance in solving them. However, a problem-oriented approach may be difficult to sell to those outside policing. There is no unit, equipment, or other physical evidence to which the police can point as evidence of problem solving. Some critics will assume the police department has been solving problems all along. These difficulties put a burden on police executives to begin teaching local government officials, members of civil organizations, the press, and others about the nature of the changes as soon as they decide to make them.

This process of educating the department and the public will continue once the police executive has committed the department to problem-oriented policing. Aside from education, the most important task for the police executive will then be to provide leadership and direction to street-level supervisors. Sergeants and lieutenants are especially important to the success of problem-oriented policing, because problem-solving efforts will rarely be cut-and-dried. These supervisors must be prepared to give their officers lots of discretion, assistance, and support, but they must also be sure that officers are putting in their best efforts. Supervisors must be patient, and emphasize performance; but they must also insist that officers persist at their efforts until they accomplish what can reasonably be done. In problem-oriented policing, the first-line supervisor's job becomes one of continually balancing conflicting objectives.

Police managers at all levels will face a tension between the quantity of problems solved and the quality of problem-solving efforts. If managers set standards too high or encourage officers to take on very large problems, others may be scared off. But standards set too low may make problem solving appear trivial. If police executives can balance this tension, both quality and quantity are possible and the effectiveness of police work will increase substantially.

REFERENCES

Cordner, G. W. (1985). *The Baltimore County Citizen Oriented Police Enforcement (COPE) Project: Final Report to the Florence V. Burden Foundation.* Baltimore: Criminal Justice Department, University of Baltimore.

Dahman, J. (1975). *Examination of Police Patrol Effectiveness: High-Impact Anti-Crime Program*. McLean, VA: Mitre Corporation.

Davis, K. (1975). *Police Discretion*. St. Paul, MN: West.

Eck, J. (1979). *Managing Case Assignments: The Burglary Investigation Decision Model Replication*. Washington, D.C.: Police Executive Research Forum.

———. (1982). *Solving Crimes: The Investigation of Burglary and Robbery*. Washington, D.C.: Police Executive Research Forum.

Eck, J. and W. Spelman (1987). *Problem Solving: Problem-Oriented Policing in Newport News*. Washington, D.C.: Police Executive Research Forum.

Fienberg, S.; K. Larntz; and A. Reiss, Jr. (1980). "Redesigning the Kansas City Preventive Patrol Experiment." Pp. 109–124 in Stephen E. Fienberg and Albert J. Reiss, Jr. (eds.), *Indicators of Crime and Criminal Justice: Quantitative Studies*. Washington, D.C.: U.S. Government Printing Office.

Fogelson, R. (1977). *Big City Police*. Cambridge, MA: Harvard University Press.

Goldstein, H. (1977). *Policing a Free Society*. Cambridge, Massachusetts: Ballinger.

———. (1979). "Improving Policing: A Problem-Oriented Approach." *Crime and Delinquency*, 25:236–258.

Goldstein, H. and C. Susmilch (1982). *Experimenting with the Problem-Oriented Approach to Improving Police Service: A Report and Some Reflections on Two Case Studies*. Madison, WI: Law School, University of Wisconsin.

Goldstein, J. (1960). "Police Discretion Not to Invoke the Criminal Process: Low-Visibility Decisions in the Administration of Justice." *Yale Law Journal*, 69:543–594.

Greenberg, B.; O. Yu; and K. Lang (1973). *Enhancement of the Investigative Function, Volume 1, Analysis and Conclusions, Final Report, Phases 1*. Springfield, VA: National Technical Information Service.

Greenwood, P. (1970). *An Analysis of the Apprehension Activities of the New York City Police Department*. New York: Rand Institute.

Greenwood, P. and J. Petersilia (1975). *The Criminal Investigation Process—Volume 1: Survey and Policy Implications*. Santa Monica, California: Rand Corporation.

Hoare, M.; G. Stewart; and C. M. Purcell (1984). *The Problem Oriented Approach: Four Pilot Studies*. U.K.: Metropolitan Police, Management Services Department.

Isaacs, H. (1967). "A Study of Communications, Crimes, and Arrests in a Metropolitan Police Department." Pp. 88–106 in *Institute for Defense Analysis, Task Force Report: Science and Technology*. A report to the President's Commission on Law Enforcement and the Administration of Justice. Washington, D.C.: U.S. Government Printing Office.

Kansas City Police Department (1980). *Response Time Analysis: Volume II—Part 1, Crime Analysis*. Washington, D.C.: U.S. Government Printing Office.

Kelling, G.; T. Pate; D. Dieckman, and C. Brown (1974). *The Kansas City Preventive Patrol Experiment: A Technical Report*. Washington, D.C.: Police Foundation.

Larson, R. (1986). "What Happened to Patrol Operations in Kansas City? A Review of the Kansas City Preventive Patrol Experiment." *Journal of Criminal Justice*, 3:267–297.

Lewis, R.; J. Greene; and S. Edwards (1977). *Special Police Units in Michigan: An*

Evaluation. East Lansing, MI: Criminal Justice Systems Center, Michigan State University.

Mastrofski, S. (1986). "Police Agency Accreditation: The Prospects of Reform." Paper presented at the annual meeting of the American Political Science Association, Washington, D.C., August 28–31.

New York City Police Department (1988). *Community Patrol Officer Program: Problem Solving Guide*. New York: New York Police Department.

Pate, T.; R. Bowers; and R. Parks (1976). *Three Approaches to Criminal Apprehension in Kansas City: An Evaluation Report*. Washington, D.C.: Police Foundation.

Schnelle, J.; R. Kirchner, Jr.; J. Casey; P. Uselton, Jr., and M. Patrick McNees (1977). "Patrol Evaluation Research: A Multiple-Baseline Analysis of Saturation Police Patrolling during Day and Night Hours." *Journal of Applied Behavior Analysis*, 10:33–40.

Schnelle, J.; R. Kirchner, Jr.; J. Lawler, and M. P. McNees (1975). "Social Evaluation Research: The Evaluation of Two Police Patrol Strategies." *Journal of Applies Behavior Analysis*, 8:232–240.

Spelman, W. and D. Brown (1984). *Calling the Police: Citizen Reporting of Serious Crime*. Washington, D.C.: U.S. Government Printing Office.

Wagner, W. (1978). *An Evaluation of a Police Patrol Experiment*. WA: Washington State University.

10

Community-Oriented Policing in Baltimore

Antony Michael Pate

In an effort to insulate police departments from political interference, early reformers proposed that the police be organized according to a "military model" (Richardson, 1974). Applying this model, three basic reforms were broadly adopted:

- Departmental operations were centralized under the control of chiefs largely independent of external control;
- The function of the police was narrowed to focus on crime prevention; and
- The quality of police personnel was upgraded.

Although at least some of these reforms undoubtedly produced improvements in the efficiency and effectiveness of the police, in many cases they were achieved at a considerable cost—often at the expense of relations with the public. To achieve centralization, for example, local precinct stations were consolidated or closed completely. To reduce the opportunities for graft and corruption, patrol officers were now rotated among beats instead of being assigned to one neighborhood over time as they previously had been. While savings may have been realized and managerial control increased, such changes also created greater isolation between the police and the public. As a result, in many neighborhoods the familiar "cop on the beat" became just another nameless official in a uniform working in a community of strangers.

By eliminating such responsibilities as supervising elections, operating ambulances, inspecting boilers, and censoring movies, reformers also made it possible for the police to devote their energies more directly to crime fighting and reduction. However, as the newly declared "war on crime" was waged, this reform too had unanticipated consequences. As more aggressive tactics were encouraged and officers and their departments became involved in situations they would previously have ignored, considerable resentment towards the police began to grow in some communities.

Combined with centralization, this focus on aggressive crime fighting created special problems in minority communities. By applying a common standard to nonviolent crimes—especially "moral offenses" such as gambling and drinking—the police often found themselves enforcing prevailing norms in areas where those norms had not yet been accepted. To the citizens of those areas (often poor and minority), the police soon came to be seen as an "army of occupation" (Wilson, 1983, p. 90). Even the efforts to improve the quality of police personnel may have had deleterious effects. As educational requirements were raised, stipulations that officers live within the city for which they work were dropped, and proof of no prior arrests or convictions was required, the reformers made it more difficult for members of minority groups to become police officers.

Other advances had equally significant impact as well. With the advent of motorized patrol, the area an officer could cover was greatly expanded. In too many cities, however, these motorized officers (made even more rapid by radio dispatching, 911 emergency telephone systems, and computers) spent much of their time driving from call to call, emerging only to contact crime victims, arrest suspects, or give traffic citations—hardly situations in which enduring trust and understanding are developed. The creation of specialized units provided valuable new resources to police operations, but again at a cost. Many in these units (e.g., planning and research, internal affairs, intelligence, crime analysis, and crime laboratories) had no direct contact with citizens, while members of other units, such as detectives and missing-persons investigators, usually had contact limited to citizens who were distraught or confronted with personal emergencies.

The cumulative effect of these several changes over the last several years has been succinctly summarized by Henig (1984, pp. 5–6):

By reducing social contact between police and citizens, and by limiting contact to emotionally charged situations in which crimes had occurred, these changes increased the likelihood that citizens and police would regard each other as strangers.

As a result, police officers assigned to an area may have little understanding of the priorities and concerns of people living or working there. This lack of information about neighborhoods causes some officers to be unaware of, and therefore unresponsive to, important neighborhood problems and may, in turn, cause citizens to feel that police neither know nor care about them. At best, such a situation limits cooperation between the police and the public they are hired to serve. In its most aggravated form, as The Report of the National Advisory Commission on Civil Disorders (1968) pointed out, such "stranger policing" may serve as a catalyst to urban riots.

This increased distancing between police and the public is, in itself, a problem demanding redress. This problem, however, can also have far-reaching law enforcement consequences, since, as much recent research has shown, to be effective, crime prevention and fear reduction must be a joint effort between citizens and the police (Lavrakas and Herz, 1982; Rosenbaum, 1982; Waller, 1979; Yin, 1979). Therefore, reductions in mutual trust which result from this distance can be expected to contribute to increases in both fear and the incidence of crime.

THE EVOLUTION OF THE COMMUNITY-ORIENTED CONCEPTS

During the 1970s, many programs to redress the problem of police isolation from citizens were developed. Most can be characterized as what Wilson (1983) called "community service" strategies: programs designed to encourage officers to become more familiar with their beats while developing contacts with citizens that might lead to higher arrest rates and better intelligence about crimes. With few exceptions, however (Boydstun and Sherry, 1975, for example), most of these programs demonstrated results that were less than had been hoped for—either because they were not fully implemented, were not properly evaluated, or both.

More recently, "community policing" has become one of the most popular topics among police scholars and practitioners. As Skolnick and Bayley (1988) have pointed out:

Among the world's industrial democracies, community-oriented policing represents what is progressive and forward-looking in policing. In Western Europe, North America, Australia-New Zealand, and the Far East, community policing is being talked about as the solution to the problems of policing. Papers exploring it have become a cottage industry.

Despite, or perhaps because of, its burgeoning popularity, the phrase "community policing" has been used to describe a wide array of programs, few of which have been subjected to rigorous evaluation. Skolnick and Bayley (1988) note that the term has been used to describe Neighborhood Watch, mini- and shopfront-police stations, liaison with gay communities, specialized attention to the problems of women and children, unsolicited visits by patrol officers to homes, media campaigns to improve the image of the police, foot patrols, village constables, designation of "safety houses" for schoolchildren, strategies for reducing the public's fear of crime, directed patrol, police-sponsored discos and athletic leagues, horse patrols, the creation of citizen auxiliary police, senior citizen escorts, lectures on self-protection and home security, and conflict mediation panels.

Still, in her review of the concept, Wycoff (1988) concludes that despite the multitude of manifestations, community policing programs "... have in common the belief that police and citizens should experience a larger number of nonthreatening, supportive interactions" that should include efforts by police to:

1. Listen to citizens, including those who are neither victims nor perpetrators of crimes;
2. Take seriously citizens' definitions of their problems, even when the problems they define might differ from ones the police would identify for them;
3. Solve the problems that have been identified.

The two versions of community policing that have been subjected to the most careful evaluations have been foot patrol and having patrol officers initiate contacts with citizens to determine their problems and attempt to work cooperatively to address those problems.

After many years of being out of fashion, foot patrol has been revived in many of the nation's cities. Although much has been written about the possible advantages and disadvantages of such patrol (Adams, 1971; Gourley, 1974; Iannoe, 1975; Payton, 1967; Brown, 1973) there is little empirical evidence concerning its effectiveness. Bloch and Ulberg (1972), for example, reported that, in a team policing experiment of which foot patrol was an integral part, it appeared that such patrol was especially popular with business people. Prefecture de Police (1973) suggests that foot patrol in Paris was useful in dealing with public-nuisance problems and stolen vehicles; but these conclusions were based on notably meager data. Hogan and Fagin (1974) suggest that supplementing motor patrol with foot patrol reduced crime and improved the attitudes of citizens— but no empirical basis for this conclusion is provided.

Bright (1970), after analyzing a British study, found that reported crime rates were significantly affected by an increase from no foot patrol in an area to the use of one foot patrol officer over a three-month period. Pendland and Gay (1972) reported that foot patrol in a high-crime area of Fort Worth, Texas led to reductions in recorded crime and increases in citizen satisfaction. Because of the lack of controls and the limited-outcome measures in both of these studies, their validity must be questioned.

Other studies were both limited and inconclusive in their results. Arlington County, Virginia Police Department (1976) found no strong effects from the implementation of a foot patrol program. Kinney (1979) found strong citizen support for foot patrol but no clear effects on crime. Schnelle et al. (1975) found that recorded crime *increased* significantly in foot patrol areas, largely as a result of an increased willingness of citizens to report crime directly to the foot patrol officers.

The best-known studies of foot patrol were conducted in Newark, New Jersey and Flint, Michigan. In Newark, the Police Foundation conducted an experimental evaluation of the effectiveness of foot patrol (Police Foundation, 1981). In brief, that evaluation found that introducing foot patrol:

- Was readily perceived by residents;
- Produced a significant increase in the level of satisfaction with police service;
- Led to a significant reduction in the level of perceived crime problems; and
- Resulted in a significant increase in the perceived level of safety of the neighborhood.

Despite these generally favorable results, there were certain limitations to this study that left important questions unanswered. Foot patrol, for example, was limited to mostly commercial areas during evening hours. Indications of the effectiveness of such patrols in residential areas, or during the day, cannot be drawn from this research. In addition, the samples of residents were relatively small, and no panel of respondents was included, reducing the statistical power of the analyses. Furthermore, although the introduction of foot patrol produced generally favorable results, the relative effects of maintaining and eliminating foot patrol showed no consistent pattern.

An evaluation of a foot-patrol program in Flint, Michigan, indicated that:

- The crime rate in the target areas declined slightly;
- Calls for service in the target areas dropped by 43 percent; and
- Citizens indicated satisfaction with the program, suggesting that it had improved relations with the police.

This study (Trojanowicz, 1982), however, also had several features that greatly limit its value as a source of conclusions about the effectiveness of foot patrol. For example, foot patrol as practiced in Flint was quite dissimilar to that in most jurisdictions. Although the officers involved in the study patrolled on foot, they had a number of responsibilities not normally part of such an assignment:

• Establishing personal contacts with the residents of the target areas;
• Conferring with residents and employees concerning problems in their neighborhood;
• Making security inspections of residences and businesses;
• Meeting with the families of juveniles with whom the police had contacts;
• Assigning priorities to and referring to other agencies complaints made by local residents;
• Writing a monthly article for a community newspaper; and
• Attending neighborhood block clubs and School Advisory Council meetings.

The evaluation also had several characteristics that restrict its validity. First, the 14 target areas were selected as a result of the requests of residents for a foot patrol program, thus limiting the generalizability of the findings. Second, there were no analyses of survey data from control areas, making it impossible to disentangle the effects of the program from those of other factors. Third, the panel samples used were extremely small, averaging only about three persons per target area. Fourth, many of the items included in the resident questionnaire were worded in such a way as to potentially bias responses. Fifth, recorded crime data were not collected or analyzed in such a way as to control for trends. Finally, analyses of such outcomes as the perceived seriousness of crime or the effect of fear on behavior did not reveal desirable results.

Studies of the effectiveness of having patrol officers initiate contacts with citizens to determine their problems and attempt to work cooperatively to address those problems are even more rare than those dealing with foot patrol. The Flint "foot patrol" study described above serves better as an example of this type of evaluation, in fact, than it does as a study of typical foot patrol.

An early precursor of this approach can be found in the San Diego Community Profile Project (Boydstun and Sherry, 1975). In this study, officers were trained to produce profiles of their beats that included a description of institutional life and an analysis of community problems and priorities as well as the resources that could be brought to bear on the identified problems. They were also asked to develop strategies to solve those problems. Unfortunately, the evaluation dealt only with the effect of the program on the officers involved, not on members of the community.

The Community Patrol Officer Program (CPOP), first instituted by the New York City Police Department in 1984, is similar in many respects to the Flint, Michigan foot patrol program (Farrell, 1988). Officers involved in this program are responsible for:

- Getting to know the residents, merchants, and service providers in their beat area;
- Identifying the principal crime and order maintenance problems confronting the people within their beat, based upon their observations, analysis of statistical records, and information provided by the people within the area; and
- Devising strategies for dealing with the problems identified.

Although the Vera Institute of Justice is conducting an evaluation of the effectiveness of the CPOP approach, the results are not yet available. Nevertheless, the initial pilot model in one beat produced such favorable responses, both from the community and the department's command staff, that it has been replicated throughout the city (Farrell, 1988).

In Houston, Texas, "citizen contact patrol" was recently tested in one target neighborhood. This approach called for the officers in the experimental area to contact persons living in residences or working in businesses and ask if there were problems in the area that the police should know about. The officer then left a business card with his or her name and the station telephone number where the officer could be reached. The problems mentioned, along with information about the contacted person, were recorded on a card, which was filed at the district station. Officers worked individually to solve the problems identified in this way (Pate et al. 1986).

Using both panel and cross-sectional samples for analysis, evaluators found the program associated with statistically significant:

- Reductions in perceived social disorder,
- Increases in satisfaction with the neighborhood, and
- Reductions in property victimization.

Using the cross-sectional samples only, the evaluators additionally found significant reductions in:

- Fear of personal victimization,
- Perceived personal crime,
- Perceived property crime, and
- Perceived police aggressiveness.

In the panel sample, a significant improvement in the evaluation of police service was found. Overall, the number of burglaries and thefts dropped by 23 percent in the program area during the year of the experiment compared to the previous year. Unfortunately, data for earlier time periods were not available, making it impossible to determine if this decrease was part of a preexisting trend. Finally, analyses of possible differential program effects on subgroups of panel respondents disclosed that black respondents and those who rented their homes were significantly less likely than whites and home owners to report awareness of this program—and therefore to benefit from it.

From these previous efforts we see that although community policing has emerged as an attractive alternative to those approaches that have created distance between citizens and the police, there is little empirical evidence to indicate how effective the various types of community policing can be in different kinds of neighborhoods. In this chapter we will explore one such program as we report on a community-oriented policing program recently undertaken by the Baltimore, Maryland Police Department. Specifically, we will compare the effectiveness of foot patrol and "ombudsman policing"—an effort by police officers to ascertain and address the problems identified by residents of particular neighborhoods.

THE METHODS USED IN BALTIMORE

The evaluation of the Baltimore community policing experiment was based upon the comparison of attitudinal and victimization measures collected from a panel of the same individuals, before (Wave 1) and twelve months after (Wave 2) the introduction of the experimental treatments. These measures were obtained by conducting in-person interviews with random samples of residents in each of the project's six experimental areas. In addition, monthly calls for service and recorded crime data were collected for all six areas for the 29 months prior to and 12 months during the implementation of the experiment. Following is a brief discussion of how the program and comparison areas, the sampling procedures, and the outcome measures were selected for use.

The Selection of Experimental Areas

A multistage selection process was used to ensure that the experimental areas were both comparable to each other and representative of a broad range of socioeconomic neighborhoods. First, 1980 census data were collected for 277 Baltimore neighborhoods. These data were analyzed to determine the underlying dimensions upon which these neighborhoods could be differentiated. The variables analyzed were the following:

—housing value percentile score;

—household income percentile score;

—percent of labor force in white collar, managerial, or professional occupations;

—percent of adult population with high school degree;

—percent of population below fourteen years of age;

—percent of households that were married couples;

—percent of households that were one-unit structures;

—percent of households that were occupied by their owners; and

—percent of population that was black.

Three basic factors emerged from this analysis:

—status, with high loadings for housing value, income, employment status, and education;

—stability, with high loadings for married couples, one unit structures, and owner occupancy; and

—race/youth, with high loadings for percent black and children under 14.

Subjecting factor scores from these three dimensions to cluster analysis indicated a total of 12 clusters of neighborhoods. In order to maximize the generalizability of the findings, we decided to implement the community policing experiment in two highly different clusters. Besides the criterion of variability, we also excluded the highly transient clusters— in order to improve the chances of being able to reinterview large numbers of residents in our panel design. Based on these standards, we selected the two largest clusters—South Baltimore and New Northwood/ Howard Park. The former cluster is located in the southeast part of Baltimore—a working/middle-class area of rowhouses inhabited primarily by immigrants from Central Europe and Greece who had resided there for several years and who have few children. The latter cluster is in northwest Baltimore—a middle-class area of single-unit homes inhabited mostly by blacks, many with young children.

We selected three experimental areas in each cluster for the experiment. In each case, we sought to identify areas that had not had foot patrol or any other special police treatment during the last several years. Furthermore, we sought areas that contained approximately 500 to 600 occupied units on approximately 16 square blocks. After consulting with police officials and making extensive tours of several neighborhoods in both clusters, we chose the Callaway, Hanlon Park, and Northeast Windsor areas in the Howard Park cluster and the Ellwood Park, Highlandtown, and Linwood areas in the South Baltimore cluster. Table 10.1 presents selected 1980 population and housing data from each of the six

Table 10.1
Summary of 1980 Census of Population and Housing Block Statistics for
Experimental Areas in Baltimore

| | Number of Persons | | | | | | | Year-Round Housing Units | | | | Owner | | Renter | | |
	Total	Black	Asian Pacific	White	Spanish	Under 18	65+	Housing Total	Single Family	10+ Units	Mean Rooms	Owner	Mean Value	Renter	Mean Rent	Mean Persons Per Unit
Callaway	2022	1937	0	76	0	541	157	664	386	5	6.0	362	33337	259	173	3.2
NW Windsor	2129	2094	2	32	1	681	143	629	387	2	6.1	344	26100	251	166	3.6
Hanlon Pk.	1764	1748	4	9	3	427	208	623	440	1	5.9	384	31400	206	175	3.0
Ellwood	1221	5	0	1199	17	239	276	549	515	-	5.3	440	21100	86	169	2.3
Linwood	1609	1	5	1568	30	359	308	643	553	0	5.7	460	21315	150	155	2.6
Highland Town	1302	29	6	1253	14	305	217	519	457	2	5.5	377	19600	124	145	2.6

areas. Within each cluster, the three areas were then randomly assigned to receive either foot patrol, ombudsman policing, or no new police programs at all.

Sampling Procedures

Police Foundation staff used updated 1980 census block maps to compile the sampling frames for each area. Site supervisors then conducted an areal listing by walking the streets and recording all addresses within the defined boundaries. Each residential address was assigned an identification number. Selection of sample addresses was accomplished by dividing the universe (the number of addresses listed) by the desired sample size to arrive at a sampling interval. Starting with a random number and selecting every Nth case (where N was equal to the sampling interval), this procedure was used to produce random samples of addresses in all six areas.

Once the samples of addresses were selected, the final step was the selection of a respondent within each household. This selection was accomplished during the first visit of an interviewer by listing all household members who were 18 years old or older and assigning them numbers, starting with the oldest male to the youngest female. The interviewer then referred to a random-selection table assigned to that household to determine who should be the respondent. No substitution was permitted for the selected respondent.

At Wave 2, attempts were made to reinterview all persons interviewed at Wave 1, producing a panel sample.

Contacting Sampled Households. One week before interviewing began, an advance letter from the Mayor of Baltimore was mailed to the selected households. The letter, addressed to "Resident," outlined the general objectives of the research effort and encouraged cooperation with it.

The Wave 1 interviewing began on April 10, 1986; interviewing was completed on May 30. Interviewing for Wave 2 began on May 15, 1987 and continued until July 17. All interviewing was conducted in person. Telephone contacts were made only after an initial household visit had been made, in order to arrange an appointment for an in-person interview with the selected respondent.

Call-Back Procedures. Interviewers made a minimum of five attempts to complete an in-person interview. Each attempt was recorded on a Call Record Sheet. The attempts were made at different times of the day and different days of the week to maximize the chances of finding the respondent at home. Approximately 40 percent of the interviews were completed on the first and second visits.

A Non-Interview Report (NIR) was completed for each selected household in which an interview could not be completed. The supervisor reviewed each NIR to decide whether or not a refused case should be reassigned to another interviewer for conversion; in most cases, such a reassignment was made. Interviewers were successful in converting nearly 40 percent of the initial refusals to completed interviews.

Outcome Measures

Survey questionnaires were designed to collect information about exposure to the programs as well as to measure the effects on each of the dimensions on which those programs were hypothesized to have some impact. A brief summary of the outcome measures used is presented below.

Recalled Program Awareness. Both before and after the program, respondents were asked questions indicating whether they had seen a police officer within the past 24 hours, within the past week, or within the past year. These responses were combined to form a scale indicating the perceived level of police visibility. In addition, respondents were asked if they thought that the level of police presence in the experimental area had increased, decreased, or remained the same during the year of program implementation.

Respondents also were asked to indicate whether they knew a police officer in the experimental area by name, and whether a police officer had come to their door to ask them about problems in their area.

Evaluation of Police Service in Area. Two scales were created to measure respondents' evaluations of the police in their neighborhoods. The first scale, designed to measure attitudes about police effectiveness, was composed of the responses to the following individual items:

—How good a job the police in the area do at preventing crime,
—How good a job the police in the area do in helping victims,
—How good a job the police in the area do keeping order on the street.

A second scale, designed to measure the nature of police in the experimental area, was created by combining the responses to the following individual items:

—How polite are police in the area in dealing with people,
—How helpful are police in the area in dealing with people, and
—How fair are police in the area in dealing with people.

Perceived Area Social Disorder Problems. To measure perceived social disorder problems, residential respondents were asked a series of questions about how much of a problem they perceived each of the following activities to be:

—Groups hanging around on corners,

—People saying insulting things or bothering people,

—Public drinking,

—Gangs, and

—Sale or use of drugs in public.

The responses to each of these questions were combined to form one composite scale.

Perceived Area Property Crime Problems. This scale combined responses to three questions which asked about the extent to which each of the following were perceived to be problems in the area:

—People breaking in or sneaking into homes to steal things,

—Cars being vandalized, and

—Cars being stolen.

Perceived Area Personal Crime Problems. This scale combined responses to two questions which asked about the extent to which each of the following were perceived as problems in the area:

—People being attacked or beaten up by strangers, and

—People being robbed or having their money, purses, or wallets taken.

Perceived Likelihood of Area Crime. This scale was composed of the responses to the following individual items:

—How much crime is there in this area;

—In the past year, has the amount of crime in this area increased, decreased, or stayed about the same;

—How likely is it that someone will harm you in the coming year;

—If you were outside in this area after dark, how likely is it that someone would try to rob or steal something from you;

—How likely is it that a car parked on the street at night would be broken into; and

—Is there any place in this area where you would be afraid to go out alone either during the day or after dark?

Perceived Safety of Area. A scale was created by combining the responses to the following items:

—How safe do you feel walking alone in this area at night;

—How safe do you feel when you are walking alone in this area during the day?

Worry About Crime in Area. The response to the following items were combined to create a scale:

—How worried are you that someone will try to rob you or steal something from you while you are outside in this area;
—How worried are you that someone will try to attack you or beat you up while you are outside in this area;
—How worried are you that someone will try to break into your home while no one is home; and
—How worried are you that someone will try to break into your home while someone is home?

Crime Avoidance Behaviors in the Area. To measure the extent to which respondents use restrictive, crime-avoidance behaviors to protect themselves against crime, the answers to the following questions were combined:

—The last time you went out after dark in this area, did you stay away from certain streets or areas to avoid crime; and
—When you last went out after dark in this area, did you stay away from certain types of people to avoid crime.

Utilization of Crime-Prevention Devices. To measure the extent to which respondents had taken precautions to prevent household crime, the responses to the following questions were combined:

—Have any special looks been installed in this home for security reasons;
—Have any special outdoor lights been installed here to make it easier to see what is going on outside your home; and
—Have special windows or bars been installed for protection?

Familiarity with Neighbors. The responses to three items were combined to create a scale:

—How easy is it to tell a stranger on your block from someone who lives here;
—How many people on your block do you know well enough to ask a favor of; and
—Do any of your good friends live in this area?

Cohesiveness of Neighborhood. The responses to these items were combined to create a scale:

—In some areas, people do things together and help each other. In other areas, people mostly go their own way. In general, what kind of area would you say this is? Is it mostly one where people help each other, or where people go their own way?

—If you were sick, could you count on your neighbors to shop for you at the market or go to the drug store for you?

—When you are away from home, can you count on your neighbors to keep their eyes open for possible trouble?

—If you had to borrow $25 for an emergency, could you expect to get it from one of your neighbors? and

—Do the people in this area work together to solve problems?

Satisfaction with Area. Responses to the following items were combined to create a scale:

—In general, in the past year, would you say this area has become a better place to live, a worse place to live, or stayed about the same?

—All things considered, what do you think this area will be like a year from now? Will it be a better place to live, have gotten worse, or stayed about the same? and

—On the whole, how satisfied are you about this area as a place to live?

Victimization in Area. Residents were asked whether they had been victims of various types of attempted and successful crimes during the year prior to being interviewed. In particular, they were asked if, during the past year, they had been a victim of a burglary, larceny from their person, larceny from auto, auto theft, vandalism, assault, or a robbery.

To provide a general measure of victimization, a composite measure was created to indicate whether each respondent had been a victim of any crime in the area within the past year.

Awareness of Victimization in Area. Respondents were asked whether they knew of anyone living in the experimental area who had been a victim of a burglary, larceny from person, larceny from auto, auto theft, vandalism, assault, or a robbery within the past year.

A composite measure was also created indicating whether each respondent was aware of any crime occurring to someone else in the experimental area during the past year.

Calls for Service and Recorded Crime Data Collection

Data concerning each call for police service recorded as having been received by the Baltimore Police Department from the six experimental areas from January 1984 through June 1987 were extracted from the department's computer. After eliminating duplicates, these calls were aggregated by month and categorized into the following types:

—Calls concerning complaints of personal harm, including possible crimes such as assault, robbery, and larceny, as well as calls indicating an armed person, a cutting, a shooting, or other incidents involving possible harm to individuals.

—Calls concerning complaints of property theft, including possible crimes such as burglary, auto theft, larceny, and vandalism, as well as calls indicating possible property damage or prowlers.

—Calls concerning disorderly behavior, such as juvenile disturbances, curfew violations, disorderly persons, gambling, street disturbances, and intoxicated persons.

—Calls concerning alarms of any type.

—Calls concerning traffic problems or complaints.

—Calls concerning automobile accidents.

—Calls concerning service, including storm damage and complaints about sanitation and street maintenance.

—All other calls.

A separate data base was created for all calls found by the police to involve either a Part 1 or a Part 2 crime. These data were also aggregated by month.

ANALYSIS AND RESULTS

Although analyses utilizing panel data provide strong tests for possible effects on those individuals in the panel, such data inevitably are biased against (a) persons who move out of the area and are lost from the sample, (b) recent in-movers who could not have participated in the first wave survey, and (c) those who refuse to be reinterviewed. Losses from a panel due to various forms of attrition usually bias the data in predictable ways, in favor of more affluent, older, home-owning, long-term residents. It is possible that such residents are more likely than others to be aware of, if not affected by, area-level programs like those evaluated here. Thus, positive panel results may be difficult to generalize to the entire population of the treatment area.

In response to this issue, analysis began by comparing the demographic characteristics of all respondents in the Wave 1 survey in each area to those of the subset of respondents who could be located and reinterviewed one year later. If those two groups differ significantly, the ability to generalize from the panel to the areas as a whole is limited by the resulting attrition bias. Fortunately, no attrition effects were statistically significant. As a result, it is reasonably safe to generalize the results of these regression analyses to the general population of the experimental areas.

Recalled Program Awareness

The analysis revealed sharp increases in police visibility in both the foot patrol and ombudsman program areas when data from all six experimental areas are combined. For both experimental programs, these increases were statistically significant. The same results were replicated in the three areas of the Northwest District. However, in the Southeast District, although there was a slight increase in visibility indicated in the foot patrol area and a large increase in the ombudsman policing area, neither increase was statistically significant.

Based on the data from all six experimental areas, there were notable increases in perceived police presence in both the ombudsman and foot patrol areas. Here, however, the increases observed in both the Northwest and the Southeast areas were found to be quite large. All of those increases were statistically significant except that produced in the foot patrol area in the Northwest District.

As shown by Table 10.2, enormous, and highly significant, increases in the percentage of residents who knew a police officer by name occurred in both the ombudsman and foot patrol areas. At the district level, it is clear that the largest contribution to these effects came from the areas within the Southeast District, where dramatic, and highly significant, increases in both the foot patrol and ombudsman areas were demonstrated. In the Northwest District, on the other hand, there was a significant increase in the ombudsman policing area but no significant change in the foot patrol area. The differential effect may well be due to the fact that foot patrol in the Southeast District was provided by the same officer throughout the year of program implementation, while in the Northwest District foot patrol was provided by a series of different individuals.

Evaluation of Police Service in Area

Table 10.2 reveals that large and statistically significant increases in evaluations of police effectiveness were produced in both ombudsman policing areas, as well as overall. No other change in this measure was notable or approached the level of statistical significance.

Further, an enormous increase in evaluation of police behavior occurred in the ombudsman area in the Southeast District. No change in any of the other three areas was nearly as notable; none approached the level of statistical significance. Because of the highly significant improvement in the Southeast ombudsman area, the overall ombudsman program effect also proved to be statistically significant.

Table 10.2
Program Effects

MEASURE	BOTH		NORTHWEST		SOUTHEAST	
A. PROGRAM AWARENESS:	FP	OP	FP	OP	FP	OP
Visibility	+**	+*	+**	+*	+	+
Change/Police Presence	+**	+**	+	+**	+	+**
Know Officer's Name	+**	+**	+	+**	+**	+**
Officer Came to Door	+	+**	+	+**	+	+**

MEASURE	BOTH		NORTHWEST		SOUTHEAST	
B. EVALUATION OF POLICE:	FP	OP	FP	OP	FP	OP
Effectiveness	−	+**	−	−	+	+**
Treatment of Citizens	−	+**	−	−	+	+**

MEASURE	BOTH		NORTHWEST		SOUTHEAST	
C. PERCEPTION OF AREA PROBLEMS:	FP	OP	FP	OP	FP	OP
Disorder	+*	−*	+	−	+	−*
Property Crime	−	−	−**	−	+	−
Personal Crime	−	−	−	−	+	−

MEASURE	BOTH		NORTHWEST		SOUTHEAST	
D. ATTITUDES ABOUT CRIME:	FP	OP	FP	OP	FP	OP
Likelihood of Crime	−	−	−	−	+	−
Safety of Area	+	+	+	+	+	+*
Worry About Crime	+	+	+	+	+	−

MEASURE	BOTH		NORTHWEST		SOUTHEAST	
E. CRIME AVOIDANCE:	FP	OP	FP	OP	FP	OP
Crime Avoidance	−	−	−	−	−	−
Protective Devices	−	+	−	+**	−	−

 * = Significant to 0.05 Level.
** = Significant to 0.01 Level.

Table 10.2 (continued)

F. NEIGHBORHOOD ATTITUDES:	BOTH		NORTHWEST		SOUTHEAST	
	FP	OP	FP	OP	FP	OP
Familiarity with Neighbors	-	-	-	-	-	-
Cohesiveness of Neighbors	-	-	-	+	-	-
Satisfaction with Neighborhood	+	+	+	+	+	+

G. VICTIMIZATION:	BOTH		NORTHWEST		SOUTHEAST	
	FP	OP	FP	OP	FP	OP
Burglary	+	-	+	-	+	-
Larceny from Person	-	+	-	+	+	+
Larceny from Auto	-	-	+	-	-	-
Auto Theft	-	-**	+	-**	-	-
Vandalism	-	-	+	-	-	-
Assault	+	-	+	+	+	-
Robbery	-	+	-	+	-	+
Any Crime	-	-	+	-	-	-

H. VICARIOUS VICTIMIZATION:	BOTH		NORTHWEST		SOUTHEAST	
	FP	OP	FP	OP	FP	OP
Burglary	+	-	-	+	+	-
Larceny from Person	-*	-	-**	-	+	-
Larceny from Auto	-*	-	-	-	-	+
Auto Theft	-	-	-**	-	+	-
Vandalism	-*	-	-	+	-**	-**
Assault	-**	-**	-	-	-*	-**
Robbery	-*	-	-	-	-	-
Any Crime	-	-	-	-	+	-

 * = Significant to 0.05 Level.
** = Significant to 0.01 Level.

Table 10.2 (continued)

I. CALLS FOR SERVICE:	BOTH		NORTHWEST		SOUTHEAST	
	FP	OP	FP	OP	FP	OP
Personal	+	-	+	-	+	-
Property	-	-	-	+	-	-
Disturbances	-	-	-	-	-	+
Alarms	+	-	-	-	+	-
Traffic	-	+	+	+	-	-
Service	+	+	+	+	+	-
Other	-	-	-	-	-	-

J. RECORDED CRIME:	BOTH		NORTHWEST		SOUTHEAST	
	FP	OP	FP	OP	FP	OP
PART 1	-	-	-	+	-	-
PART 2	-	-*	-*	-	+	-

* = Significant to 0.05 Level.
** = Significant to 0.01 Level.

Perceived Area Disorder Problems

As revealed in Table 10.2, there was a statistically significant reduction in perceived disorder problems in the Southeast ombudsman policing area; although there was no significant effect in the Northwest, the reduction demonstrated in the combined data set was also statistically significant. There was a significant increase in perceived disorder problems in the foot patrol areas in the combined data set, reflecting a significant increase in the Southeast foot patrol area and an almost-significant increase in the Northwest.

Perceived Area Property Crime Problems

Although sizable decreases in the level of perceived property crime problems were observed in the Southeast ombudsman area and in the combined data set, Table 10.2 indicates that neither of these effects quite reached the .05 level of significance. As shown in the table, there was also a statistically significant reduction in perceived property crime problems in the Northwest foot patrol area. When combined with the Southeast data, however, where there was an increase in perceived problems, the overall effect was not statistically significant.

Perceived Area Personal Crime Problems

Reductions in perceived area personal crime problems in the ombudsman areas occurred in both the Southeast and the Northwest; however, neither effect reached the .05 level of significance. The overall ombudsman effect, as shown in Table 10.2, did not quite reach the level of statistical significance. No foot patrol effects were notable or statistically significant.

Perceived Likelihood of Crime in Area

No program effects were found to be statistically significant, although the Northwest ombudsman program achieved effects close to the .05 level.

Perceived Safety of Area

As shown in Table 10.2, the Southeast ombudsman program was associated with a statistically significant increase in perceived safety. This was accomplished at the same time that perceived safety in the other two areas declined. No other tests for program effects were statistically significant.

Worry About Crime in Area

No program effects approached the .05 level of significance.

Crime Avoidance Behaviors in Area

No significant program effects were observed.

Utilization of Crime Prevention Devices

Although a significant increase in the use of crime-prevention devices occurred in the Northwest ombudsman policing area, neither the Southeast ombudsman program effect nor the overall program effect reached the .05 level of statistical significance. No foot patrol effect approached significance.

Familiarity with Neighbors

No significant program effects were found to be associated with either foot patrol or ombudsman policing.

Cohesiveness of Neighborhood

No significant program effects were observed.

Satisfaction with Neighborhood

No program effects reached the .05 level of statistical significance, although the ombudsman program approached that level both in the Northwest and overall.

Victimization in Area

No program effects reached the .05 level of statistical significance, although the reduction in victimization in the Northwest foot patrol approached that level.

Awareness of Victimization in Area

Several statistically significant program effects were discovered. Among the combined data, the foot patrol program was associated with significant reductions in awareness of six types of crimes: assault, robbery, larceny from persons, larceny from automobiles, damage to automobiles, and vandalism. Within the foot patrol area in the Northwest District, significant reductions in awareness of larceny from persons, auto theft, and damage to automobiles was indicated, with the reductions in awareness of larceny from automobiles and robbery coming close to meeting that criterion. The foot patrol program in the Southeast was associated with a significant reduction in awareness of vandalism and assault—but also with a significant increase in awareness of burglary.

Overall, the ombudsman policing was associated with a significant reduction in the awareness of assault, an effect that was also significant within the Southeast ombudsman area. The Southeast ombudsman program was also associated with a significant reduction in the awareness of vandalism. Within the Northwest District, the ombudsman program was associated with a significant increase in awareness of crimes of any type.

Recorded Crime Data Analysis

Monthly recorded crime data were analyzed according to the following categories:

—Total Part 1 crimes,

—Burglaries,

—Personal crimes (robbery, assault, rape),

—Outside incidents,

—Larcenies, and

—Auto thefts.

These data were subjected to interrupted time-series analysis to determine if, at month 45, there was a significant change in either the levels or trends of these series.

The results show that there was statistically significant decreases in the program area in (1) total Part 1 crimes, (2) personal crimes, (3) thefts, and (4) outside incidents. These produced decreases of from 24 to 41 percent in the monthly incidences of these types of crime. No significant effects of any kind were indicated in these comparison areas.

Such findings, although interesting, are difficult to interpret clearly, because of the intrinsic ambiguity of recorded crime data (see Skogan, 1976). These results, therefore, could well represent a change in the reporting behavior of the residents and in the recording practices of the officers. McCleary and Riggs (1982) have developed statistical models for controlling for such effects but these time series, unfortunately, are too short for correction. No matter what effect on reporting or recording may have led to these differences, however, the reader is strongly warned *not* to interpret them as changes in actual victimization, as further demonstrated by the fact that no significant effects were noted with respect to the survey measurement of victimization.

REFERENCES

Adams, T. F. (1971). *Police Patrol Tactics and Techniques*. Englewood Cliffs, NJ: Prentice-Hall.

Arlington, Virginia Police Department (1976). Unpublished internal study of foot patrol programs.

Bloch, P. and C. Ulberg (1972). "The Beat Commander Concept." *The Police Chief*, 39(9).

Boydston, J. and M. Sherry (1975). *San Diego Community Profile: Final Report*. Washington, D.C.: Police Foundation.

Bright, J. (1970). *Beat Patrol Experiment*. London: Home Office, Police Research and Development Branch.

Brown, W. (1973). "Patrol Deployment: An Analysis." *Canadian Police Chief*, 62(3).

Farrell, M. (1988). "The Development of the Community Patrol Officer Program: Community-Oriented Policing in the New York City Police Department." In *Community Policing: Rhetoric or Reality*. New York: Praeger.

Gourley, G. (1974). *Patrol Administration*, 2nd Edition. Springfield, IL: Charles C. Thomas, Inc.

Henig, J. (1984). *Citizens Against Crime: An Assessment of the Neighborhood Watch Program in Washington, D.C.* Washington, D.C.: Center for Washington Area Studies, George Washington University.

Hogan, E. and J. Fagan (1974). "Integrating the Policeman into the Community." *Police Chief*, 41.

Iannoe, N. (1975). *Principles of Police Patrol*. New York: McGraw-Hill.

Kinney, J. (1979). *Isla Vista Foot Patrol*. Paper presented at American Society of Criminology Annual Meeting, Philadelphia, Pennsylvania.

Lavrakas, P. and E. Herz (1982). "Citizen Participation in Neighborhood Crime Prevention." *Criminology*, 20(3–4).

Pate, A.; Wycoff, M. A.; Skogan, W.; and Sherman, L. (1986). *Reducing Fear of Crime in Houston and Newark: A Summary Report*. Washington, D.C.: Police Foundation.

Payton, G. (1967). *Patrol Procedures*. Los Angeles: Legal Book Corporation.

Pendland, M. and W. Gay (1972). "Foot Patrols: The Fort Worth Experience." *Police Chief*, 39(4).

Police Foundation (1981). *The Newark Foot Patrol Experiment*. Washington, D.C.: Police Foundation.

Prefecture de Police, Paris (1973). "The Beat System in Paris." *International Criminal Police Review*, 271 (October).

Richardson, J. F. (1974). *Urban Police in the United States*. Port Washington, NY: Kennikat Press.

Rosenbaum, D. P. (1982). "Police Responses: Conventional and New Approaches to Local Crime Problems." Paper presented at the American Psychological Association annual convention, Washington, D.C.

Schnelle, J.; R. Kirchner; M. McNees; and J. Lawler (1975). "Social Evaluation Research: The Evaluation of Two Police Patrolling Strategies." *Journal of Applied Behavior Analysis*, 4.

Skolnick, J. and Bayley, D. (1988). *Community Policing: Issues and Practices Around the World*. Washington, D.C.: National Institute of Justice.

Trojanowicz, R. (1982). *An Evaluation of the Neighborhood Foot Patrol Program in Flint, Michigan*. East Lansing, MI: School of Criminal Justice, Michigan State University.

Waller, I. (1979). "What Reduces Residential Burglary?" Paper presented at the Third International Symposium on Victimology, Muenster, West Germany.

Wilson, J. Q. (1983). *Thinking About Crime*. New York: Basic Books.

Yin, R. (1979). "What is Citizen Crime Prevention?" In *How Well Does It Work? Review of Criminal Justice Evaluation, 1978*. Washington, D.C.: U.S. Government Printing Office.

11

ROP: Catching Career Criminals

Susan E. Martin and
Lawrence W. Sherman

Two facts stand out in modern crime control police debates. First, a small proportion of criminals commit a disproportionate number of crimes. Second, most prisons are overcrowded. Together, these facts have generated growing interest in selectively focusing criminal justice system resources on the most active and dangerous chronic offenders.

While police have rarely adopted a proactive targeting approach to apprehending repeat offenders, the Washington, D.C. Metropolitan Police Department adopted precisely this approach in May 1982 when it established an 88-officer (later reduced to 60) Repeat Offender Project (ROP).

The Repeat Offender Project offered a unique opportunity to assess the problems and effectiveness of a proactive police unit formed to carry out a selective apprehension strategy. Between January 1983 and December 1984, the Police Foundation, in cooperation with the D.C. Metropolitan Police Department, conducted a multifaceted evaluation to assess ROP's effectiveness and costs. A controlled experiment sought to determine whether "repeat offenders" identified by ROP were more likely to be arrested by ROP than they were in the absence of ROP activities. A comparative component examined prior arrest histories and current cased dispositions of a sample of persons arrested by 40 ROP

From "Catching Career Criminals: The Washington, D.C., Repeat Offender Project," (1986). Reprinted with permission of the Police Foundation.

and 169 non-ROP officers, as well as arrest productivity rates for both groups of officers.

The Police Foundation study addressed the following questions:

1. How does ROP operate and what strategies do officers use in selecting and apprehending their targets?
2. Do ROP's tactics increase the likelihood of arrest for targeted repeat offenders?
3. Are offenders arrested by ROP officers more active and serious than offenders arrested under routine police operations?
4. Are ROP arrestees more likely to be prosecuted, convicted, and incarcerated? and,
5. How does ROP affect the arrest productivity of its officers?

While it is premature to conclude that all police departments would benefit from a proactive repeat offender unit, large departments should consider creating such units, given the magnitude of the repeat offender problem and the findings of this study.

ROP'S DESIGN AND INITIAL IMPLEMENTATION

When Maurice Turner, chief of the Washington, D.C. Metropolitan Police Department, requested innovative proposals from senior officers on ways to reduce crime in the nation's capital, Captain (now Inspector) Edward Spurlock responded with a plan to establish a proactive, "perpetrator-oriented" unit. The unit would identify and apprehend two types of active recidivists: those already wanted on one or more warrants who could be arrested on sight, and those believed to be criminally active but not currently wanted. The former were called "warrant targets"; the latter "ROP-initiated" targets.

ROP's Initial Organization

ROP's criterion for selecting both types of targets was "the belief that the person is committing five or more Part–1 offenses per week." The unit's time and effort would be divided equally between the two types of targets. Active apprehension efforts were limited to a 72-hour-or-less time period. This enabled ROP to focus its resources on the most active criminals, since only very active offenders were likely to be observed committing a crime within a three-day period.

ROP's command staff selected a team of 88 officers who varied in age, race, sex, appearance, and previous police experience. The officers were organized into seven-member squads, each including a female and a detective. The squad was led by a sergeant, and became the basic work group to which targets were assigned and credit for arrests given. While officers were allowed ample discretion over their routine activities, the sergeant was responsible for selecting squad targets and worked on the street with officers. A Target Committee of three experienced investigators was responsible for developing new targets and reviewing candidates generated by the squads.

The unit's resources included 20 old cars, other surveillance and investigative equipment, and a computer terminal linked to the department's on-line information system. To aid in target selection, ROP routinely received copies of the department's daily major violators list, criminal histories of recent arrestees, daily crime reports from each district, and specially prepared weekly printouts listing all persons wanted on three or more felony warrants.

To reduce rivalry with other police units that could inhibit the flow of information needed to function effectively, ROP adopted an internal arrest log. This log listed all arrests for which ROP officers were responsible, even if the arrest was formally booked to another officer. This enabled ROP officers to assign formal arrest credit to other officers, while obtaining recognition from their supervisors for the work they had performed.

Prior to commencing operations, ROP's proposed procedures were reviewed by the department's general counsel, the U.S. Attorney, and the local American Civil Liberties Union (ACLU). The ACLU was concerned that ROP would be a "dragnet" operation that harassed and entrapped people. These concerns were satisfied when the ROP commander explained that ROP would use no formula or profile for target selection and that places where citizens have a right to privacy would be put under surveillance only with the permission of the court (Epstein, 1983).

Operational Changes

Difficulties during the first several months led to several modifications of ROP's targeting practices, squad operations, and apprehension tactics. The ROP design anticipated that surveillance would be the principal tactic for apprehending ROP-initiated targets. When constant surveillance failed to produce arrests, and therefore, frustrated ROP officers, the squads increased their proportion of warrant targets to about 75 percent of those selected. The command staff also gradually broadened the officer's repertoire of investigative and undercover infiltration strategies and skills. After several months, surveillance became one of a number of tactics. In addition, the rule that work on a target be terminated after 72 hours was relaxed when it proved difficult to implement.

Target development practices also changed. Initially, the Target Committee selected and developed all targets, mostly on the basis of official record information. However, this information typically was incomplete and an unreliable indicator of criminal activity, and, therefore, was far less desirable than "street' information. With strong encouragement from the ROP command staff, ROP officers built informal information networks and fostered cooperative relations with other units and agencies.

After several months, the unit acquired a reputation for responding to suggestions for targeting and "hot tips" from other police units and informants. Information sources in other departmental units and neighboring police agencies and street informants increased the proportion of targets generated by ROP squads. These squads also initiated a number of joint target investigations with other agencies.

These changes had both positive and negative effects. They allowed ROP to expand its resources and become a center of information about criminal activities in the metropolitan area. But they also resulted in targeting persons who did not meet ROP's selection criteria, diverting limited resources away from a focus on persons committing many Part 1 offenses.

After six months, to streamline operations, ROP was reduced from 88 to 60 officers, the 12 squads were reorganized and reduced to eight, and administrative procedures were tightened. In January 1983, a new theft statute (The District of Columbia's Theft and White Collar Crime Act of 1982[4–238]) went into effect. At that time, ROP's target selection criteria were expanded to include "persons believed to be trafficking in stolen property."

ROP IN ACTION

Target Selection

Although officers were expected to select criminally active targets, ROP did not establish formal indicators of activity or any system for prioritizing among potential candidates. Selection was based on informal understandings about what makes a "good" target.

Common considerations affecting selection became the target's catchability, deservedness, longer-term yield, and the squad's working style. "Catchability" depended primarily on the quality, recency, type, and amount of information about a warrant target's whereabouts and a ROP-initiated target's activities. ROP officers preferred to use information provided by other officers or an informant. Police recognize that most offender arrest records fail to reflect the full extent of criminal activities. They believe that only criminals in the criminal environment really know what is going on, and that this information helps reduce the amount of preliminary investigation required.

"Deservedness" was related to an officer's belief that the target deserved to be arrested and punished. The primary factors contributing to deservedness were the seriousness and length of the target's criminal history and alleged current criminal activity. Another factor was the target's apparent contempt for the law and police. The former was exemplified by failing to appear in court; the latter encompassed those who were armed or belligerent when arrested on a previous occasion. Concern with "deservedness' helps explain why ROP officers tended to select older persons and suspected fences as targets. Older persons showed a clearer commitment to crime and had an observable modus operandi (in addition to being more likely to be incarcerated if convicted). Fences, although generally not violent, support and facilitate street crime by providing a market for stolen property.

"Yield" was measured by a target's contribution to ROP's information network and public visibility, and the likelihood that the target would result in additional targets and arrests, or in the immediate incarceration of the arrestee. For example, those persons already on pretrial release for another offense and/or on parole were desirable targets because they were more likely to be kept in jail.

ROP squads tended to use three styles for meeting informal pressures to make arrests, and these styles became factors that affected target selection. "Hunter" squads focused almost exclusively on warrant targets, particularly those wanted for violent crimes. "Trapper" squads, which accounted for most ROP initiated arrests, preferred to initiate their own longer-term investigations. These investigations focused on one key target and were designed to close a large number of cases, recover large amounts of stolen property and, subsequently, arrest as many of the target's criminal associates as possible. While an investigation was proceeding, "trappers" also "filled in" with warrant targets, particularly those requested by officers from other units with whom they were working. "Fisherman" squads did not specialize. They made some ROP-initiated arrests on quick buy/bust operations, followed up on "hot tips," arrested some warrant targets, and made many "serendipitous" arrests by street cruising.

Apprehension Strategies

The primary task in apprehending warrant targets was *locating* the target. This was simple if the squad had a current address. But when the officers did not have a good address, the process became more complex. Finding the target usually involved reviewing police and other records or contacting persons likely to know the target's whereabouts.

While some contacts were straightforward, others involved deception. For example, a target's relatives might have been told that the target had just won a contest or was being considered for a job and must be contacted. Records to be checked included those at the post office (e.g., mail-forwarding requests), the Department of Motor Vehicles, and the phone company (after getting a court order to gain access to the latter). If these efforts failed, officers sometimes placed the target's girlfriend or close associates under surveillance.

Most warrant targets were wanted in Washington, D.C. as fugitives from justice in neighboring jurisdictions or on felony bench warrants for probation or parole violation or for failure to appear in court. Such targets were frequently selected because they met all informal targeting considerations. They were more catchable than other targets for two reasons. First, D.C. residents being sought by officers from neighboring jurisdictions could be easily located through information provided by these officers. Second, non-ROP D.C. officers were less likely to seek out fugitives and persons wanted on bench warrants than those wanted for Part 1 crimes, despite the seriousness of the underlying charges against the former. In addition, these arrests strengthened cooperative ties between ROP and other units.

To arrest persons not wanted on a warrant, ROP officers had to develop evidence about a specific crime in which targets had participated. This involved a variety of vice and investigative activities such as buy/busts, cultivating informants, investigating "tips," placing targets under surveillance, and tracing stolen property found in the target's possession to its rightful owner. A few prolonged investigations involved undercover penetration of fencing operations. While quite diverse, ROP-initiated target investigations generally focused on property crimes that were more highly organized and, therefore, more easily penetrated through informants and undercover tactics.

Analysis of the ROP-apprehension activities and their outcomes indicated that there was no consistent formula for or primary tactic associated with arrests. Most ROP arrests were made quickly (80 percent within one week of targeting) and did not involve extensive investigative efforts.

RESEARCH DESIGN

Experiment

Three research components were used to assess ROP's effectiveness. First, an experiment was conducted to determine whether those selected by ROP as "repeat offenders" were more likely to be arrested because of ROP efforts than they would otherwise. The experiment's design required ROP officers to identify their constantly changing pool of targets, pair any two of the same target type (warrant targets or ROP-initiated targets) and, by coin toss, assign one target to the experimental group and the other to the control group. Experimental targets were investigated by ROP squad officers over a seven-day period. Control targets were off-limits to ROP officers but could be arrested by any other police officer during the seven-day period. The experiment lasted 26 weeks, during which time 212 pairs of randomly assigned targets were investigated.

As is common in field experiments, evidence suggests that some ROP officers manipulated the coin toss (which research staff did not always control) to ensure immediate assignment of desired targets. Others avoided the coin toss by getting the Target Committee to treat the target as an authorized exception even though it did not always fit the rules for exception. In addition, there were difficulties in locating non-ROP arrests, suggesting that some arrests were missed by the researchers. Nevertheless, statistical adjustments designed to eliminate the potential impact of manipulation of random assignment and missed non-ROP arrests did not alter the significance of the experimental outcome.

Comparative Study

The second research component compared ROP officers with a sample of other officers on three factors: 1) criminal histories of those arrested; 2) court dispositions of those arrests; and 3) overall arrest productivity of the officers. ROP officers in this study included 40 officers previously assigned to patrol, tactical/crime prevention, vice, and detective units. The comparison group included a random sample of 95 officers drawn from patrol, vice, and detective assignments; all 60 officers in tactical/crime prevention units; and 14 officers with warrant squad duties. Data were collected on each of the three factors for both groups over two time periods: April 1 to September 30, 1981 (prior to the 1982 establishment of ROP), and April 1 to September 30, 1983.

Information regarding all arrests made by ROP and comparison officers during both time periods was collected from station house arrest logs and a special ROP arrest log. Samples of about 300 ROP–1981, Comparison–1981, and Comparison–1983 arrests were then randomly selected for comparison with all 263 ROP–1983 adult arrests. Arrest histories were obtained from the Metropolitan Police Department. Information on case dispositions was obtained from the Criminal Division of the Superior Court.

Observation and ROP File Data

A third research component involved extensive observation of ROP officers at work, and provided information about ROP target selection, investigative techniques, and apprehension strategies. Various data items also were collected from case jackets of all persons targeted by ROP during the study period. This included 289 persons involved in the experiment, 100 targets that were authorized exceptions, and 85 persons whom ROP officers serendipitously arrested while working on other assigned targets.

FINDINGS

Experiment

The experimental results clearly showed that *ROP increased the likelihood of arrest of targeted repeat offenders*. ROP arrested 106 (50 percent) of the 212 experimentals. In contrast, only 17 experimentals (8 percent) and 8 controls (4 percent) were arrested by officers in other units. This difference was statistically significant.

Differences in ROP and control arrest rates were found for both warrant and ROP initiated targets. Fifty-five percent of the warrant targets eligible for ROP arrests were arrested by ROP, while only 9 percent of warrant targets eligible for non-ROP arrests were arrested by non-ROP officers. For ROP-initiated targets, the comparable figures were 47 percent and 6 percent. *The magnitude of this finding suggests that despite several problems in implementing and sustaining the experimental design, ROP made a difference by increasing the likelihood of arrest for both warrant and ROP initiated targets.*

Prior Arrest Histories of Arrestees

The study next examined the criminal histories of the samples of 1981 and 1983 ROP and comparison officers' arrestees, after making adjustments for officer's district and assignment and arrestee's age. In 1981, differences between the number of prior arrests for each group's arrestees were minor. *However, in 1983, ROP arrestees had twice as many prior arrests per arrestee as comparison officer arrestees*. ROP 1983 arrestees had an adjusted mean of 8.4 total prior arrests, while comparison officers' arrestees had only 4.2, a statistically significant difference. Assignment to ROP thus led to the expected change in criminal history characteristics of those arrested by ROP officers. The prior arrest records of ROP officer arrestees between 1981 and 1983 became significantly longer and more serious, while the criminal records for [comparison officers'] arrestees became somewhat less serious.

Arrest Seriousness and Case Dispositions

In examining ROP arrests and their outcomes, the study first looked at the seriousness of the arrest charge. There was little difference between ROP and comparison arrest charges in 1981. In 1983, while charges by officer group did not differ in most categories, two categories did differ. Twenty-six percent of ROP arrestees were charged as fugitives, escapees, or probation or parole violators in contrast to only 8 percent of comparison arrestees. Fifteen percent of ROP arrestees and 30 percent of comparison arrestees faced such minor "other" charges as sexual solicitation, gambling, disorderly conduct, unlawful entry, violating vending regulations, and traffic offenses. *Overall, ROP arrests tended to be for more serious offenses.*

The dispositions of the samples of arrests made by ROP and comparison officers were then examined to determine if ROP officer arrestees were more likely to be prosecuted, convicted, and incarcerated. In 1983, there were substantial differences between case outcomes of ROP and comparison officers' arrests, after adjusting for offense type, offender's age, and arrest history. These differences were not found in 1981 cases.

Although the proportion of cases accepted for prosecution did not change between 1981 and 1983, *there was a substantial increase in the proportion of the ROP officers' new cases accepted for prosecution as felonies.* At the same time, the proportion of the sample of comparison officers' cases prosecuted as felonies fell for officers in all assignments except casual clothes tactical units. As a result, 49 percent of ROP's new cases were accepted for prosecution as felonies while comparison cases charged as felonies in 1983 ranged from 24 to 33 percent.

Total convictions increased from 49 percent of case outcomes in 1981 to 63 percent in 1983 for both ROP and comparison officer groups. The proportion of misdemeanor convictions increased for both groups as well. *However, the proportion of felony convictions resulting from ROP officer cases increased from 19 to 24 percent of all prosecuted cases,* whereas the proportion of felony convictions in comparison officers' case outcomes decreased for officers in patrol, vice, and detective assignments and increased for those assigned to tactical units and the warrant squad.

Finally, incarceration rates for 1983 ROP arrestees remained at about the 1981 level. The rates for comparison officers in all other assignments fell, except for the warrant squad. Although warrant rates rose substantially in 1983, the number of cases involved was quite small.

After statistically controlling the data for offense type, age, and criminal history, the study found that ROP arrestees sentenced to serve time in 1983 appear to have received longer sentences than comparison officer convictees. This apparent effect on sentence length is probably a result of the more serious conviction offenses of ROP arrestees within each of the broad categories of offenses used in this study.

Effects on Officer Arrest Productivity

The third component in the comparative study explored an issue of particular importance to many police administrators: the effect of ROP assignment on officers' productivity as measured by total and specific types of arrests. Changes in the individual arrest rates of each ROP and comparison officer were examined by using two different measures for ROP arrests, and by statistically controlling for differences in district, assignment, time in ROP, and 1981 arrest productivity.

Both measures revealed that *assignment to ROP decreased the total number of arrests made by an officer*. Using the more conservative measure, the study found that in the six-month period in 1983, ROP officers made an adjusted mean of 5.7 arrests per officer and comparison officers an adjusted mean of 12.4 arrests, a statistically significant difference. While ROP officers also made significantly fewer Part 1 arrests than comparison officers in 1983, there was no difference in the number of "serious" arrests (i.e., arrests for Part 1 crimes plus those for distribution and possession with the intent to distribute drugs, weapons charges, and arrests on a felony bench warrant), based on the conservative measure of arrests.

CONCLUSIONS

By most measures used in this study, the ROP unit appears to have achieved its goals of selecting, arresting, and contributing to the incarceration of repeat offenders. It increased both the likelihood of arrests of targets, the seriousness of the criminal histories of its arrestees, the probability of prosecution for a felony, the chance of a felony conviction, and the length of the term of those sentenced to incarceration. However, several factors suggest a cautious interpretation of these findings, and the need for other departments to recognize the potential dangers in adopting the ROP model of perpetrator-oriented proactive policing.

Costs

Creating and operating ROP involves costs that cannot be overlooked. First, it took approximately $60,000 in direct expenses to equip the unit. Second, ROP decreased its officers' arrest productivity and, in all likelihood, other aspects of police service as well. Most forgone arrests, however, tended to involve minor offenses such as disorderly conduct and traffic charges. The rate at which ROP officers made "serious" arrests was unaffected, however, and may have increased if the less conservative measure is a more accurate indicator. Thus, the trade-off appears to be reduced-order maintenance activities in exchange for a focus on crime-fighting activities.

The Criminal Activities of Targets

Although ROP arrestees had longer criminal records than comparison arrestees, it cannot be assumed that ROP arrestees are the most active 20 percent of all offenders or are committing five or more Part 1 offenses per week. Other studies have found that prisoners with longer criminal records are more likely than those with short records to be among the highly active group. But prediction instruments, particularly those using official record information, are often unreliable when selecting high-rate criminals (Chaiken and Chaiken, 1982; Greenwood with Abrahamse, 1982; Cohen, 1983; Chaiken and Chaiken, 1985).

Chaiken and Chaiken (1985), for example, used prisoners' self-report of their criminal activities to distinguish three groups of prisoners: "high-rate winners," "high-rate losers," and "low-rate losers." Most of the self-admitted high-rate criminals were "losers" who were often caught and had long criminal records. A small group of "high-rate winners" had avoided apprehension for many years, however, and had official records that made them appear to be low-rate criminals. At the same time, a group of inept "low-rate losers" were not very active but were apprehended nearly every time they committed a crime. The Chaikens suggest that while it is not possible to distinguish accurately among these three groups solely on the basis of criminal record, police and prosecutors have access to additional knowledge that may help them make more accurate distinctions.

This is likely to have been the case with many ROP targets. Criminal history data were generally supplemented by street information upon which ROP officers heavily relied, as well as by data regarding drug use, information from criminal associates, and confessions by targets to many crimes cleared by police but not charged by prosecutors. These sources of information enhanced their ability to select the most criminally active targets. Nevertheless, it was impossible to determine what proportion of ROP targets actually met that unit's targeting criterion of five or more Part 1 crime per week. More important, the ultimate goal of the ROP unit is to reduce crime, and the data from this study do not permit us to determine whether changes in the D.C. crime rate during the study period were related the the program or to other factors.

Legal, Ethical, and Police Issues

ROP activities also pose dangers to civil liberties, especially because of the use of undercover tactics. A proactive plainclothes unit using a variety of unorthodox tactics gives officers an enormous amount of discretion. Without careful supervision, there will be opportunity to harass, entrap, and otherwise violate a citizen's rights.

These problems appear to have been minimized through the ROP supervisors' and officers' careful attention to legality. ROP officers recorded undercover transactions whenever possible and frequently consulted with the U.S. Attorney's office when preparing warrants and carrying out covert operations. Both Inspector Spurlock of the ROP unit and Leslie Harris of the ACLU reported that between May 1982 and September 1985, ROP avoided lawsuits and major complaints of harassment and violation of due process. Nevertheless, the same degree of care may not prevail in other jurisdictions. Nor is it certain that the procedures used by the D.C. ROP unit will stand the test of time.

Proactive units must also make difficult policy choices, either deliberately or by default. These include finding comfortable balances between the emphases to be placed on quantity and quality of targets and arrests, between warrant and unit-initiated targets, and among various types of targets and offenses.

Informal pressure to "put the meat on the table" (i.e., make more arrests) has implications for the type of targets and arrests produced. Emphasis on the number of arrests made results in greater temptations to pick "easy" targets that fail to meet ROP's targetary criteria. An exclusive focus on selecting and arresting only the most active targets, however, is likely to increase the quality of each arrest but decreases their number. Because such a strategy also increases the amount of personnel and other resources devoted to each target, a "failure" (i.e., selection of a low-rate offender or failure to make an arrest) has higher costs and makes accuracy an even more critical part of the target selection process.

Similarly, there is no formula for finding a balance between warrant and unit-initiated targets. The amount of emphasis put on the former must rest, in part, on the effectiveness of existing warrant service procedures and an examination of the types of offenses and offenders left at large in the community due to a failure to serve outstanding warrants. Additionally, warrant targets already "wanted" by the system are likely to pose fewer legal challenges than those initiated by the unit. Warrant targets also are more likely to be a source of violent-offense arrests and to require less officer time and fewer resources per arrest. An emphasis on warrant targets wanted for violent crimes is also likely to yield a greater proportion of targets detained prior to trial, prosecuted for felonies, and incarcerated if convicted given the greater seriousness of the charges underlying these arrests.

Warrant targets also entail several disadvantages relative to unit-initiated targets. They "belong" to the officer who obtained the warrant and, therefore, yield the unit less information about other crimes and criminal associates upon which to base subsequent targeting activities. The quality of a warrant case depends on evidence developed by another officer. Conversely, proactive investigations enable the police to develop eye-witness evidence and penetrate organized criminal activity networks. Only through systematic proactive efforts are the police likely to develop cases against major fences, professional thieves, and other "high-rate winners."

Difficult police choices also must be made when a proactive unit decides on which types of criminal activities to focus. For example, ROP initiated an investigation of area-wide shoplifting activities that resulted in closure of more than 40 cases in five jurisdictions, recovery of more than $100,000 in stolen property, and more than a dozen arrests. The targets clearly fit the selection criteria; there was ample evidence that they were committing more than five Part 1 offenses per week. Yet, most of the drug-addicted professional shoplifters arrested were neither armed nor violent. The question is thus balancing potential crime control and other community benefits achieved when apprehending organized, active property offenders against the benefits of apprehending fewer persons believed to be committing violent crimes.

Applicability of the Findings to Other Settings

There are also problems in generalizing from the findings of a single case study. What worked for ROP may be related to the unique characteristics of Washington, D.C., its police department, and ROP's personnel and leadership. In the absence of other comparative units or groups, it is difficult to determine which aspects of ROP's organization and tactics are idiosyncratic, which may be effectively replicated in a different setting, and which might better be altered.

REFERENCES

Chaiken, J. and M. Chaiken (1982). *Varieties of Criminal Behavior*. Santa Monica: The Rand Corporation.

Chaiken, M. and J. Chaiken (1985). *Who Gets Caught Doing Crime?* Unpublished report. Los Angeles: Hamilton, Rabinovitz, Szanton and Alschuler.

Cohen, J. (1983). "Incapacitation as a Strategy for Crime Control." Pp. 1–85 in

M. Tonry and N. Morris, eds. *Crime and Justice: An Annual Review of Research*, Volume 5. Chicago: University of Chicago Press.

Epstein, A. (1983). "Spurlock's Raiders." *Regardies*, 3:41–42.

Greenwood, P. with A. Abrahamse (1982). *Selective Incapacitation*. Santa Monica: The Rand Corporation.

12

Repeat Calls for Service: Policing the "Hot Spots"

Lawrence W. Sherman

Three percent of the estimated 115,000 addresses and intersections in Minneapolis were the subject of 50 percent of the 321,174 calls to police between December 15, 1985 and December 15, 1986. Sixty percent of the addresses and intersections produced no calls to police at all. Of the 40 percent with any calls, the majority (52 percent) had only one call, while 84 percent had less than five. The top 5 percent of locations with any calls produced 48.8 percent of the calls.

This highly skewed concentration of all police calls in relatively few locations raises substantial questions about current police strategies and suggests the need for focusing police resources on the chronic repeat call locations. This chapter reflects the first step in a research and development effort to create such a strategy, under National Institute of Justice (NIJ) funding, of a collaborative project of the Crime Control Institute and the Minneapolis Police Department.

From "Repeat Calls to Police in Minneapolis," *Crime Control Reports* (4). Reprinted with revisions by the author with permission of the Crime Control Institute. This report was conducted under Grant #86-IJ-CX–0037 from the National Institute of Justice. Points of view or opinions expressed in this document do not necessarily represent the official position of the U.S. Department of Justice.

Acknowledgments

In collaboration with: Alva Emerson, Duane Goodmanson, David Martens, Steven Revor, David Rumpza, David Dobrotka and Ron Jensen of the Minneapolis Police Department and David Doi, Robert Dell'Erba, Carol Bridgeforth, Anne Beatty, Samuel Engel, and Christina Tetreault of the Crime Control Institute.

911 RUNS THE POLICE DEPARTMENT

Much of the work sponsored by NIJ since 1982 has attempted to develop a variety of strategies for accomplishing police objectives. Prompted in part by Professor Herman Goldstein's landmark proposal for "problem-oriented policing" (Goldstein, 1979), NIJ's work has created and tested strategies focusing resources on specific, high-priority police targets. Implicit in these new strategies is a strong critique of the prevailing "dial-a-cop" system of allocating most police resources on the basis of the phone calls police receive.

With the recent growth of 911 systems and the steady increase in the number of calls to police, a virtual coup d'etat has taken over American policing. Gradually, with little public notice, police managers have lost control over how police spend their time. The usurper is the telephone, and a common policy that requires all calls to be answered rapidly.

In the words of one police chief, "911 runs the police department." This means that for all the orders headquarters may make, most police effort is directed simply on the basis of telephoned citizen requests for immediate service, almost all of which are now received in many cities at the emergency "911" number. This system is neither rational nor fair.

The dial-a-cop system is irrational because it prevents police from setting priorities and controlling crime more effectively. By letting each citizen decide whether a matter is appropriate for police work, we make it impossible for police to decide which matters deserve the most attention. In some cities, homicides literally go uninvestigated while police cars respond rapidly to help people locked out of their cars.

Of all the calls to police in the city of Minneapolis in 1986, for example, 5 percent were for car lockouts, 4 percent were for noise complaints, and 25 percent were for domestic and other arguments which generally had no violence (see Table 12.1). Meanwhile, scarce police resources permitted only limited efforts against narcotics pushers, repeat offenders, and serious domestic violence.

Dial-a-cop is irrational because, as NIJ-sponsored research has shown, rapid response by police makes little contribution to the apprehension of criminals or the prevention of victim injury, in the overwhelming majority of calls (Spelman and Eck, 1986). Other NIJ research shows that the calling public is generally happy to wait for a police response, or to receive no police car dispatched at all, as long as the telephone operators politely and accurately explain to the callers exactly what is going to happen (McEwen et al., 1984).

The dial-a-cop system also allocates resources unfairly across the problems that generate calls. Because all calls must be answered quickly, very little time can be spent on each call. The chronic locations are not given extra attention to try to reduce their heavy demands on police.

Table 12.1
Nature of Calls to Police in Minneapolis, All Addresses, 1986* (unadjusted data)

CATEGORY	NUMBER	PERCENT**
Conflict Management:	104,354	32.5%
Domestics	24,948	7.8
Other Disturbances	55,568	17.3
Noise	12,204	3.8
Assault	11,634	3.6
Property Crime-Related:	91,055	28.4%
Theft	35,741	11.1
Burglary-related	33,384	10.4
Vandalism	11,197	3.5
Alarms	10,733	3.3
Traffic Problems:	59,630	18.6%
Traffic Enforcement	27,992	8.7
Property Damage Accident	10,296	3.2
Parking	8,007	2.5
All Other Traffic	13,335	4.2
Service:	42,473	13.2%
Lockouts	17,389	5.4
Medical Aid	9,008	2.8
Emergencies	6,986	2.0
Assistance	6,308	2.0
Persons -- Lost/Found	1,578	0.5
Fires	1,204	0.4
Miscellaneous:	17,591	5.4%
Arrests and Bookings	5,059	1.6
Other	12,532	4.0
Stranger to Stranger Crime Against Persons:	6,071	1.9%
Robbery	4,219	1.3
Criminal Sexual Conduct	1,852	0.6
TOTALS:	321,174	100.0%

*December 15, 1985 to December 15, 1986.
**Percentages do not total 100 due to rounding.

Each call at the chronic locations receives the same limited attention that a call to a once-in-five years location receives. Dial-a-cop goes on putting out the fire, but it never takes away the matches.

Recognizing these problems, the National Institute of Justice has funded tests of a variety of police efforts to focus resources proactively (Reiss, 1971)—not waiting for telephone calls for direction—on high-priority police problems: repeat offenders (Martin and Sherman, 1986), unjustified community fear of crime (Pate, Wycoff, Skogan, and Sherman, 1986), and area patterns of street crime (Spelman and Eck, 1986).

We now add to the list of these proactively policed, high-priority targets the chronic repeat-call locations that generate the majority of police patrol dispatches.

The purpose of this chapter is to demonstrate the concentration of police work at a small number of locations, and the justification for assigning extra resources to those locations as a way of reducing total calls to police. While it is true that much of that concentration may simply reflect concentrations of people using or living at those locations, that does not alter the logic of police identifying and focusing their efforts on those locations. Whether extra resources can succeed in reducing repeat calls will be the subject of a later report on the Minneapolis RECAP (repeat call address policing) experiment.

RESEARCH METHODS

In order to develop the RECAP alternative to the dial-a-cop system, the Crime Control Institute obtained NIJ support for two tasks. One task was analyzing the patterns and concentrations of repeat calls. The other task was selecting, training, and evaluating the effectiveness of a small RECAP unit of police officers devoting full time to proactive policing of the most chronic locations in the city.

The analysis was intended to identify those locations as the targets for the unit's efforts. But it also serves to demonstrate the need for the unit, which would have been abandoned if the analysis showed little concentration of calls.

The analysis proved to be far more difficult than anticipated. Most police departments will experience similar or greater difficulties in undertaking the same analysis. The problem is that a full year of call data is needed to develop a reasonably complete picture of the distribution of repeat calls. But such a large data base seems to be beyond the current capacity of most big-city police departments.

We have not surveyed this issue systematically, but we can offer some examples to illustrate the problem. The minimum requirement for this kind of analysis is that police call records must be computerized. In some big cities like Milwaukee, this is still not the case (although it is changing rapidly). Even among the computerized dispatch systems, few if any have sufficient data storage capacity for analyzing a full year of calls.

The subject address and call nature code data punched into the computer—as distinct from a tape recording of the words exchanged between the caller and the police telephone operator—is generally removed from the computer and recorded on tape as soon as the computer's capacity is reached. In Minneapolis, the data are removed to tape about every seven days, depending on the volume of calls. In Colorado Springs, with an advanced computer-aided-dispatch system, the on-line storage capacity is reportedly three months. Other cities, like Dallas, have multiyear storage and retrieval capacity.

In order to identify the most active Minneapolis addresses over the course of a year, a new data base had to be constructed specifically for that purpose. Such an extensive task was not something the Minneapolis city government computer programmers had time to do. Nor, with a high hourly use cost, was it economical for the Crime Control Institute to use the city's mainframe computer. Both of these problems were handled, at the city's recommendation, by the Crime Control Institute's buying a microcomputer and retaining a programming firm familiar with the city's dispatch system.

The Unadjusted Data Base

The analysis proceeded by our agreeing on a few data "fields" in the computerized "record" of each call that would be transferred from the weekly tapes into the microcomputer data base. The fields included street name, address, floor number, apartment number, nature code of call, date and time of call, and officer's disposition (which would tell whether a report was filed from the call). The total information taken from each record was 80 "bytes." With an estimated 300,000 calls, we purchased a microcomputer that could handle at least 24 million bytes. We then used a tape drive attached to the micro to read those fields off of each weekly dispatch tape and into the hard disk data file.

The original plan had been to define addresses down to the level of apartment, but the programmers advised us that the complications involved in creating that definition would be enormous and very expensive. The "address" in the data base is no more specific than the building address, and the data base is thus biased towards addresses with large resident or user populations.

The data base was limited to calls to police, thus excluding fire department and ambulance calls. It also excluded administrative calls recorded in the system, such as police officers notifying the dispatcher that they are "out to lunch." We asked that calls be excluded if there was no police car dispatched. Finally, we directed that the address in question would always be an address where the problem was located, not the address from which the call came (if that was a different address).

Both of the last two definitions were difficult to impose, given the nature of police-dispatching systems. The address employed in the data base was generally the address to which a police car was dispatched; but there was no way to insure that the problem had actually occurred at that address. Thus the "unadjusted" number-one call location in the city is the Hennepin County Medical Center, because police respond there to take a crime report whenever medical staff notify police (as required by law) that a crime victim has arrived in the emergency room. The crime, of course, happened elsewhere, but the dispatch computer does not record the address of occurrence.

The address in the data base is only "generally" the address to which a car is dispatched because some of the included calls—we do not know how many, but believe it to be relatively few—did not result in a police car being dispatched at all. There was an exclusion made of one code indication showing that the call was screened out, or handled by the telephone operator. But other non-dispatched calls slipped in because they had a "closed" disposition at the time they were received.

The "closed" disposition means that the purpose of the call is to create a record of an event rather than to request police service. When an off-duty police officer working as a retail security officer apprehends a shoplifter, for example, he can fill out all the paperwork to charge and release the suspect right at the scene. But he must still call the police operator to receive a case number for the arrest report. Such a call is listed as a closed call under the "event" disposition field, as distinct from the "officer" disposition field, on each call record.

At the time the data base fields were selected, we were not aware of this distinction. It only emerged as we analyzed the preliminary report from the last six months of 1986. We had omitted it in trying to conserve computer storage space, since including it would have taken close to a million bytes. But when we discovered how crucial it was to determining whether cars were actually dispatched, we decided to rebuild the data base from scratch. That effort will begin shortly and will provide the basis for the final evaluation of the RECAP unit's effectiveness at reducing calls to which police are actually dispatched.

The data base as described to this point will be defined as the "unadjusted" data base, which included 321,174 calls. The following exclusions describe how the "adjusted" data base was constructed for the purposes of identifying the most active addresses in the city.

The Adjusted Data Base

In order to limit the target list more closely to addresses where problems actually occurred, the RECAP commander and officers went through a printout of the top 2,000 addresses in the last six months (approximately) of 1986. The time period was selected merely on the grounds of moving speedily, at a time when the data base was only half built. They tried to eliminate all addresses, such as all hospitals, city hall, police precinct stations, the St. Joseph's Shelter for lost, abandoned, and abused children, and the courthouse, which were clearly not the locations of the problems but rather the locations to which police were dispatched to take a report. (Unfortunately, two small hospitals slipped through, but were deleted from the target list described below.)

They also decided, after a three-day planning retreat with Crime Control Institute staff and extensive debate for a week thereafter, to eliminate *intersections*. The problem with intersections from the standpoint of proactive police work is that there is very little chance of finding a stable group of people who generate or deal with the problems. Recurrent traffic accidents at bad intersections are already being mapped by another unit; so the remaining problems of muggings, fights, car lockouts, etc., could not be dealt with conveniently by a small unit.

For similar reasons, the RECAP unit also decided to eliminate parks and schools (which have their own special police units), and the one-block area downtown in which an enormous amount of vice consumption is concentrated: pornography stores, movies, and the most active bar in the city for calls to police. The city council was debating the future of that block heavily at the time, and even considered condemning it and tearing it down. When this analysis found that the twelve addresses and four intersections of the "E" block, as it is known, were the subject of 3,230 police calls in the unadjusted data base—more than 1 percent—the finding was the subject of a detailed story in the Minneapolis *Star and Tribune* (January 15, 1987).

The fact that 0.001 percent of the addresses and intersections produced 1 percent of the calls, or 1,000 times more calls than would be expected by an equal distribution, is a striking part of the overall concentrations reported here. But it also suggested a problem so major that it was prudent for the RECAP unit to exclude it from its work.

The final categorical exclusion was the check-cashing establishments, which generate many calls for arrests of felonious bad-check passers. These arrests have a high conviction rate, and the RECAP officers did not want to discourage the arrests. One such establishment, however, slipped by into the adjusted data base reported here.

In addition to these categorical exclusions, the officers dealt with two other issues. One issue, which will affect any police department attempting to identify repeat call locations, is the fact that police telephone operators enter the same address in different ways on different occasions. A good example comes from the most active bar on the "E" block, Moby Dick's, which is entered in at least these different ways:

- 620 Hennepin Ave.
- 620 Hennepin Ave.—Moby's
- 620 Hennepin Ave.—Moby Dick's
- 620 Hennepin Ave.—Moby's Bar

These different listings made the address appear to have fewer calls than it actually had, because the true total was split among the different ways of labeling the address.

Other buildings may have entrances and addresses on different streets, or have similar variations in the description of the premises following the address. We had asked the programmer to suppress those descriptions in the analysis, but it was not possible to combine the multiple listings without far more complex programming. Thus, both the unadjusted and adjusted data bases show *less* concentration of calls than actually exists.

The problem was somewhat reduced for the top 2,000 addresses. The RECAP officers read the address listings for the full year data set. They instructed the programmer to merge the remaining addresses that were presented under multiple labels, to the extent that they were able to detect them.

In addition, less than twenty addresses were deleted for reasons related to the evaluation research design, which will be described in later reports.

Commercial and Residential Addresses

The preliminary inspection of the top 2,000 addresses showed that they were predominantly commercial addresses. In order to insure that the RECAP experiment would have enough residential addresses to explore the full range of police problems, we decided to stratify the study sample. The officers went through the top 2,000 locations, using the reverse telephone directory to supplement their formidable knowledge of city addresses, and labeled each location as residential or commercial.

Once the designations and all the exclusions were complete, the programmers rank-ordered the commercial and residential addresses in separate lists. The top 250 addresses in each category were then identified as the project targets. It is this final, adjusted list that is the basis for the data presented in Tables 12.2 and 12.3. For the purpose of the experimental phase of the unit, only half of each list will be assigned to RECAP. The other, randomly selected half of each list will be left alone as a control group against which to compare the frequency of calls at the experimental locations.

LETTING CALLS SET PRIORITIES

Table 12.1 presents the overall distribution of calls by nature code in the unadjusted data base of 321,174 calls. The distribution is a regrouping of 114 separate nature codes into six more general categories. The cat-

Table 12.2

Nature of Police Calls to the 250 Most Active Commercial and to the 250 Most Active Residential Addresses in Minneapolis, 1986* (adjusted data)

CATEGORY	Commercial Number	%**	Residential Number	%**
Conflict Management:	6,357	32%	11,427	59%
Domestics	462	2	3,703	19
Other Disturbances	4,919	25	5,560	29
Assault	919	5	1,254	6
Noise	57	--	910	5
Property Crime-Related:	7,857	40%	3,640	19%
Theft	5,757	29	1,583	8
Burglary-related	940	5	1,432	7
Vandalism	425	2	587	3
Alarms	735	4	68	--
Traffic Problems:	985	5%	519	3%
Traffic Enforcement	131	1	131	1
Property Damage Accident	130	1	130	1
Parking	251	1	251	1
Service:	3,006	15%	2,584	13%
Lockouts	1,993	10	706	4
Medical Aid	700	4	1,025	5
Emergencies	435	2	940	5
Assistance	486	2	640	3
Persons -- Lost/Found	88	--	206	1
Fires				
Miscellaneous:	756	4%	882	4%
Arrests and Bookings	304	2	460	2
Other				
Stranger to Stranger				
Crime Against Persons:	722	3%	548	2%
Robbery	616	3	371	2
Criminal Sexual Conduct	106	1	177	1
TOTALS:	19,564	100%	19,462	100%

*December 15, 1985 to December 15, 1986.
**Percentages do not total 100 due to rounding.

egories are guided by the prior literature on the nature of police work (e.g., Wilson, 1968; Goldstein, 1977). The results show what police work becomes when police priorities are determined by the calls that come in.

There is no question that police are needed to deal with angry conflicts that can erupt, or have already erupted, into violence. It is hard to criticize the fact that one-third of all calls fall into this category. It is also hard to argue that police should not attend to calls about actual or

Table 12.3
Distribution of Calls to Police by Locations Generating Police Calls in
Minneapolis, 1986* (unadjusted data base)

Percentile of Call Addresses	# of Calls	Raw % of Calls	Cumulative % of Calls**
5	156,076	48.58	48.58
10	40,040	12.46	61.04
15	24,142	7.51	68.55
20	17,106	5.32	73.87
25	13,216	4.11	77.98
30	10,449	3.25	81.23
35	8,456	2.63	83.86
40	6,966	2.17	86.03
45	6,966	2.17	88.20
50	5,845	1.82	90.02
55	3,483	1.08	91.10
60	3,483	1.08	92.18
65	3,483	1.08	93.26
70	3,483	1.08	94.34
75	3,483	1.08	95.42
80	3,483	1.08	96.50
85	3,483	1.08	97.58
90	3,483	1.08	98.66
95	3,483	1.08	99.74
100	3,352	1.04	100.78

*December 15, 1985 to December 15, 1986.
**Percentages do not total 100 due to rounding.

potential property crime, which comprise 29 percent of calls, or traffic control at 19 percent, or even some of the service calls, at 13 percent.

It is possible to argue that police should not be providing a free car lockout service (5 percent of calls), when private locksmiths could do the same on a fee-for-service basis, a plan that is under much discussion in Minneapolis. But there are few such categories of calls that police could reasonably abandon altogether. The problem is not one of need, but one of balance.

The fact that only 2 percent of all calls concern the most serious crimes, stranger-to-stranger crimes against persons, suggests that the balance does not match citizen priorities. The Minneapolis police do expend other resources on street crime besides patrol car responses to citizen calls. But the total resources dedicated to stranger crime are probably minimal in comparison to the high priority many citizens would place on such offenses.

Bittner (1980) has defended the picture of police work presented in Table 12.1 by defining policing as the intervention in "situations-about-which-somebody-must-do-something-now." That is no doubt the common theme that runs through all of these calls. But it is arguable that police work can and should be more than just immediate responses. A good analogy is found in medicine, which is increasingly moving away from just treating the sick towards the preventive maintenance of health.

The analogy of public health is even more compelling, with the recent growth of proactive efforts to identify carriers of Acquired Immune Deficiency Syndrome (AIDS) to stop them from spreading the disease. Far more lives may be saved by such efforts than by doctors treating sore throats and the flu. Similarly, far more lives may be saved by focusing police resources on serious crime problems than by simply waiting for calls on minor crime problems to come in.

Whatever the merits of the priorities reflected in this distribution of calls in the unadjusted data base, it is important to note how it differs from the nature of calls about the top 250 commercial and residential locations in the adjusted data base. As Table 12.2 shows, both commercial and residential addresses are relatively free of traffic problems. But commercial addresses have proportionally more property crime calls than addresses in general, and residential addresses have proportionally twice as many conflict management calls as addresses in general.

Solving the problems that produce the high concentrations of repeat calls at these locations will not necessarily reduce street crime, but they may free up other police resources to concentrate on such crimes.

THE CHRONIC CALL LOCATIONS

And the concentration is substantial indeed. Each of the locations in the two adjusted lists of most active addresses generates an average of about 80 calls per year, slightly less than two a week. Each list of 250, with only two-tenths of one percent of the city's addresses, produces 6 percent of the calls in the city. These addresses are thus 30 times more likely to produce a call to police on any given day than the average address in the city.

The concentrations are even more clearly demonstrated by the data from the unadjusted list. Analysis shows a steep decline in the total percentage of calls produced by addresses ranked below the top 5 percent of addresses in call frequency. The second 5 percent of addresses produce only 13 percent of the calls, the third 5 percent of addresses only 7 percent of the calls, and so on.

Table 12.3 shows a similar distribution among the 60 percent of addresses and intersections that had any calls at all, with almost 49 percent of the calls concentrated in the top 5 percent of those addresses.

Table 12.4 shows the distribution of places with calls by the number of calls at each place. The majority of those addresses had only one call, and 85 percent had less than five. Thus, the concentration of most calls in the few most active addresses is clearly intense.

These statistical concentrations raise the obvious question: What kinds

Table 12.4
Number of Locations Responded to by Number of Police Calls per Address in Minneapolis, 1986* (unadjusted data base)

Number of Calls	Number of Locations
0	45,353
1	35,926
2	11,329
3	5,691
4	3,511
5	2,304
6	1,680
7	1,253
8	964
9	817
10	655
11	508
12	417
13	358
14	302
15	301
16	260
17	203
18	225
19	175
20	162
Over 20	2,606

*December 15, 1985 to December 15, 1986.

of locations are consuming the lion's share of police patrol responses? The answer is not just low-rent apartments or tough bars, although they are well represented. The lists also include major commercial locations, which attract large numbers of people for many hours of the day.

Table 12.5 lists in rank order the top 50 addresses, both commercial and residential, in the adjusted list, showing the frequency of calls and the generic type of location at each address. An analysis of these locations shows that 21 are apartment buildings, of which four are public housing projects. Twelve are retail or grocery stores, and the grocery stores are generally open 24 hours a day. Five are bars, three are 24-hour convenience stores with the same national company, three are hotels, one is a fast-food hamburger chain (not McDonald's), and five others are of varied character.

It is fairer to say that these addresses usually attract trouble rather than cause it. The role of the late-night hours, when many people are intoxicated and more vulnerable to committing or being victimized by crime, appears to be substantial. Yet, the profits from all-night operations are also reported to be substantial and a strong incentive for businesses to stay open.

Table 12.5

Top 50 Addresses in Minneapolis by Nature of Location and Number of Calls, 1986* (adjusted data base)

Rank	Nature of Location	Number of Calls
1	Large discount store	810
2	Large department store	686
3	24-Hour convenience store and bar	607
4	Apartments -- Public housing	479
5	Large discount store	471
6	Large discount store	449
7	Homeless center -- former hotel	379
8	Transportation center	343
9	Large department store	319
10	Downtown business mall	251
11	Bar	244
12	Large department store	242
13	High-priced hotel	240
14	Bar	237
15	Apartments	233
16	Bar	222
17	Community center	209
18	Apartments	208
19	Apartments	207
20	Apartments	195
21	Grocery store -- 24-hour	195
22	Medium-priced hotel	193
23	Supermarket	192
24	Apartments	190
25	Supermarket	190
26	Small apartment	187
27	24-hour convenience store	183
28	Apartments -- high rise	181
29	Apartments	177
30	Apartments	175
31	Apartments	168
32	Halfway house	163
33	Bar	158
34	Apartments	156
35	Apartments	156
36	Low-priced hotel	152
37	Apartments	149
38	Apartments -- public housing	149
39	Apartments -- public housing	148
40	Bar and 24-hour restaurant	147
41	Social service center	147
42	Fast food restaurant	146
43	24-hour convenience store	145
44	Grocery store -- 24-hour	145
45	Liquor store	143
46	Apartments	142
47	Apartments	142
48	Apartments	142
49	Apartments	142
50	Apartments -- public housing	136
	TOTAL CALLS	11,870

*December 15, 1985 to December 15, 1986.

It is also interesting to note the role of big business in these demands for local police service. While many of the locations are owned by local small businesses, especially the apartments, six of the top ten are operated by Fortune 500 companies.

User Fees

Whether they simply attract trouble along with large numbers of customers by offering the public a needed service, or in the case of certain bars, cause trouble by serving intoxicated customers, these addresses do place major demands upon the police. Whether they pay disproportionately larger taxes than other police users is unclear. If not, then one implication might be to create a system of user fees for calling the police, restricted to commercial addresses—just as garbage collection is charged to commercial, but not residential, addresses in many cities.

THE RECAP STRATEGY

A less extreme approach is simply focusing police resources on the chronic use locations, in order to reduce their use. The goal of such a strategy should not be merely to reduce calls to police, and certainly not to discourage people from making calls in emergencies. The goal should be solving or reducing the problems generating the repeat calls.

One way to accomplish that goal might be to assign a small unit of officers to spend full time on proactive police work at these locations. These officers would not answer radio calls, but would work flexible hours to accomplish the following tasks at the high-volume locations identified through the computer-generated analysis described in this report:

• Description of the nature and use of the premises.
• Diagnosis of the problems generating the calls.
• Planning police or user action for reducing those problems.
• Implementing the action plan.
• Following up on repeat call rates to measure success.

The description can generally be done on the basis of existing officer knowledge or merely driving by the location. The diagnosis should be based upon a review of a computer printout of the nature, days, and time of the calls at the location, as well as the narratives in the crime and arrest reports previously filed for those locations. The diagnosis may also include personal contact with owners, managers, users, or residents of the locations.

The planning could be done after discussion with colleagues or supervisors, and possibly after consultation with other community resources, such as social service agencies. The action plan can then be implemented by the RECAP officers, other police units, social welfare organizations, or persons on the premises. The important point of departure from conventional police work is the *follow-up*: the RECAP officers' efforts to insure that the action plan was indeed implemented, and their monitoring of weekly computer reports on subsequent calls at the addresses they have worked upon. These reports, ideally, will take the form of a trend line showing how many calls were dispatched each week, with a vertical line through the trend showing the date the action plan was implemented.

This RECAP strategy began in Minneapolis in 1987 with four hand-picked volunteer officers and one sergeant commanding them. These officers were among the most experienced, hardest-working and creative officers in the department. Two were college graduates in social science, and they averaged over fifteen years of patrol experience. They were intentionally chosen for their excellence, as they would be in normal operational circumstances.

Whether even such a high-quality team can implement the complex strategy described here remains to be seen. If it is implemented properly, the experimental design being employed will give a fairly clear answer to the question of whether such a unit can reduce repeat calls at these chronic locations.

The ultimate success of such a strategy may depend as much upon the tactics used as upon the strategy itself. Negative results would not necessarily disprove the value of the strategy. But it would show that the methods used by the Minneapolis RECAP team failed to deal with the problems producing the calls, and raise serious doubt about whether any tactics could have made a difference.

The Minneapolis RECAP team is well aware that, perhaps for the first time in the history of the department, there is a "bottom line," profit-or-loss statement that they will show at the end of the experiment. With approximately 400 patrol officers handling 321,000 calls a year, each officer on patrol will handle roughly 800 calls per year, or about four per day worked. In order to justify their removal from patrol to RECAP, the officers must reduce calls by five times 800, or 4,000 calls, on an annualized basis. Anything more than that will be considered "profit"; anything less can be considered a "loss."

An annualized reduction of 4,000 calls amounts to about 20 percent fewer calls at the target addresses than in the previous year. Such a goal is not easy to attain, but neither does it seem unrealistic. Given the high quality of the group, there is good reason for optimism.

REFERENCES

Bittner, E. (1980). *The Functions of the Police in Modern Society.* Cambridge, MA: Oegelschlager, Gunn and Hain.

Goldstein, H. (1977). *Policing a Free Society.* Cambridge, MA: Ballinger.

———. (1979). "Improving Policing: A Problem-Oriented Approach." *Crime and Delinquency,* 25:236–258.

McEwen, J., E. Connors, and M. Cohen (1984). *Evaluation of the Differential Response Field Test.* Alexandria, VA: Research Management Associates.

Martin, S. and L. Sherman (1986). "Selective Apprehension: A Police Strategy for Repeat Offenders." *Criminology,* 24(1).

Pate, A., M. Wycoff, W. Skogan, and L. Sherman (1986). *Reducing Fear of Crime in Houston and Newark.* Washington, D.C.: Police Foundation.

Pierce, G., S. Spaar, and L. Briggs (1984). *The Character of Police Work: Implications for the Delivery of Services.* Boston: Northeastern University.

Reiss, A. (1971). *The Police and the Public.* New Haven: Yale University Press.

Spelman, W. and D. Brown (1981). *Calling the Police: A Replication of the Citizen Reporting Component of the Kansas City Response Time Analysis.* Washington, D.C.: Police Executive Research Forum.

Spelman, W. and J. Eck (1986). *Problem Oriented Policing.* Washington, D.C.: National Institute of Justice.

Wilson, J. (1968). *Varieties of Police Behavior.* Cambridge, MA: Harvard University Press.

_____IV

Policing the Police

13

Policing the Police

Robert Blecker

When "We, the People of the United States," adopted a Constitution in 1788, our goal was liberty—the freedom to develop our talents, to become most fully ourselves. Toward that end, in federal and state constitutions we allocated power among three coordinate branches: an executive, a legislature, and a judiciary. The legislature would enact laws—general rules ordinarily reflecting the will of the majority that must not run counter to fundamental rights. The courts would expound on and apply these laws to do justice. But primarily the executive, including police and prosecutors, would ensure that the legislature's general rules were faithfully translated into reality. We depend upon the executive principally to maintain order and punish crimes so that we may cooperate and compete within limits, striving for scarce rewards according to posted rules. Still, from our infancy as a nation we have understood that public officials are human beings. "Ambition must be made to counteract ambition," declared Madison (*51st Federalist*); each branch would help check the others from expanding individual power at the cost of the People's liberty. Lest we become a police state, the executive must be kept in check, and policing the police includes restraining them from overzealousness.

The Founders feared not only that the executive would seize power, but also that they would sell it. Powerful public cheats corrode our constitutional core, for the Plan works only as long as most citizens believe that legal commands mostly translate into facts of life, that by and large public officials honestly enforce laws and carry out orders.

When the people lose this faith; as we catch on that official cheating pays; when we come to believe that really two systems of rules operate— one on the books for ordinary citizens and another, more favorable code, for the powerful—we become cynical and calculating, clawing in a world of hypocrites, doing whatever we can get away with. When corruption becomes rampant, we may pledge, but we feel no allegiance.

CORING THE ROTTEN APPLE: CORRUPTION IN NEW YORK CITY

"The policeman is convinced that he lives and works in the middle of a corrupt society, that everybody is getting theirs and why shouldn't *he*, and that if somebody cared about corruption, something would have been done about it a long time ago," Officer David Durk concluded in his publicly televised Knapp Commission testimony. Through the efforts of Durk's partner, Officer Frank Serpico, as well as Robert Leuci, a narcotics detective who voluntarily confessed his own corruption and agreed to document that of his former friends and associates, a dismal portrait emerged of a widely fixed New York City criminal justice system.

During the investigative stage, prior to arrest, cases were sold out, corrupt cops warning targets of wiretaps and warrants. At the *time of arrest*, defendants would pay to be released on the spot. Or evidence could be altered later, especially in narcotics cases with confiscated contraband resold. Arresting officers could write open-ended complaints enabling them to testify consistently with the facts, even while making the arrest appear to violate constitutional guarantees. Those cases were then thrown out. *After arrest*, awaiting trial, defendants, often through their lawyers, paid assistant district attorneys—ADAs—to reduce the bail, or register their clients as informants, crediting them with cases they never made. Because of the defendant's reported "cooperation," charges would be reduced or dismissed.

After indictment cases were fixed through court clerks who moved them before the "right" judges, who decided motions improperly, accepted reduced pleas, or dispensed light sentences.

The local criminal justice system was a mess. Everyone knew it. The only citizens who complained, however, were those who couldn't prove it. Certainly not all judges, prosecutors, or police officers were corrupt— far from it. But when corruption is at every level of the system, we have been cheated on the basic promise we have made to ourselves. When the criminal justice system itself is corrupt, the Republic exists only on paper. How do we attack a *system* that is fixed? Who will police the executive when it will not police itself?

In this instance the federal government investigated New York City. United States Attorneys sent DEA Agent Sante Bario undercover to pose as Salvatore Barone, an out-of-town mob hit man arrested with two unlicensed guns, looking to fix his gun possession case. Initially "arrested" by a cooperating New York City police officer, "defendant Barone" was processed through the system. False papers were filed, unsuspecting judges were deceived, and eventually, under orders, but under oath, a *federal* agent lied to an unsuspecting *state* grand jury.

By adopting our federal republic in 1788, we partitioned power between a single central federal government and several states. State sovereignty essentially includes each state's internal police power—a power to define, detect, prosecute, and punish crime. With very few constitutional prohibitions (such as against cruel and unusual punishment) each state is free to define crimes and mete out punishments as it sees fit. This task falls to local legislatures, courts, and executives—local prosecutors, local police.

Yet here, the federal government had manipulated the state's criminal justice system. Federal law enforcement power has greatly expanded since the adoption of the United States Constitution. Under expansive definitions of "interstate commerce," mail fraud, and other areas of national interest, the federal executive, supported by the federal courts, have policed many areas traditionally reserved to the states. But policing the state's own police? A small but growing chorus who reject overexpansive federal power nevertheless find support for this in a little-used provision of the Constitution: Article IV, section 4 which "guarantees" the people of every state republican government. When state legislators secretly sell their votes to special interests, the people are not fully, fairly, or equally represented. If the essence of representative government is free elections, that is, occasions for meaningful choices, then undetected corruption seriously undercuts our ability to assess candidates. Undetected corruption denies us truly representative government. When the police, district attorneys, and judges routinely fix cases, the will of the people, as expressed in the legislatively adopted penal law, is not translated into actual fact. Under such conditions, there is no true republic.

In the end, this federal probe was prematurely exposed but still revealed that the Grand Jury Bureau Chief of the Queens District Attorney's Office accepted part of a $15,000 bribe (paid by Bario to his defense attorney) to steer the phony gun-possession case before a pliable grand jury who, after the corrupt prosecutor's presentation, would decide not to indict. At the time of this federal intrusion, the only office with jurisdiction to investigate and prosecute corruption in the Queens County District Attorney's Office was, in fact, the Queens County District Attorney's Office. Yet, when the investigation prematurely became front-page news, the questions of who was corrupt were dwarfed by questions of who was to police the police, and how?

POLICING WITHOUT ENTRAPMENT

Experience shows that to expose corruption best is to simulate it, to send undercover agents into the system to monitor and participate in it. In short, the most effective way to police the police and the rest of the executive is to sting them. Simulate the environment, offer the bait, and someone will bite!

Stings and scams have always worked. In Shakespeare's *Measure for Measure* the Duke efficiently tested the faithfulness of his deputy by going undercover. Long before him, Odysseus went undercover to see who had remained faithful in his absence. Earlier, in Eden, Eve, pressured repeatedly by the serpent, had yielded. But the Garden was wired. And when God confronted Adam, he instantly gave up Eve, who in turn replied: "The Serpent beguiled me and I did eat." This, the first recorded entrapment defense, failed, although the case reporter doesn't tell us exactly why. Perhaps the snake was on its own mission.

Future defendants fared little better before the United States Supreme Court until another prohibition agent, posing as a tourist, had dropped in on an unsuspecting veteran—Sorrels—swapping old war stories, asking repeatedly for booze. Finally, Sorrels yielded, was prosecuted, and convicted. A unanimous Supreme Court reversed the conviction but divided as to why.

Thirty years later Sherman, a narcotics addict under treatment, was befriended at the doctor's office by a government informant who begged for narcotics. Sherman avoided the issue but his new "friend," the informant, pressed. Finally, Sherman yielded, abandoning his attempt to go straight and purchased narcotics for both of them. A federal appellate court affirmed his ten-year prison sentence, but again the United States Supreme Court unanimously reversed, finding entrapment. Once again, however, the court was split 5–4 as to why.

A bare majority, per Chief Justice Warren, focused upon Sherman's mental state: "When the criminal design originates with government investigators and they implant in the mind of an innocent person the disposition to commit the alleged offense and induce its commission in order that they may prosecute . . . then stealth and strategy become as objectionable police methods as the coerced confession and the unlawful search" (*Sherman v. United States*). The fact that government agents "merely afforded opportunities or facilities for the commission of the offense" did not constitute entrapment, which occurred only when the criminal conduct was "the product of the creative activity" of law enforcement officials.

The key question for these "subjectivists" was the defendant's "predisposition." Was the defendant otherwise "ready and willing"? The government could not "play on the weaknesses of an innocent party and beguile him into committing crimes which he otherwise would not have attempted," said Chief Justice Warren. "To determine whether entrapment has been established, a line must be drawn between the trap for the unwary innocent and the trap for the unwary criminal."

Was the defendant, although induced, *predisposed* to commit that crime, and therefore not innocent? This, the key question, rarely allows a simple yes or no. Predisposition lies on a continuum, as Judge Fullam observed in an ABSCAM opinion:

At one extreme is the defendant who customarily engages in this type of criminal activity as a way of life, and who enthusiastically embraces any additional opportunities for such activities. At the other extreme is the resolute individual who would not commit a crime of this type under any circumstances. In between are many gradations: the person who occasionally commits crimes of this type, and would be willing to do so again only if a particularly favorable opportunity should present itself; the person who has previously succumbed to temptation, but is making a sincere and concerted effort to resist such temptations; the previously innocent person who is weak and easily influenced. (*United States v. Jannotti*)

If few of us are corrupt, most of us are corruptible. In a moment of need, most of us are predisposed to some degree to violate some rules, especially when no one gets hurt, the chances of detection are small, and the rewards are great. If everyone has their price, the essence of honesty might consist of pricing yourself out of the corruption marketplace. But to avoid entrapment by ensuring that a particular target *is* predisposed, the executive need merely make an offer so tempting that almost everyone, including the target, would be predisposed to accept it.

For the concurring minority of the Supreme Court in *Sorrels* and *Sherman*, the stakes were larger than a particular defendant's guilt or innocence: "The crucial question, not easy of answer, to which the court must direct itself is whether the police conduct revealed in the particular case falls below standards, to which common feelings respond, for the proper use of governmental power. For answer it is wholly irrelevant to ask if the 'intention' to commit the crime originated with the defendant or government officers" (*Sherman v. United States*). For these objectivists like Justice Frankfurter, the proper focus is not whether this particular defendant was predisposed but whether an average law-abiding citizen would succumb to the type of pressure exerted. An entrapment defense should protect the purity of the criminal justice process. By threatening to release an otherwise guilty defendant, it should check prosecutorial overzealousness. So conceived, this defense of entrapment would help police the police.

This objective standard, too, has its flaws. Who is a "normally law-abiding citizen"? A wealthy, very cautious public official, thoroughly predisposed to corruption but only through intermediaries, is almost certain to decline all but the most substantial bribes. Government agents can reveal this corruption only by offering inducements sufficient to cause other, less well positioned citizens to violate the law.

Independent of an entrapment defense—however conceived—conduct of law enforcement agents may be "so outrageous that due-process principles would absolutely bar the government from invoking the judicial processes to obtain a conviction." First enunciated by Justice Rehnquist in 1973 (*United States v. Russell*), this doctrine continues to command the support of a bare majority of the United States Supreme Court if not of Rehnquist himself. The problem, of course, is to determine just what is sufficiently "outrageous" to violate due process.

In 1976, the United States Supreme Court refused to find it "outrageous" that government undercover agents supplied *and* purchased the very heroin that the defendant was convicted of selling. "There is certainly a constitutional limit to allowing government involvement in crime," the court declared in affirming Hampton's conviction. "It would be unthinkable, for example, to permit government agents to instigate robberies and beatings" (*United States v. Hampton*).

Would it necessarily be unconstitutional for government agents while penetrating the mob to participate in robberies and beatings? Would it be a violation of due process to inject phony crimes into a criminal justice system, and to institute bribe attempts? How far is too far? Where does effective policing end, and overzealous policing begin? It's a nagging question.

Many who seek to specify limits on proper investigatory techniques look to Justice Brandeis' classic, stirring call:

Decency, security, and liberty alike demand that government officials shall be subjected to the same rules of conduct that are commands to the citizen. In a government of laws, existence of the government will be imperiled if it fails to observe the law scrupulously. Our government is the potent, the omnipresent teacher. For good or for ill, it teaches the whole people by its example. Crime is contagious. If the government becomes a lawbreaker, it breeds contempt for law; it invites every man to become a law unto himself; it invites anarchy. To declare that in the administration of the criminal law the end justifies the means—to declare that the government may commit crimes in order to secure the conviction of a private criminal—would bring terrible retribution. (*United States v. Olmstead*)

Government shall commit no crimes: This sounds appealing but actually begs the question. While investigating narcotics, gambling, and other "victimless" crimes, government agents routinely engage in generally forbidden transactions, yet are held to commit no crimes. And although Bario, the federal undercover agent, and Murano, the cooperating New York City police officer who "arrested" him, did intentionally lie under oath, they did not thereby commit the crime of perjury.

The New York Penal Law declares under its "justification" provision that "conduct which would otherwise constitute an offense is justifiable and *not criminal when . . .* performed by a public servant in the *reasonable exercise* of his official powers, duties and functions." Acts which would be criminal when done by a private citizen are justifiable and *not criminal* when done by a government agent in the reasonable exercise of law enforcement power. We can't know, then, whether the government commits crimes unless we first determine whether the conduct of undercover agents is a reasonable exercise of police power.

Some critics of undercover operations seek other bright line tests to constrain the executive. But in covert activities, domestic and foreign, it is probably impossible to erect in advance a workable, comprehensive set of rigid rules to constrain police power. Judge Bryant offered one such rule in an ABSCAM opinion: "If after an illegal offer is made, the subject rejects it in any fashion, the government cannot press on" (*United States v. Kelly*). Judge Pratt anticipated the flaw in this rule:

It would provide a corrupt politician easy insurance against any undercover investigation, for when the suggestion of improper conduct was raised, all the subject would have to do would be to invoke the magic incantation, "I desire to act within the law" and then plunge into his nefarious activities. Such a per se rule would soon frustrate virtually all undercover law enforcement (*United States v. Myers*).

Other critics have drawn an active/passive bright line test and urge that government stay on the passive side: Like an undercover agent posing as an elderly citizen on a park bench, waiting to be attacked by muggers, government agents should offer only passive opportunities but not make the initial approach. Of course, active/passive is less a dichotomy than a continuum. More active than the park bench mugging victim, the government establishes a legitimate business, awaiting demands for protection money and payoffs. More active is an *illegitimate* business awaiting those approaches. Government is more total when its undercover operation is a fully fashioned world, in which people unwittingly play their parts, relationships are formed, targets are initially contacted and actively enticed with inducements.

The point is that no point is obviously out of bounds always. Passive stings won't uncover judges and D.A.s fixing cases. Rarely will those public officials make the first approach. If we are committed to cleaning up corrupt criminal justice systems, we cannot be passive.

On the other hand, some advocates of unrestricted undercover operations criticize any restraint on the police and prosecutors. Investigate fully and vigorously, they urge. Conversations secretly taped, and the intrusion of an undercover operation can be judged afterwards on a case-by-case basis. An entrapment defense, supplemented with due-process protections, will check the executive. "The tapes will speak for themselves," they insist.

As linguist Roger Shuy demonstrated before a House Oversight Committee investigating ABSCAM abuses, that assumption, that "the tapes speak for themselves" is too facile. "In normal everyday conversation, the listener is expected to give feedback to the person who is talking. . . . The most commonly used signals for such feedback are what linguists call 'lax token.' The positive lax tokens usually take the form of 'uh-huh,' 'all right,' 'yeah,' or 'OK.' Since the function of the lax taken is to provide feedback to the speaker, its meaning cannot be taken as agreement. Yet prosecutors, courts, and juries often mistake these as agreement. If an indictment is made on the basis of a presumed agreement when, in fact, the response meant 'I hear you, keep talking,' a false indictment has been made" (Subcommittee on Civil and Constitutional Rights).

Securing the appearance of agreement was only the first of seven distinct FBI strategies that Shuy identified—strategies that agents used to manipulate their targets, strategies of which the agents themselves were not always conscious. Taken together, they challenge the idea that the tapes speak for themselves.

But suppose at trial we could review each case and determine from testimony and tape the predisposition of each defendant, and whether the government's inducement threatened the average law-abiding citizen with overwhelming temptation. Suppose we could prevent under-cover agents from needlessly engaging in otherwise prohibited acts. If we freed every subjectively or objectively entrapped defendant, and made certain each defendant's due-process rights were protected, wouldn't we then sufficiently police the police?

No! Perhaps the most troubling aspect of undercover operations is that they work so well in combating crime. Barely a week goes by now without some new revelation of a successful undercover operation. We snicker when, during the 1987 Constitutional Bicentennial, United States Attorney Rudolph Giuliani announces that an FBI agent posing as a salesman of steel products had offered bribes to municipal officials 106 times and "on 105 of these occasions the public official accepted the bribe. And on the other occasion he turned it down because he didn't think the amount was enough" (*New York Times*, 1987). We chuckle at a supermarket scam in which the government printed coupons for non-existent items that stores fraudulently submitted for repayment. We applaud the headline in the newspaper next to pictures of eagle, elk, big horn sheep, and grizzly bears: "Wildlife Agents Shift Tactics to Trap Poachers" and the accompanying story of how agents are posing as out-of-town commercial hunters. We cheer the ingenuity of undercover agents posing as Asian businessmen to trap taxicab drivers who overcharge foreigners. Would we also chuckle at undercover agents as taxicab drivers picking up conversations of their unsuspecting passengers? Perhaps we applaud undercover agents sent into school systems to pose as janitors, to reveal drug-dealing among students. But what message do we convey to our children if undercover agents in their schools include teachers and fellow students? Stings and scams have proliferated wildly these past fifteen years, as vigorous, honest police and prosecutors have come to appreciate their power. But however effective at attacking crime, including executive corruption, however justifiable individually, collectively they are taking a hidden toll—perhaps irreversibly polluting our most precious national resource—a free, open society.

Twenty-four hundred years ago, Aristotle observed that the tyrant must "endeavor to keep himself aware of everything that is said or done among his subjects." Aristotle listed "tyranny's three aims in relation to its subjects, namely that they shall: 1) have no minds of their own, 2) have no trust in each other, and 3) have no means of carrying out anything." George Orwell's *Nineteen Eighty-Four* updated Aristotle's vision. Big Brother was everywhere, and a person lived from birth to death under the eye of the police. Everywhere agents were testing morality, testing thought itself, testing predisposition for crime. Every aspect of a person's life was subject to inspection, every relationship suspect. But at least Winston Smith, Orwell's protagonist who rebelled, saw the telescreens and other signs that reminded him that Big Brother was watching. At least he knew the game.

We, the People of the United States, may be threatened more subtly but no less seriously. We watched 1984 come and go with a certain relief that we were immune. At the office, the gym, we feel at liberty to talk openly, act openly, express and expose ourselves. We trust that persons are who they seem. In private, we quickly open up to new friends whose acquaintance we "chance" to make.

"In totalitarian countries, undergoing liberalization, a major demand is the abolition of secret police and secret police tactics. Subterfuge, infiltration, secret and intrusive surveillance, and reality creation are not generally associated with United States law enforcement," sociologist Gary Marx warned in his ABSCAM testimony. "However, we may be taking small, but steady steps toward the paranoia and suspiciousness that characterize many totalitarian countries" (Subcommittee on Civil and Constitutional Rights, 1982).

The "critical question," testified law professor Geoffrey Stone, is "whether and to what extent law-abiding citizens in a free society should be entitled confidently to assume that their supposed friends, confidants, lawyers, and other associates are in fact what they appear to be, and are not in reality clandestine agents of government secretly reporting their activities and conservations to the authorities" (Subcommittee on Civil and Constitutional Rights, 1982).

The debate continues beyond 1984 while undercover operations spread, occasionally to surface and splash corruption into view. Are we steadily but unwarily embracing totalitarianism to rid ourselves of anarchy?

In private, We, the People, should be able to feel free and secure, but in a healthy republic, public officials entrusted with public power must always feel somewhat insecure. How then can we achieve honest government, government-tested, government-monitored, while maintaining a free society? If the dangers of using and not using undercover operations are so great, what are we to do?

Maintaining the quality of life in the United States may require double standards—double standards that promote a vigorous attack on public corruption while safeguarding privacy. Double standards have a bad ring; "equal protection under law" seems their very antithesis. We reject an unfair society where the rich and powerful live more or less by their own private set of rules, while the ordinary citizen is subject to the rules on the books, or worse, to arbitrary targeting by individual law enforcement agents because of race, sex, poverty, politics, or whim. But achieving honest republican government may require multiple standards: special protection of *private* citizens acting in a *private* capacity.

To apprehend a vicious mugger, a decoy cop should pose as a helpless elderly citizen. But if a garrulous stranger should share the park bench and make conversation, the agent must not establish a "friendship" nor ever record how the retiree illegally supplements social security, nor how his successful daughter doesn't report all her income. However, an undercover agent posing as a fellow crooked cop or ADA, should encourage free-ranging conversations about other abuses of the public trust.

Suppose those conversations lead to an invitation to dinner. Is it proper for an undercover agent to begin an intimate relationship with the target's child? How much of the private life of targeted police is out of bounds?

After the North Muskegon Police Department dismissed a police officer for violating an adultery statute by cohabiting with a married woman not his wife, a federal district court in western Michigan rejected the city's argument that the officer's off-duty conduct at least potentially affected his job performance. In doing so, the court rejected the town's claim that as a condition of their employment law enforcement officers can be required to be totally law-abiding citizens (*Briggs v. North Muskegon Police Department*). On the other hand, we do have a right to know whether officials entrusted with national secrets are subject to blackmail for sexual misconduct or gambling habits. The public/private distinction is further complicated when private citizens for private gain corruptly contract with public officials: some lawyers do pay for favorable rulings, some businesses do routinely bribe inspectors. In thousands of ways we private citizens seek personal benefits from public officials. Are we all subject to stings and scams? Per se rules are not obvious, and finer distinctions between public and private await collective wisdom, but in the end we may be forced to adopt variable standards.

Here we are today in the United States, powerful abroad, free at home, celebrating a constitutional system based upon the Founders' bleak view of human nature which experience seems only to confirm: Power unchecked encroaches on liberty; liberty unchecked degenerates into anarchy. Government cannot be trusted to police others, and no one can be trusted to police themselves (*51st Federalist*). Yet, We the People look to legislators for rules and exceptions by which they too will be governed, to judges to judge their own jurisdiction, and ultimately to executive investigators and "special" prosecutors to investigate and prosecute the executive. We are mired in paradox. Simulated criminality—the most effective technique against corruption itself corrupts. It corrupts the undercover agents whose sense of self, of right and wrong, erode as they become their roles. It corrupts the prosecutors who look with mixed distaste and bemusement at the folly of trusting creatures scurrying about in a manufactured world. And most important, it corrupts the citizenry who must approach each other with suspicion.

To promote trust we must be suspicious; to promote freedom we need control; to preserve genuine self-government, we must inject the phony; to attack hypocrisy, we need double standards. Contrary to what we know of human nature—that people cannot be fair judges in their own cases—suppose in a moment of trust, We the People nevertheless declare that henceforth the police shall police all and only those who do not police themselves. Who, then, would police the police?

When this Republic was founded, Madison said it best: "Provision for defense must in this, as in all other cases, be made to counteract ambition. . . . If men were angels, no government would be necessary. If angels were to govern men, neither external nor internal controls on government would be necessary. In framing a government which is to be administered by men over men, the great difficulty lies in this: you must first enable the government to control the governed; and in the next place oblige it to control itself" (*51st Federalist*).

REFERENCES

Briggs v. Muskegon Police Department, 563 F. Supp. 585 (W.D. Michigan 1983).

"F.B.I. Undercover Operations: Hearings Before the Subcommittee on Civil and Constitutional Rights of the House Committee on the Judiciary." 97th Congress, 2d Session (1982).

Madison, J. *The 51st Federalist*. New York: Mentor Books, 1961.

New York Penal Law, Article 35.05(1).

People v. Archer, 68 AD2nd 441 (2nd Dept), 417 NYS 2nd 507 (1979).

Sherman v. United States, 356 U.S. 369, 372 (1958).

United States v. Hampton, 425 U.S. 484, 493 (1976).

United States v. Jannotti, 501 F. Supp. 1182; 1191.

United States v. Kelly, 539 F. Supp. 363, 374–376 (D.D.C. 1982) rev'd 707 F2nd 1460 (D.C. Cir.) cert denied, 104 U.S. Ct 264 (1983).

United States v. Myers, 527 F. Supp. at 1231–32.

United States v. Olmstead, 277 U.S. 438, 485 (1928).

United States v. Russell, 411 U.S. 423, 431–432 (1973).

14

The Process of Erosion:
A Personal Account

Robert Leuci

My memory is of color and of light and shadow, of inked-in outlines and clearness of vision, of seeing things I'd never seen before and of aromas that came in the late silent nights when the music of the street had died, and when it seemed that the only person out and about was me in my blue uniform with a silver shield that was bright as sunshine on my chest and cap. It came early, this simple realization. The world of the policeman would be my home, my anchorage, the place I belonged. And now, twenty-six years later—five years after my official retirement from the New York City Police Department—I am still not ready to go away forever from that part of myself. The part that is, and always will be, a cop.

Back then, my ineradicable belief was that the world was divided between good and evil; there were no gray areas. White was white and black was all around. Gray was the discredited philosophy of those who hadn't stood near the spreading pool of a victim's blood. For hours I'd stand in the street and watch the large and small injustices that people constantly delivered to one another. As I watched, I was sure that the police, and those who stood with them, were good; everyone else, it seemed, was evil.

This is in preface to remarking that during these past five years I've lectured to and listened to police officers from Seattle to Maine, from New York to Texas. These men and women all carry themselves and think like police officers. Most burn with a love for the profession. And

I've found that a large portion of the community today continues to view the world in the very same way that I did so many years ago.

And who can blame them.

Legitimately, self-defense occupies much of the police officer's energy. Instinctively, police officers know they are in harm's way; it's the nature of the profession. Police work is, after all, a contact sport. But perhaps the most sinister peril that confronts the police is not physical at all. Physical threats are both expected and trained for and, in truth, are rarely encountered by the vast majority of officers. On the other hand, almost all officers, from the moment they put on the uniform, are attacked by insidious forces that invade their morality, integrity, and sense of right and wrong. And there is little, if any, training that can prepare them for such an attack.

At age twenty-one, I was keenly aware of the world surrounding my profession. Although I worked with individuals, the world I saw existed in terms of them and us. I would soon learn, however, that this way of thinking is a trick—a way to trap you into a strategic collapse of your own sense of integrity. It is a major signpost along a road of moral erosion. On this road, damage is slow but thorough. Like a form of gangrene, ultimately it will kill all that is good and leave only corruption.

Early in a career, this them-vs.-us perception leads officers to turn inward and join secret covenants of their profession that are as powerful and beguiling as any the Mafia can create. They build fences in order to hold in friends and keep out what they view as an unjust and threatening world. Only on themselves, their partners, and other police officers they will depend.

FROM THE BEGINNING

The sixties were not easy years for a New York City police officer. It was one barricade after another. Antiwar demonstrators spit and called you pig. And on the hot nights, there were the riots. Believe it when I tell you that a brick makes one loud bang when thrown from the roof of a six-story tenement. I trained myself to be vigilant and whenever possible I walked my foot patrol under the protective overhang of fire escapes. Rooftop bombardiers were out there, the enemy was everywhere. But there was a sweet feeling in the knowing that you were part of something much larger and stronger than yourself. The clear sounds of sirens in the night were thrilling to me. While the enemy was there, my police friends were around too. It was a good feeling. I was twenty-one years old and felt the full weight of being part of something special.

At the time, I was certain that my colleagues, the others on my side of the barricade, were capable of little worse than fraternity pranks. And so, during my first year, when I happened to walk in on a patrol sergeant struggling to remove a ring from the finger of an old man who had had his final heart attack and lay dead on his bedroom floor, I panicked. I knew that police officers didn't do such things. Still, I had not been a cop for a year for nothing. I was aware of the stories about corruption in the department. But in my mind, at least until that moment, I was sure that our society was far more corrupt than anything that might occur in the police department.

Try as I could, I was unable to keep panic in its place. I need only tell you that I had knelt for a half hour giving mouth-to-mouth to that poor old man. Emergency service units had arrived with the sergeant and literally dragged me from him. He was dead, they said, a long time dead. I had done all that could be expected. The emergency service units left, and the sergeant took over.

He was hardly quick enough to conceal what he was doing. I remember standing, looking at him, watching him lie. I would never be totally the same again. What had once been a solid wall of white and black developed a hairline crack of gray. In time it would grow to be a chasm. But that was later. First there was my assignment to the Detective Division.

THE SUBTLETY OF THE EROSION PROCESS

I argue that if you could gauge the integrity and morality of police departments in this country you would find that 5 percent of all officers would have been criminals had they not chosen a career in law enforcement. At the other extreme, 5 percent will remain totally honest, no matter what the temptation. The remaining 90 percent of officers will yield to the weight of the aura of their particular agencies and the towns and cities they police.

History is a powerful force that can easily influence. Simply put, if the prevailing morality of a particular city and its police department is racist, abusive, and fundamentally dishonest—and those abuses and dishonesty do not outrage those in positions of power and influence— the chances are that the agency will be heavily corrupted. Naturally, the opposite is also true. If the leaders of a city, and the superior officers of a department, set a high standard of morality and integrity, those standards will be reflected by the rank and file of the police department. When that is the case, you will have an honest and law-abiding police force. It is true that our police officers reflect the towns, cities, and counties they police. But it is even more true that they will reflect the expectations, fears, and fashions of their departments. No one wants to be an outsider; very few are willing to play a different game.

For me, this became significant after two years in the New York City Police Department. I had come to realize by then that I had a gift: joining the rhythms of the street came naturally to me. It was only a matter of perfecting the technique of appearing extremely young and very dumb.

In those days, for New York City police officers there was a height requirement, a requirement that I barely made. And, I did look young, really young. In fact, I would turn thirty before I was no longer required to show I.D. at bars. Since the drinking age in New York was eighteen at the time, you can be sure that I looked nothing like a police officer.

This genetic gift, I figured, could be my real value to the department. In retrospect, I had no real understanding of what going into the streets really meant. I was, in those days, absolutely fearless, and a bit of an egomaniac.

As a member of the Tactical Patrol Force, I sometimes was required to participate in "decoy" operations. Simply put, as a decoy cop you sometimes dressed as a woman, an Orthodox Jew, whatever. You wore a costume of sorts, then went to the streets as a target for criminals. Backed up, I might add, by sturdy cops who hid waiting for you to be set upon. Backup cops were there to make sure the decoy, though threatened, would not be overrun. At just the right moment (you hoped) they would jump from ambush and lay a whole lot of woe on whoever had "hit" on the decoy. It was fun, cop games, there was nothing better.

When it was my turn to play "decoy," it always struck me as nothing short of amazing to see the number of street drug dealers that marched over to me and, with little more than a "how are ya?" asked if I wanted to buy some drugs. It was the sixties, after all, a time when drug-taking was exalted. Still, my superiors were not amused. I was meant to be mugged, I was not a narcotics officer. I, on the other hand, looked at myself as a cop out to stop crime—any kind of crime. It wasn't my fault that dealers came to me pushing drugs, forcing me to take action. In the neighborhoods that we worked, I could hardly get a block without running into a dealer. They'd hit on me, I'd arrest them. My backups and I were making tons of arrests. It was easy, no contest.

Eventually, the police department decided that I should be doing this full-time. I was gifted, after all, a natural. I could play junkie as well as anyone so they transferred me from the Tactical Patrol Force to the Narcotics Division. I was twenty-two years old, unsure which way was up, and they were going to make me a detective.

I had learned little about myself and the way I really was. For me, this transfer offered a prospect of great adventure. I wanted to be at the center of things going on in the street. I longed to be a part of it all. Perhaps most important, I had a need to belong, to be liked, to be accepted as a member of the greater group.

My first year or so in narcotics was not particularly bad. I continued to do what had made me successful in the Tactical Patrol Force's decoy units. I stood around on street corners and continued to appear young and dumb. In no time, I was buying drugs from street-level dealers at record rates. But slowly I was also sucked into a whirlpool of street life. For an undercover officer, those streets can be sensual and seductive. The distinctions between good and evil that were so clear to me earlier slowly began to blur.

My life centered around my work. In the Narcotics Division we were free to make our own hours, and results were all that counted. Since results were measured by arrest numbers, when I wasn't on the streets, I was in court.

A complex process of inclusion took place at the courthouse. Relationships were developed with district attorneys, defense attorneys, and bail bondsmen. And of course, there were the judges—they seemed to be friendly with everyone.

The courthouse was viewed as a clubhouse. The place itself closed the multiple gaps of generation, education, and social background. It was a world of its own, with its own language and secret signals. The courthouse was a community of elders with a long and corrupt history.

Anyone with eyes to see and a nose to smell could lift the shade and move the screen and see that the system had been perverted. Assistant district attorneys pushed for testimony that assured conviction. Truth was hardly a consideration. Defense attorneys offered money for changed testimony after giving you their cards with a request that you give them to potential clients for a percentage of the fee. The courts had become a reflection of the streets. A reflection driven by power plays and sleezy deals.

The clear distinction between good and evil became every more blurred. No one, it seemed, played by the rules.

I make perhaps too much of the involvement of others. We are, after all, masters of our own thoughts and actions. But it is so important to understand that people, including those that gravitate to police work, are social beings. I'm convinced that for most officers, nothing could be worse than not being accepted by their peers. And so it goes; personal values take a back seat to the values of the group. It was his ability to resist such pressures that marks the true heroism of Detective Frank Serpico.

As for me, I came from a different place. Some would describe it as a land of misplaced loyalty; others, less kind, would say personal cowardice. I could not maintain the courage to remain an individual. I could not divorce myself from the group. To exist without acceptance, for me, was to exist without roots. In short, I found the rationalizations to go along.

STEPPING INTO THE VOID

I had worked as an undercover officer—mostly alone, sometimes with backup—for a number of years when I began to realize that I needed an informant. Although making buys was not particularly difficult, many of the bigger dealers were inaccessible to me. An undercover officer must have access, which meant that I needed someone who would be willing to bring me to places that I could not get to alone. Knowing my need, an older, more experienced detective introduced me to Lefty.

Lefty, a true pro, was twice my age and I soon learned that his life was endless acres of disaster. A heroin addict who was well-worn, Lefty had worked for the department for many years. Still, he remained an effective informant. For months we worked together as a team. I had always viewed addicts as parasites and villains, but spending day and night on the street with Lefty had made me see the world through his eyes.

At this moment, I can say little in my own defense about my ultimate relationship with Lefty. I certainly cannot blame him; he was powerless over his addiction. It was my own action that changed my destiny; it was Lefty's need that brought me from one place to quite another.

Lefty and I had been making heroin buys from a house in the Red Hook section of Brooklyn. "House connections" were rare and valued. After buying from a street dealer, it was often difficult to find him two or three weeks later to effect the arrest. But a "house connection" was always there, always around.

On this night, Lefty and I were to return to the house connection to "double up" (make a second buy). Sitting in my car, however, Lefty told me that he couldn't go, that he wouldn't go—he was too sick. Nor could I get access to the house alone. It was Lefty who was known there and welcomed; I needed him. I pointed out to him that he was always sick—that he was, after all, a junkie.

He told me that I was a fool, that I had no understanding of the difficulties, or of the unfairness of my treatment of him. He was my informant, he put his life on the line for me daily. He told me that I was responsible to see to it that he would not be sick. Other detectives he'd worked with made certain of that. I never did.

"What is it you want me to do?" I asked.

"Get me some drugs, get me some heroin. My God," he cried, "can't you see how sick I am. You use me, now I'm asking for a little help."

A year earlier, had this same request been made, I would have beaten him and thrown him from the car. Six months earlier, I would have simply thrown him from the car. But months had gone by. Lefty and I had spent those months together on the streets where only the strong survived. In that time, reality had somehow changed and become distorted. My erosion had already begun.

I can still imagine Lefty sitting in the back seat of my car. This man, twice my age, crying out in pain like a child. And for what, a tiny glassine envelope of white powder that I bought every day from whomever? The police department gave me an expense account of $100 a month that I gave to Lefty. But Lefty had a $250-a-day habit. The $100 I gave him monthly lasted not quite one morning. Meanwhile, he had delivered pushers to me by the score. We were responsible for hundreds of arrests. So what was the big deal . . . ? In law enforcement, I rationalized, we were all unconscionable hypocrites.

I need not tell you that I did for Lefty what he asked.

It was, by later comparison, minor.

What it did do, that particular act, was to bring me by the hand to a place I was never meant to be. I moved from being a professional police officer to a reflection of the people I was policing. Then, and since, I've seen it happen scores of times to others: to police officers, lawyers, judges, district attorneys. Once we lose sight of what we are, who we are, and what we're all about—once we take the first step toward what is truly foreign to our nature, away from our better self—we walk, head bowed, into an abyss from which it is most difficult to return.

That first step is a killer. The rest is an escalator going down to nowhere.

15

Maintaining Control in Community-Oriented Policing

David Weisburd, Jerome McElroy, and Patricia Hardyman

In recent years, community policing proposals and programs have captured the interest of police scholars, administrators, and public officials
in metropolitan areas across the country (Wilson and Kelling, 1982; Kelling, 1985; Goldstein, 1987; Greene and Taylor, 1987). Yet, there is little
consensus on what the term denotes. For us, community policing refers
to a philosophical position that holds that the goals of policing, the
conditions it addresses, the services it delivers, the means used to deliver
them, and the assessment of its adequacy, should be formulated and
developed in recognition of the distinctive experience, mores, and special structures of local communities.

A number of community policing programs have been described and
research on the actual operations and effects of such patrol strategies is
well under way (e.g., Police Foundation, 1981; Cordner, 1985; Farrell,
1986; Spelman and Eck, 1987). The research focuses primarily on program impact on crime, fear of crime, the degree of community involvement in crime control and order maintenance strategies, the morale of
community policing officers, and the ways in which they and their activities are perceived by other police personnel. While most commentators have recognized that the community policing philosophy has
serious implications for police managers, researchers have not focused
their attention on this issue.

From "Challenges to Supervision in Community Policing: Observations on a Pilot Project."
American Journal of Police, 7(2) 1988. Reprinted with permission.

The increased interaction between police and citizenry, the greater autonomy given to community policing units and the ambiguity inherent in order maintenance work are features of community policing strategies for which traditional types of line supervision are ill prepared. We need to know more about the nature of the supervisory challenges that emerge under these conditions and how first-level supervisors respond to them. This chapter describes and analyzes some of those challenges and responses using data collected during a study of the pilot phase of the Community Patrol Officer Program (CPOP) in New York City.

ORGANIZATION AND CONTROL IN POLICING

Most scholars describe police agencies as "bureaucratic" or "paramilitary" organizations (e.g., see Wilson, 1963; Goldstein, 1977; Bittner, 1980; Punch, 1983). Police departments rely for internal control on a highly articulated set of rules defining what officers should and should not do in various situations. This supervisory system is essentially negative, relying primarily upon sanctions for noncompliance with police rules and regulations.

The system evolved, in part, as a reaction against corrupt, unproductive police organizations that failed to define their obligations to the public and were often more responsive to private interests than to central authority. That evolution was facilitated by the priority given to the crime control function over the order maintenance responsibilities of the police, the emphasis on responding to incidents rather than solving problems in the community, and the heavy reliance on central dispatching of motorized units responding to discrete calls for service (McElroy, 1987).

Whatever the historical achievements of the bureaucratic, military model of organization, its shortcomings are increasingly evident to scholars and police administrators, who argue that the demands of contemporary urban society undermine the assumptions upon which traditional police structures were built (e.g., Rubenstein, 1973; Van Maanen, 1973; Goldstein, 1981; Allen, 1982; Barker, 1986; McElroy, 1987). While the military model depends on predictability, many of the situations to which officers are asked to respond cannot be anticipated. Though the norms that define appropriate responses may reduce the vulnerability of officers to criticism, they often do not provide useful guides for developing effective solutions to the problems encountered. Finally, deployment patterns that treat patrol officers as if they were interchangeable parts prevent police officers from learning and responding to the distinctive problems, needs, and resources of the neighborhoods they serve.

Egon Bittner (1980) suggests that a shift of focus to order maintenance problems, such as that demanded by the community policing philosophy, leads to additional conflicts with traditional control systems in policing. He argues that as long as police officers are treated as "soldier bureaucrats" they cannot be expected to develop or value professional skills that are required for successful problem-oriented policing (see also Goldstein, 1979). Bittner indicates that the control of police behavior must address both the problem of legality, which concerns compliance with explicit regulation, and the problem of workmanship, which "involves the maintenance of minimally acceptable levels of knowledgeable, skilled and judicious performance" (1983:2–3). Bittner's insistence that the workmanship criteria must be more fully developed and more widely applied to police work seems especially appropriate with respect to community policing programs.

Murphy and Muir (1985) allude to this same issue as a potential barrier to the success of community policing strategies in Canada. They point out that the fundamental principles of the paramilitary model—a closed system, compliance with rigid formal rules, centralized decision making and specialization—are incompatible with the goals and strategies of community-oriented policing (see also Reiss, 1985). Supervision in this system does not encourage the initiative and flexibility that are essential to carrying out the community policing philosophy.

In theory, the supervision function involves a wide array of responsibilities. These include shaping the attitudes of subordinates in terms of the goals of the agency, teaching them how to apply those goals in their own work, assessing the adequacy of subordinates' performance, using available incentives and training to correct deficiencies in performance, and monitoring subordinates' actions to control various types of misbehavior (Goldstein, 1977). All too often, however, supervision is reduced in practice to deterring police abuses. This control dimension of supervision is of particular concern with respect to community policing because the role differences involved in such programs frequently constitute a challenge to traditional control techniques.

Though there is clearly strong reason for examination of field supervision in community policing, this question has not been explored in research on these new policing programs. In this chapter we focus on three control responsibilities faced by the sergeant in the New York City pilot program in community policing: monitoring how a CPO spends his or her time on patrol; overseeing proactive patrol strategies to guard against abuses of authority; and monitoring officer/citizen contacts to prevent corrupt activities. To understand the form these particular concerns take in a program like CPOP, it is necessary first to describe the program and the way it differs from conventional patrol operations.

THE CPOP PILOT PROJECT

In July 1984, the New York City Police Department (NYPD) and the Vera Institute of Justice began the Community Patrol Officer Program (CPOP) as a pilot project in one of the city's 75 police precincts. The program was designed by Vera as a means of introducing the principles of community policing without requiring restructuring of the patrol force (see Farrell, 1986). It sought to create a new role for an individual police officer to perform within the specific beat area (ranging in size from about twelve to thirty square blocks) for which he or she was assigned permanent responsibility.

In the pilot project, nine such beats were delineated within the precinct and ten police officers (CPOs) were assigned to work under the direction of a sergeant who functioned as a unit supervisor. The CPOs were taken off the regular shift rotation chart used by the department and were encouraged to establish starting and finishing times for their tours that were appropriate, given the needs and conditions of their beats. Each officer was instructed to patrol the beat on foot, making a special effort to identify himself or herself to the residents and business people and to solicit their views regarding the major crime and order-maintenance problems of the area. This information was to be entered in a Beat Book on a regular basis, along with problem-solving strategies developed by the officer (in conjunction with representatives of the neighborhood) and approved by the supervising sergeant.

Development and implementation of these strategies would constitute the core of the officer's work plan each month. In short, the CPO was to function as a planner, problem solver, community organizer, and information link between the community and the police.

Vera research staff conducted an exploratory study to the pilot project during its first year of operation to see how the officers actually attempted to implement the new role and how the sergeant supervised their work. Each of the CPOs and the sergeant were interviewed extensively, using both structured and unstructured techniques. In addition, staff spent substantial periods of time accompanying officers on patrol and making notes about what they did and why they did it.

FIELD SUPERVISION IN REGULAR PATROL

Supervision of conventional patrol operations does not provide much opportunity for goal-setting, careful performance assessment, and the patient provision of assistance to improve police officer performance. It is concerned primarily with making sure that the officers are working, and with preventing trouble for the officers, the supervisor, and the command personnel to whom the supervisor is accountable. Of course, the field supervisor is only one element in the New York City Police Department's efforts to control the behavior of police officers.

Other units provide random performance audits, full-blown investigations of suspected persons and conditions, and an opportunity for aggrieved citizens to have their complaint against police officers received, investigated, and disposed. In addition, aspects of the patrol force deployment plans and procedures are intended to keep the officers out of situations thought conducive to misbehavior. Regular tour rotation, frequent changes in sector assignments, and a plethora of regulations regarding the time, place, and length of interaction between the officer and members of the public are designed, in part, to reduce familiarity that can be the occasion for corrupt behavior. Nonetheless, the patrol sergeant, armed with the book of regulations and prepared to "write up" an officer who is not in full compliance with them, is often believed to be the department's first line of defense against misbehavior by its members.

The regulations are fairly specific for officers on regular patrol. Those in patrol cars (typically, two officers to the car) are given a specific sector in which to operate, and they are not to venture outside that sector unless directed to by the dispatcher. They are to remain in radio contact with him or her at all times and are to be available for dispatch except while responding to a call. It is understood that the average call will take no more than 30 minutes to handle and failure to inform the dispatcher of one's availability within that time, or provide an acceptable reason for continued unavailability, creates the presumption that something is wrong.

The conventional foot patrol officer's routine is even simpler. He or she is assigned to a linear post of about four or five blocks and is expected to patrol up and down the post, remaining visible at all times.

Patrol sergeants are expected to know where every unit under their supervision is operating. They must check on them personally at least once during a tour (signing the officer's memo book to record the check); report instances in which their behavior deviates from the regulations; monitor the calls to which the officers are dispatched; and respond personally to oversee the police response in a wide range of situations.

On any given tour in a precinct, circumstances may be such that only one or two patrol sergeants are available to supervise the work of as many as two dozen or more patrol units (including those in cars, on scooters, and on foot). At such times, the sergeant is extremely busy and hard-pressed to see each of the officers during the tour. Thus, rules specifying where the officer should and should not be and what he or she should or should not be doing, are an important aid to the sergeant's supervisory performance. They provide predictability and clarity with respect to behavioral expectations, are presumably applicable to all patrol officers, provide predictable sanctions for violations, and may actually reduce the prevalence of opportunities for misbehavior.

OPERATIONAL DIFFERENCES BETWEEN CPOP AND REGULAR PATROL

There are several important differences between the CPO and regular patrol roles that require modifications to be made in the conventional assumptions and practices of the supervisor. While regular motor patrol officers operate in pairs, responding to "runs" given them by a radio dispatcher, CPOs operated alone (on foot) and were not dispatched in response to calls for service. Unlike the small commercial foot patrol posts common in the NYPD, CPO beats were large, roughly rectangular, and generally residential in character. CPOs might legitimately patrol anywhere in those beats and they worked flexible as opposed to rotating tours, often with odd starting and ending times.

Regular patrol officers are discouraged from leaving their cars and spending time in conversation with neighborhood residents and business people. In contrast, CPOs were encouraged to identify and interact with residents of the areas they patrolled. Indeed, they provided phone numbers through which they could be reached, and spent time in homes, stores, and offices, and at community meetings discussing the concerns of the community and enlisting people to assist in correcting its problems.

Regular patrol officers address incidents as they arise and have neither the opportunity nor the obligation to follow through with solutions. CPOs, on the other hand, were encouraged to tackle beat conditions by marshaling police and nonpolice resources needed to deal with them and following through on the effects of applying those resources. Among other things, this meant that CPOs had a greater exposure to some of the misbehaving people on the beat and a more persistent need to "do something" about the chronic problems of the communities they patrolled.

Finally, traditionally used indicators of productivity among regular patrol officers, such as response time and time in service on radio runs, were irrelevant to the work of the CPO. Moreover, since the CPOs were expected to develop a working rapport with the people in the neighborhoods in order to address their particular problems, it could not be assumed that the volume of the officer's arrest and summons activity was a useful indicator of the officer's productivity and effectiveness.

Let us now look at the nature of the challenges posed by these operational differences and the ways supervision in the CPOP pilot project responded to them.

MONITORING THE CPO'S TIME ON PATROL

CPOs are neither in a radio-dispatched patrol car nor walking a conventional foot post; so the first challenge to a CPOP supervisor is to monitor the officer's location and how he spends his time on the street. As the CPO sergeant noted:

I was worried at the beginning, especially about the control. You know, 10 or 11 cops out there in an area that size. I mean . . . to control somebody in a fifteen-block area and control ten different people in a regular authoritarian type of supervision is impossible.

The sergeant discovered other techniques to monitor the officers' whereabouts. They carried radios and were expected to respond to him when he called. They used their memo books and other forms to note when they went indoors for meetings or discussions with store owners or local residents. The sergeant reviewed these entries regularly. He established monthly work plans with each officer in which they agreed on the priority problems on which the officer would focus and on what strategy and tactics he would use to address them. The sergeant would review these work plans on a regular basis as a means of assessing progress with respect to the problems while checking to see that the officer was doing what he or she was supposed to be doing.

The supervisor was also concerned with what the officer does while on patrol. The agreed-upon work plans that set objectives and described actions to be taken against beat problems were an important supervisory tool in this regard. However, because the CPO's relationship to the community was to be different from that of the conventional patrol officer's, traditional criteria for judging officer contacts with citizens were largely inapplicable. As one CPO indicated:

On "normal" (motor) patrol they have what's called unnecessary conversation. You know, you get a boss that comes by and sees you're talking with someone. He figures—ten minutes, you were talking to the person for ten minutes—he figures that's five minutes too long. So he'll give you a "rip" (disciplinary report) for unnecessary conversation. Whereas in this program, they emphasize communicating with the public. They want you to go out there and talk and get to know these people.

Thus, the contacts themselves were no longer seen as wasted patrol time or an indicator of an officer's desire to "goof off." The CPOs saw quickly that such contacts were important to building goodwill in the community. They claimed to be a bit more surprised to find that those conversations could actually contribute directly to maintaining order in the neighborhood.

When someone comes out of there at the end of the day drinking beers and you walk up to him and call him by name, and say, "Listen Jose, no Cervesa on the street," the guy now says "Okay, okay," and shakes my hand. This is because he'll feel bad, like I've caught him and I have to say it to him. I've caught a lot of people in stuff like that, just people I've met who ended up doing things for me.

While the sergeant sought to prevent the officers from "goofing off" on duty, in CPOP he could not rely on bureaucratic supervisory tools which discourage informal contacts with the public. In the pilot project, the sergeant tried to establish a standard of reasonableness with the CPOs. When he reviewed the time spent in meetings off the street, he would ask for further explanation regarding those which appeared excessively long. As he said in discussing a hypothetical extreme:

It means they must have had a real good reason to be there for two hours. There's nothing to stop me from going to talk to that store owner about whatever the problem was that he was discussing for two hours. Twenty minutes would be a reasonable amount of time to talk about neighborhood conditions or whatever. Hours assumes a major problem.

OVERSEEING PROACTIVE PATROL STRATEGIES AND TACTICS

Regular motor patrol is incident-based, reactive, and time-regulated. It is also governed by a set of priorities that limit the dispatching of police units to many kinds of order-maintenance situations. CPOP was in part a response to these limitations. However, it was not intended to function merely as a supplemental responding patrol unit. CPOP was designed as a proactive, problem-solving resource for the community. Functioning in this capacity, CPOs were encouraged to assume responsibility for addressing chronic problems that had defied previous corrective efforts. But it was also considered important that their zeal not lead to tactics that constitute abuse of authority or provoke confrontations that result in excessive use of force.

Concerns in this area go first to the issue of when the police should and should not intervene. This is not an easy question since, as Wilson (1968) pointed out, ambiguity is the hallmark of the order-maintenance function. In the CPOP pilot project, these officers' activities were directed to a wide variety of beat conditions including: groups of disorderly youths; street narcotics use and sale; adults who congregate on street corners drinking beer; loud radios; illegal parking that prevented the Sanitation Department from keeping the streets clean, and various disorderly conditions within vacant lots and parks.

The most difficult and potentially controversial of these problems was the concentration of open, street-level narcotics dealing in specific parts of selected beats. When the pilot project began, regular patrol officers in the NYPD were discouraged from enforcing the drug laws against low-level sellers and buyers. This policy was perceived by the CPOs as an obstacle to their effectiveness. In the words of the unit sergeant:

Even though a normal cop wouldn't be that much involved with drug enforcement, we got pushed into it by the community. The reason we got pushed into it by the community was that we went to community meetings and we asked them: "Tell us your problems. We're not going to tell you what your problem is, you tell us what your problem is!" Ninety-nine percent of the people, that's what their problem was—low-level street drugs and it was affecting the quality of life in the neighborhood.

In light of that definition of the situation, the CPOs believed that they would lose credibility if they refused to get involved in combating the problem. Thus, the unit did begin to concentrate attention on two or three significant narcotics locations in different beats.

In general, the strategies adopted by the CPOP unit consisted of three parts. In the first place, they provided a great deal of intelligence information to the Narcotics Unit which had jurisdiction and responsibility for narcotics enforcement throughout the patrol borough. Secondly, the officers and supervisor went to community meetings to explain that they could not use aggressive enforcement tactics against the street narcotics trade without the understanding and support of the community. Thirdly, the unit applied aggressive patrol tactics on the streets on which the drug sales were concentrated. Frequently, several CPOP officers would work together, along with the sergeant, in carrying out these tactics.

Although there were few public outcries against the unit's use of these tactics during the pilot project, the officers were aware that their use might make the CPOs the subject of citizen complaints, and that such tactics might be judged improper in some instances. Generally, the officers believed that they were acting within the department's regulations and satisfying the community's demand that actions be taken against drug trafficking. However, the department guidelines in this area are themselves ambiguous, and CPOs realized that the propriety of their actions might be judged differently by different people. Indeed, more than once, certain of the officers in the unit suggested to researchers that other CPOs had on a number of occasions overstepped their authority.

The sergeant was aware that aggressive enforcement tactics could be controversial. However, he believed that their use was sometimes needed to attack certain problems. The sergeant argued that the familiarity of officers with people in the community helped them to prevent situations from becoming confrontational and led community residents to be more willing to accept CPO interventions. He believed also that he and his officers were aware of the kinds of behaviors that were clearly impermissible. Indeed, he pointed out that he often had to explain to individuals and groups of citizens that the police were prohibited by law from using some of the tactics that the citizens encouraged them to use. Finally, he indicated that a focused strategy of aggressive patrol directed at a particular problem had to be approved by him and was usually implemented by using a part of the unit as a task force under his operational direction.

MONITORING POLICE/CITIZEN CONTACTS TO PREVENT CORRUPTION

Putting patrol officers in cars, rotating working shifts, and breaking continuity in the assignment of officers to particular units and neighborhoods, were policies intended not only to increase efficiency but also to reduce the likelihood of familiarity and special relationships developing between the officers and the public. Such relationships were thought to increase the likelihood of corrupt behavior. Today, such concepts lead some police administrators to look with caution on the movement toward community policing, which seeks to increase and strengthen interaction and familiarity between the police and the public.

The suspicion that familiarity between police officers and neighborhood residents is directly associated with corrupt activities seems impossible to test empirically. The logic of that suspicion is surely not compelling, however, when one thinks of gross forms of corruption, such as extorting payoffs from legitimate business people or even from known "hustlers" in a community. On the contrary, citizen familiarity with police officers may very well serve to make those officers more visible and vulnerable to discovery and complaint. Indeed, such thinking is reflected in the fact that the sergeant in the pilot project let his officers know that he would be talking regularly with people in each of the beats to get an independent sense of the community's needs and of how well the officers were operating.

On the other hand, it is reasonable to believe that frequent friendly contact with local residents and merchants may increase the temptations toward softer forms of corruption such as the free lunch, the "professional" discount, or the gift of appreciation for effective service. People often wish to express their appreciation, perhaps especially when the officer is known and liked personally. It should be noted that officers often devoted extraordinary time and effort toward assisting individual citizens in their beats. Sometimes, such efforts led to citizen attempts to express their appreciation in concrete terms. In one such incident, for example, a CPO was offered a monetary reward from a community resident who reclaimed lost property through the CPO's efforts.

The New York City Police Department uses a wide range of auditing and investigative techniques to deter soft corruption. While the CPO role may increase the risks of such corruption, the CPO supervisor indicated that he did not develop any special techniques to check such behavior. The sergeant did say that he made an effort to be on the scene whenever his officers were making arrests. However, he added that he did the same as a regular patrol supervisor.

Importantly, there appeared to be control mechanisms special to the CPO program that served to deter soft corruption. These included: the special nature of the selection process for officers; the extraordinary visibility of the pilot project to the department, the community, and the media; and the sense of reciprocal trust that existed between the supervisor and the members of the CPO unit. While these mechanisms served also as deterrents to other forms of misbehavior, the officers and the sergeant appeared most aware of the influence in reference to corruption.

All of the officers in the pilot project had worked in the precinct before the program began. In each case they were approached by the sergeant, who had served in the precinct for several years, and interviewed before he asked them to volunteer. Thus, the sergeant had selected officers with whom he was already familiar and whom he judged to be reliable. In discussing the selection process, he indicated that his confidence in the officer's integrity and openness to close supervision were the essential selection criteria.

The officers themselves were very much aware of the special nature of the project and the fact that it was being watched closely by officials at all levels of the department. They believed in the program concept and liked the opportunity it afforded them to exercise initiative and follow through on problem solving programs. Thus, they realized that a corruption scandal could destroy any chance of this new role becoming a regular feature of the department's operation.

CONCLUSIONS

Our research on a single pilot project attempting to create a new community policing role for selected patrol officers illustrates the new supervision problems faced in community policing as well as potential adjustments that can be made to address these problems. The community policing philosophy calls for a number of operational and organizational changes that are inconsistent with the military model of police organization. The differences between the CPO role and that of the conventional motorized patrol officer do indeed pose a challenge to the line supervisor.

Our observations suggest that a community policing sergeant must use methods of supervision that are more systemic than bureaucratic in character in order to meet this challenge (Rossi and Freeman, 1982). While the CPO sergeant in the New York program continued to remind his subordinates of departmental regulations, he shifted his supervisory strategy away from a preponderant concern with controlling misbehavior to focus upon the officers' knowledge of and involvements in the community and the adequacy of their problem-solving activities. Thus, the sergeant shifted emphasis from the criteria of legality to those of workmanship (Bittner, 1983). With each officer, he helped prepare a work plan that identified priority problems in the beat, established goals for their amelioration and set forth action strategies to achieve them. These plans served as a context within which the sergeant could encourage the officers' initiative and judge the efforts made and the results achieved by them. This approach to supervision also recognized the diversity of problems, desires, and resources among neighborhoods patrolled and permitted the supervision to take account of that diversity in judging the performance of police officers.

REFERENCES

Allen, D. (1982). "Police Supervision on the Street: An Analysis of Supervisor/ Officer Interaction During the Shift." *Journal of Criminal Justice*, 10.

Barker, T. (1986). "An Empirical Study of Police Deviance Other than Corruption." *Police Deviance*, ed. T. Barker and D. Carter. Cincinnati, OH: Anderson Publishing.

Bittner, E. (1980). *The Functions of the Police in Modern Society*. Cambridge: Oegeschlager, Gunn and Haine.

——. (1983). "Legality and Workmanship: Introduction to Control in the Police Organization." *Control in the Police Organization*, ed. M. Punch. Cambridge: MIT Press.

Cordner, G. (1985). *The Baltimore County Citizen Oriented Police Enforcement (COPE) Project: Final Evaluation*. Baltimore, MD: University of Baltimore.

Farrell, M. (1986). *The Community Patrol Officer Program: Community Oriented Police in the New York City Police Department*. New York: Vera Institute.

Goldstein, H. (1977). *Policing a Free Society*. Cambridge, MA: Ballinger.

——. (1979). "Improving Policing: A Problem Oriented Approach." *Crime and Delinquency*, 25.

——. (1981). "Police Policy Formulation: A Proposal for Improving Police Performance." *Critical Issues in Law Enforcement*, ed. H. Moore. Cincinnati: Anderson Publishing.

——. (1987). "Toward Community Oriented Policing: Potential, Basic Requirements, and Threshold Questions." *Crime and Delinquency*, 33(1).

Greene, J. and R. Taylor (1977). "A Closer Look at Foot Patrol and Community

Policing: Issues of Theory and Evaluation." Paper presented at the Conference on International Perspectives on Community Policing, Temple University.

Kelling, G. (1985). "Order Maintenance, the Quality of Urban Life and Police: A Line of Argument." *Police Leadership in America: Crisis and Opportunity*, ed. W. Geller. New York: Praeger.

McElroy, J. (1987). "The Police." *The Encyclopedia of the American Judicial System: Studies of the Principal Institutions and Processes of Law*, ed. R. Janosik. New York: Charles Scribner's Sons.

Murphy, C. and Muir, G. (1985). *Community Based Policing: A Review of the Critical Issues*. Ottawa: Solicitor General.

Police Foundation (1981). *The Newark Foot Patrol Experiment*. Washington: Police Foundation.

Punch, M. (1983). "Management, Supervision, and Control." *Control in the Police Organization*, ed. M. Punch. Cambridge, MA: MIT Press.

Reiss, A. (1985). "Policing a City's Central District: The Oakland Story." Washington, D.C.: National Institute of Justice.

Rossi, P. and Freeman, H. (1982). *Evaluation: A Systematic Approach*. Beverly Hills, CA: Sage.

Rubinstein, J. (1973). "The Dilemmas of Vice Work." In *City Police*. New York: Farrar, Straus and Giroux.

Spelman, W. and Eck, J. (1987). "Problem Oriented Policing." *NIJ Research in Brief* (January).

Trojanowicz, R. (1983). *An Evaluation of the Neighborhood Foot Patrol Program in Flint, Michigan*. East Lansing: Michigan State University.

Van Maanen, J. (1973). "Observations on the Making of a Policeman." *Human Organization*, 32(4):407–418.

Wilson, J. (1968). *Varieties of Police Behavior*. Cambridge: Harvard University Press.

Wilson, J. and Kelling, G. (1982). "Broken Windows." *Atlantic Monthly* (March).

Wilson, O. (1963). *Police Administration*, 2nd ed. New York: McGraw-Hill.

V

Citizens in the Law
Enforcement Process

Community Crime Prevention: A Review of What Is Known

Dennis P. Rosenbaum

Growing interest in community crime prevention was not simply the result of academic and professional dissatisfaction with traditional crime control strategies. Beginning with the Kennedy administration and the civil rights movement in the early 1960s, the United States federal government has encouraged citizen participation in policy decisions regarding community action, health, and the environment. During this period, there was a major increase in the number of community organizations in the United States (Bell and Held, 1969). Citizen interest in the crime issue was a logical extension of this grass roots activity because of changes in the magnitude of the crime problem. In the United States, rising crime rates during the 1970s meant that more people were victimized by crime than ever before. Not surprisingly, public concern about crime and fear of crime were also on the rise (DuBow, McCabe, and Kaplan, 1979), thus providing more citizens with a motivation to seek some type of effective preventive action. Also, because fear of crime is believed to accelerate neighborhood decline and increase crime rates (Skogan, 1986), numerous fear-reduction programs have been developed recently that are strongly oriented toward citizen-police partnerships in the coproduction of public safety.

Community crime prevention is a field that has continually evolved from the standpoint of the practitioner. In the late 1960s and early 1970s,

From *Justice Quarterly*, 5(4), 1988. Reprinted with permission of the Academy of Criminal Justice Sciences.

"crime prevention" was largely a public relations tactic by law enforcement to improve the community's image of what the police were doing (DuBow and Emmons, 1981). In the mid–1970s, after the push of several national commissions and the availability of grants from the Law Enforcement Assistance Administration (LEAA), police departments began to educate the public about *individual* crime prevention measures for protecting themselves and their property. Within a few years, law enforcement officials felt comfortable promoting *collective* crime prevention measures, such as "Block Watch," but only as the "eyes and ears" of the police in a crime-reporting capacity. Not until 1977 was there a recognition, through national crime control policy, that the "community" should play the central role in defining "community crime prevention" (DuBow and Emmons, 1981; Lavrakas, 1985). Two federal initiatives—the Community Anti-Crime Program in 1977 and the Urban Crime Prevention Program in 1980—provided funds directly to community organizations (rather than to law enforcement) to help mobilize neighborhood residents in the fight against crime. To some extent, community scholars in the early 1980s rejected the role of the criminal justice system in the maintenance of order and placed their confidence in the efficacy of voluntary organizations. But we have since learned that community groups are quite limited by themselves in preventing urban crime without the support of law enforcement, adequate funding, and considerable technical assistance (Bennett and Lavrakas, 1988; Lewis, Grant, and Rosenbaum, 1988; Yin, 1986). Thus, starting in the mid–1980s, the pendulum began to swing back to a more realistic position, namely, that formal and informal means of crime reduction/order maintenance are complementary and should work together to define "community crime prevention."

COMMUNITY CRIME PREVENTION BEHAVIORS

Personal Protection Behaviors

Individual citizens have employed a variety of behaviors for self-protection, ranging from avoiding threatening situations to taking self-defensive classes to buying large dogs and handguns. Essentially, there are two basic types of individual protective measures: (1) those intended to reduce the risk of victimization by avoiding threatening situations, and (b) those measures intended to manage risk (when it is unavoidable) by either making victimization more difficult or by minimizing the loss when victimization occurs.

How effective are these behaviors in reducing the probability of victimization and/or reducing fear of crime? In the extreme, there is little doubt that risk-avoidance behavior is effective at reducing one's risk of victimization. Unless one lives with a violent family member, staying at home behind locked doors and not venturing outside should lower a person's risk of personal victimization. However, many people have little choice but to live and work in high-risk environments, and life-style patterns are often shaped by years of social influence. Even if avoidance behaviors were easily modifiable, a policy of encouraging withdrawal from social interaction would be viewed with suspicion to-day. Avoiding risk by restricting one's behavior is often viewed as a major loss of freedom and opportunity for a better life. Many elderly citizens have become prisoners in their own homes, with more than two-thirds of those studied reporting that they "never" go out at night (Rifai, 1976). Shopping, visiting friends, and attending social activities have been restricted for many older citizens. Risk-avoidance may also have a long-term detrimental effect on local crime rates. When large numbers of residents withdraw from the streets, this reaction may un-dermine the community's ability to exercise informal social control and surveillance over public behavior, thus lowering the constraints against deviant and criminal behavior. In sum, individual protection may be increased, but oftentimes there is a heavy price to pay in terms of per-sonal freedom and/or long-term collective safety.

Household Protection Behaviors

As with other prevention activities, household protection measures are intended either to prevent victimization entirely or reduce the amount of loss that occurs when victimization is not prevented. Many preventive measures create *physical barriers* to access (e.g., locks), while others are designed to create *psychological barriers* (e.g., leaving lights on). Clearly, "target hardening" is the primary strategy employed for household protection, and it has a long history of application. Target-hardening measures, whether they be locks, window bars, fences, alarms, or other devices, are designed to eliminate physical intrusion or make it more technically difficult, thus reducing the probability that a crime can be successfully committed.

A large number of studies have measured the extent and nature of home protection activities (Lavrakas, 1981; Percy, 1979; Rosentraub and Harlow, 1980; Schwartz and Clarren, 1978; Skogan and Maxfield, 1981). The following general conclusions can be made: The most common hard-ware change is the purchase and installation of better locks on doors in the "last few years" (between 25 percent and 50 percent of urban resi-dents). Most other devices—including window locks and bars, special outside lights, and alarms—are installed by a much smaller segment of the population (often under 10 percent), although 30 to 40 percent of the residents in some cities report installing special outdoor lights and window locks. A one-time supplement to the National Crime Survey found that roughly 7 percent of the U.S. households interviewed in 1984 had a burglar alarm (Whitaker, 1986). There is some evidence to suggest that persons who engage in household protection behaviors are less likely to be victimized by property crime than persons who do not take such actions. Although the evidence is not always clear about whether the relationship is causal or spurious, it is suggestive.

NEIGHBORHOOD PROTECTION BEHAVIORS: COLLECTIVE ACTIONS

Strategies to "organize" the community and provide a collective response to crime have become the cornerstone of community crime prevention activities in recent years. Neighborhood protection behaviors, as defined here, are collective attempts to prevent crime and disorder in a geographically defined residential area, such as a block or neighborhood.

There are many types of collective citizen actions and many ways of conceptualizing these responses to crime. Neighborhood-level surveys in a number of major U.S. cities indicate that between 11 and 20 percent of the population participate in *crime prevention activities* associated with these organizations (Lavrakas et al., 1980; Rohe and Greenberg, 1982; Skogan and Maxfield, 1981; Taub, 1977). National data from 1981 indicate that 12 percent of the adult population was involved in a neighborhood group with crime prevention activities (O'Keefe and Mendelsohn, 1984).

Community groups are often the mechanism for organizing community action, but there exists wide variation in their organizational structure, objectives, and approaches to crime prevention (Lewis, Grant, and Rosenbaum, 1988). Citizen groups range from stable, multi-issue organizations with "crime" as one of many items on their agenda, to single-issue ad hoc groups that focus on a particular type of criminal activity (DuBow et al., 1979; Skogan, 1987). Nevertheless, the anticrime strategies pursued by voluntary citizen groups show some degree of commonality. Two distinct approaches to crime prevention have been identified in the literature with corresponding behaviors: The most publicized orientation has been referred to as the "opportunity reduction" or "victimization prevention" approach, while the alternative orientation has been called the "social problems" or "root causes" approach to crime prevention (Bennett and Lavrakas, 1988; Lewis and Salem, 1981; Podolefsky and DuBow, 1981).

Opportunity Reduction Approach

Collective anticrime measures that emerge from the opportunity reduction approach often involve surveillance, crime reporting, and target-hardening activities designed to control or deter crime in specific settings. Neighborhood Watch is the prototype of this approach, and often serves as a vehicle for encouraging a range of opportunity-reduction behaviors. Through a national survey of 550 Neighborhood Watch programs, Garofalo and McLeod (1986) found that, in addition to being the "eyes and ears" of the police, a majority of programs included property markings (81 percent), home security surveys (68 percent), meetings to plan and exchange information (61 percent), and the distribution of newsletters (54 percent). More than one-third were also involved in crime-tip hot lines and efforts to improve the physical environment (e.g., better street lighting).

In terms of social impact, it is important to note that Neighborhood Watch is billed by program advocates as more than an opportunity-reduction program (National Crime Prevention Council, 1987). By encouraging social interaction (beginning with local meetings), this strategy is considered one of the primary mechanisms available to community residents who are interested in restoring informal social control processes or creating a sense of "community" (see Rosenbaum, 1987, 1988).

Despite widespread publicity and public awareness of Neighborhood Watch, participation levels remain rather modest. Resident surveys in areas that had been the target of substantial organizing activity indicate that attendance at a Block Watch or Neighborhood Watch meeting has been consistently reported by 15–16 percent of the households in Portland, Oregon (Schneider, 1986), Minneapolis (Silloway and McPherson, 1985), and Chicago (Rosenbaum et al., 1985). At the national level, two national crime surveys conducted in 1984 provide some reliable data on this topic: In the United States, 7 percent of the nation's households had participated in Neighborhood Watch (Whitaker, 1986), while in England, where the concept is newer, less than one percent were involved (Hope, 1988). The opportunity to participate is one factor that restricts participation levels. The U.S. data (Whitaker, 1986) show that 38 percent of the households in neighborhoods that *have* Neighborhood Watch are participants in the program. Central-city areas are more likely to have Watch programs than either suburban or nonmetropolitan areas, but people living in the latter areas are more likely to participate in the program when one is available.

For citizens who prefer a more aggressive and structured approach to area surveillance, civilian patrols have become a popular alternative to passive watching. Citizen patrols have a long history that predates the creation of public law enforcement and includes an extended period of vigilantism in the United States (see DuBow et al., 1979). Over the past 25 years, a variety of patrols have emerged in urban areas, serving a variety of functions. In the 1960s, for example, blacks used citizen patrols to protect themselves against police abuses in urban areas and against racist groups in the South (Marx and Archer, 1971; Garofalo and McLeod, 1986). In the 1970s, citizen patrols in urban areas became a popular supplement to police patrols and were initiated to deter residential criminal activity and detect crimes in progress. Patrols differ in function (e.g., community protection vs. crime prevention), types of surveillance area (e.g., buildings, neighborhood streets, public transportation, college campuses), mode of transportation (e.g., foot, bicycle, or motorized patrol), policies about intervention, and other dimensions (Yin et al., 1986).

The prevalence of civilian patrols is difficult to estimate from the available data. In 1975, a national study estimates that there were more than 800 patrols throughout the United States (Yin et al., 1976). In 1984, a national mail survey of Neighborhood Watch Programs revealed that 12 percent had a formal surveillance component and most of these were motorized patrols (Garofalo and McLeod, 1986). At the city level, Pennell et al. (1985) cite reports that an estimated 150,000 Philadelphia residents participated in mobile patrols in the first half of 1980, and a similar number in New York City. However, there is some evidence that the number of newly created citizen patrols (and Neighborhood Watches) peaked in 1983–84 and then declined significantly in 1985 (Garofalo and McLeod, 1986). But this conclusion must be viewed with caution, as it is based on a mail survey with a moderately low return rate (26 percent).

Who participates in collective anticrime activities? The pattern of participation in community crime prevention groups is quite similar to that of voluntary community organizations in general. A number of studies have found that those who participate in voluntary organizations are more likely to be middle or upper-middle class, home owners, educated, middle-aged, married with children, and less transient than nonparticipators (Greenberg et al., 1985; Skogan, 1987). Certainly, residents who participate in Neighborhood Watch fit this description, as shown in both a national survey of Neighborhood Watch programs (Garofalo and McLeod, 1986) and the one national survey of U.S. households (Whitaker, 1986). Also, unlike self-protection and even household-protection behaviors, participation in collective neighborhood anticrime activities is often motivated by "civic-mindedness" rather than by fear of crime (Lavrakas et al., 1980).

Who participates in formal citizen patrols is less well documented, but the available evidence suggests a similar pattern to that of Watch-type programs, with the exception that men are more involved in patrolling activities than women (Lavrakas et al., 1980; Pennell et al., 1985). There is also some evidence that citizen patrols are more likely to emerge in racially heterogeneous areas (Yin et al., 1976) and in gentrifying areas among newcomers (McDonald, 1986), but this latter observation can be found with participation in Watch programs as well (Henig, 1984).

Social-Problems Approach

The social problems approach to collective anticrime activities is based on the belief, held by many citizens (Erskine, 1974), that crime is caused by the "social ills" of society, especially by social conditions that cause youth to become delinquent (Podolefsky and DuBow, 1981). Hence, many citizens participate in community crime-prevention activities that address a variety of social problems or "root causes" of crime. The nature and extent of collective participation in such activities is not well documented in the literature. Two major projects at Northwestern University provide some data on this topic. The "Reactions to Crime" project collected random survey data in three large cities and ten neighborhoods, giving persons associated with voluntary organization an open-ended chance to describe anything their group had ever done about crime. Podolefsky and DuBow (1981) identified 946 activities and placed them into 47 categories. Of these 47 types of activities, the most common was "providing positive youth activities" (14 percent of the activities), followed by holding meetings to discuss crime (9 percent), improving or cleaning up the neighborhood (8 percent), and putting pressure on the police about policy (6 percent). In total, youth-related activities comprised nearly 20 percent of the total anticrime responses.

More recently, Bennett and Lavrakas (1988) have completed a process evaluation of 10 community crime prevention programs in 9 large U.S. cities as part of the Eisenhower Neighborhood Program. Four neighborhood-based programs emphasized the "causes of crime" (i.e., social problems) approach, three emphasized "opportunity reduction," and three showed an even balance. Youth-oriented activities were the backbone of the social problems approach, and communitywide surveys (including residents who were not community group members) revealed that participation in such activities ranged from 1 to 15 percent across the 10 sites (with a mode of 6 percent), and from 6 to 15 percent in neighborhoods with groups that emphasized the "causes of crime" approach. Youth activities included athletic programs, employment programs, drug prevention programs, computer clubs, troops, tutorial and literacy programs, youth councils, and many others. Generally speaking, youth-oriented programs often seek to either (a) get youths off the streets by giving them "something else" to do, under the assumption that removing them from the streets will reduce their chances of "getting into trouble," or (b) given them specific skills and opportunities that will improve their competence, self-respect, and likelihood of self-sufficiency. Boys have been the target of nearly all neighborhood-based programs, although there is a growing interest in developing programs for adolescent girls (e.g., pregnancy and drug prevention), and adults (e.g., parenting and employment skills).

THE EFFECTIVENESS OF COLLECTIVE ACTION

Social-Problems Approach

Nearly all of the evaluation research on collective anticrime strategies has focused on opportunity-reduction activities. At present, we know little about the effectiveness of neighborhood-based strategies that focus on social problems, especially youth-oriented activities organized by voluntary community organizations. The available data on the effects of the "social problems" approaches come from evaluations of large-scale government employment and training programs in the 1960s and 1970s—programs designed to improve local labor market experience and reduce crime. After reviewing this literature, McGahey (1986) concludes that "analyses of individual employment and criminal behavior show little or no effect on labor market status or recidivism" (p. 256). One exception was the Job Corps, whose success McGahey attributes to the fact that participants were "physically and socially removed from their high-crime neighborhoods and crime-prone peer groups" (p. 257).

Despite the debatable success of earlier social-problems approaches, Lynn Curtis and Betsy Lindsay of the Eisenhower Foundation (Curtis, 1987) have remodeled this strategy for the 1980s, emphasizing the importance of "bubble-up" planning by grass-roots community groups who seek "financial self-sufficiency," rather than continuing the traditional "trickle-down" approach to funding and program development. A four-year demonstration called the "Neighborhood Anti-Crime Self-Help Program" was initiated in 1982 in ten urban neighborhoods. The preliminary results from a major-impact evaluation show that local programs had little effect on official crime rates and possibly a negative effect on victimization rates (Lavrakas and Bennett, 1988; Curtis, 1987 for a more positive view of the results). Fear of crime was largely unaffected in neighborhoods served by organizations with a social-problems orientation, but showed some evidence of decline in several sites with a strong opportunity-reduction orientation, especially citizen patrols.

In summary, there is little *hard* evidence showing that the social-problems approach to community crime prevention is effective in reducing community crime rates or building community cohesion, despite the fact that several strategies are seen as conceptually attractive and lauded as model programs for helping poor neighborhoods help themselves. To say "there is little hard evidence" is not to say that this approach is ineffective; only that there have been few strong evaluations of program effects in this rediscovered policy area.

Opportunity Reduction: Interventions and Evaluations

There can be little doubt that community crime prevention, involving collective citizen actions, has been depicted as highly effective by the mass media, politicians, researchers, and program advocates. Hundreds of success stories have been told in recent years about how these programs, especially Neighborhood Watch, have reduced crime and fear of crime, and have been responsible for restoring a sense of community. What is the empirical basis for these reports of success? Sometimes, the "I-believe-it-works" testimony of surveyed police officials, community leaders, and program staff is used as "evidence" that the programs are effective in achieving these outcomes. Many of the success stories, however, are based on actual crime statistics and sometimes on fear of crime data (see Feins, 1983; Titus, 1984; National Crime Prevention Council, 1987). The literature is replete with claims that collective citizen action has reduced residential burglary anywhere from 20 to 60 percent. Unfortunately, these reports often represent a significant misuse of the terms "research" and "evaluation research." As I have noted elsewhere, many of these "evaluations" are seriously flawed on methodological grounds and, consequently, the findings should not be taken very seriously. Evidence regarding the efficacy of two types of surveillance programs is reviewed below—citizen patrols and Neighborhood Watch.

Impact of Citizen Patrols. While citizen patrols are common in urban neighborhoods, and have been praised as effective in reducing street crime (Castberg, 1980; Russell, 1982; Washnis, 1977), there is very little evaluation research that measures patrol impact. The national evaluation of citizen patrols (Yin et al., 1977) appealed to anecdotal evidence to reach the conclusion that building patrols (one of four patrol types) *may be* effective in preventing crime and increasing residents' sense of safety at home and when patrols are visible. The evidence regarding other forms of patrols was less certain at the time. Neighborhood patrols were able to report numerous crime incidents to the police, but occasionally made residents feel uneasy about the legitimacy of their activities. Although Yin and his colleagues found some evidence of vigilante-like behavior by patrols (especially when members grew bored or were recruited from youth factions in the neighborhood), generally speaking, there was little support for this common concern.

Crime and perception data have been collected in two separate studies. In Columbus, Ohio, Latessa and Allen (1980) found that a well-organized walking patrol was associated with a decline in several types of reported crime in the target area, with the largest decreases occurring in burglary and auto theft. As part of a national evaluation of the Guardian Angels, Pennell and her colleagues conducted an impact assessment in San Diego and found that this patrol group had little impact on violent crime, but may have contributed to a short-term decline in property crimes during peak visibility periods (Pennell et al., 1985). In terms of perceptions, surveys of San Diego residents and eastern transit riders showed that citizens perceive the Guardian Angels as effective in reducing crime and report feeling more safe when the Angels are patrolling.

At this point, citizen patrols have not been sufficiently studied to draw any conclusions about possible deterrent effects, but there is little reason to think that this type of formal surveillance would be more effective than uniformed police officers on foot patrol. The evidence showing crime reduction through police foot patrols is rather limited (e.g., Trojanowicz, 1986), but a more consistent finding has been a reduction in residents' fear of crime (e.g., Pate et al., 1986).

Impact of Neighborhood Watch. Several observations can be made regarding the general research on Watch-type programs. On the positive side, a number of studies have found that persons who participate in Watch-type programs are less likely to be victimized by property crime than nonparticipants, and some evidence (although considerably less) that target areas experience lower burglary rates after program implementation (Greenberg et al., 1985; Titus, 1983). Still, many of these evaluations are methodologically weak and cannot be defended against numerous threats to validity. Even some of the more carefully designed evaluations—showing positive impacts on crime and fear levels in New York (Rich et al., 1987) and St. Louis (Kohfeld, Salert, and Schoenberg, 1981)—have reported only cross-sectional data, leaving room for pre-program characteristics to account for the observed differences between treated and untreated areas. Some of the stronger evaluations of community crime prevention programs, with pretests and strong measurement, have found evidence of success in reducing property crime victimizations and fear of crime (see Rosenbaum, 1986). Unfortunately, many of these evaluations do not isolate the effect of collective citizen action, per se, because the programs were typically comprehensive in nature and often included changes in police practice, citizen activities, and/or the physical environment.

By far, the best empirical evidence regarding the efficacy of collective citizen action can be found in four large-scale quasi-experimental evaluations of Neighborhood Watch programs in the cities of Seattle (Lindsay and McGillis, 1986), Chicago (Rosenbaum et al., 1985), Minneapolis (Pate et al., 1986), and London, England (Bennett, 1987). These evaluations collected panel and/or independent sample data on residents in experimental and carefully selected control areas, and employed state-of-the-art measurement to examine program effects on a wide variety of intervening and outcome variables. In addition to rigorous evaluation designs, these projects are noteworthy because of the resources and effort devoted to systematic implementation of the program in most target areas.

Table 16.1 provides a summary of the impact results in the areas of crime, fear, and community cohesion. Clearly, the pattern of findings from these four studies is dramatically different from the hundreds of other Neighborhood Watch evaluations that claim success. The pro-

Table 16.1
Major Evaluations of Collective Citizen Crime Prevention[1]

| Authors/Sites | MAJOR OUTCOMES | | | |
	Crime[2]	FEAR Personal	Property	Social Cohesion
Bennett (1987)				
LONDON, ENGLAND				
Target Area 1	Increase	No Change	Decrease	Increase
Target Area 2	No Change	No Change	No Change	No Change
Cirel et al (1977)				
SEATTLE, WA.	Marginal Decrease in Burglary	Marginal Increase	-----	-----
Pate et al (1987)				
MINNEAPOLIS, MN	No Change[3]	No Change	No Change	No Change
Rosenbaum et al (1985)				
CHICAGO, IL				
Target Area 1	Marginal Decrease	Increase	No Change	No Change
Target Area 2	Increase	Increase	No Change	Decrease
Target Area 3	Increase	Increase	Increase	No Change
Target Area 4	No Change	No Change	No Change	No Change

[1]Findings are significant at p. < .05 unless otherwise indicated.
[2]Survey data using a composite index of property and personal crime unless otherwise indicated.
[3]Both survey and police data.

grams generally showed either no effect or increases in crime rates in the experimental areas after the intervention. Two *marginally* significant decreases in crime were found—a reduction in residential burglary in Seattle (which was based on a liberal analysis of the data) and a reduction in overall victimization rates in one of four Chicago neighborhoods. The pattern of results for fear of crime was similar. With the exception of one neighborhood in London, fear of personal crime and property crime were either unaffected by neighborhood organizing or showed significant increases relative to controls. Three of four Chicago neighborhoods experienced increases in fear of personal crime; but the more typical finding across these evaluations is one of "no difference."

Finally, social cohesion was generally not affected by the programs, and the one increase in London was offset by one decrease in Chicago.

Noteworthy is the fact that the only favorable outcomes with respect to fear of crime and social cohesion (reported in one London neighborhood) were based on the weakest subset of data, namely a pretest-posttest comparison on independent samples without a control group. All other findings were based on much stronger research designs. Finally, there was little evidence of program effects on various subgroups of the target population.

Perhaps the most important set of findings to emerge from these evaluations is that community organizing was unable to activate the *intervening* social behaviors that are hypothesized as necessary (according to informal social control and opportunity-reduction models) to produce the desired changes in crime, fear, and social integration. Specifically, the researchers reported very few changes in social interaction, surveillance, stranger recognition, crime reporting, home protection behaviors, feelings of control, efficacy, responsibility, satisfaction with the neighborhood, and attitudes toward the police.

One of the basic conclusions to be drawn from this work is that organizing the community through Watch-type programs, which emphasize surveillance and target-hardening activities, has been oversold as a stand-alone strategy in the war against crime. A more comprehensive approach that involves changes in citizen behavior, police activity, and the physical environment appears to increase the chances of impact, but the causal variables in these multifaceted interventions are difficult to isolate.

Another major lesson from these experimental programs is that organizing and sustaining community interest in activities directed at opportunity reduction and creating informal social control is considerably more difficult in low-income, heterogeneous areas that are most in need of crime prevention assistance. Participation levels are generally much lower in these areas (Bennett, Fisher, and Lavrakas, 1986), even after a much stronger organizing effort (Silloway and McPherson, 1987). Asking residents to "join together" and "watch out for suspicious persons" is asking a lot in neighborhoods characterized by high levels of fear and distrust, a disproportionate number of "strangers," and a host of other problems. In fact, local voluntary organizations in these areas often express a preference for the social-problems approach to community crime prevention rather than opportunity reduction (Podolefski, 1983; Bennett and Lavrakas, 1988), recognizing that crime is not caused by "strangers" from outside the neighborhood, but by local problems that affect local residents, such as drug abuse, unemployment, and poor housing.

CONCLUSIONS AND IMPLICATIONS

The gains achieved by citizen crime prevention behaviors often come with a price tag. At the individual level, persons who engage in high-risk avoidance behaviors are generally less likely to be victimized but this response amounts to a loss of behavioral freedom, it may enhance fear and, if widely practiced, it may contribute to a rise in community-level crime rates. Self-defense training, victim resistance, and even carrying a weapon may lower the risk of successful victimization and increase feelings of safety (although the effects of weapons are uncertain); but these actions may also increase one's risk of injury.

In terms of household protection behaviors, there is consistent evidence that target-hardening actions are associated with a lower risk of victimization for residential burglary. However, the benefits of these security measures (assuming the relationship is causal) are for those who can pay for security hardware, and participation tends to be restricted to persons with higher levels of income. Furthermore, while home protection behaviors are expected to reduce fear of crime, there is evidence that home security surveys have the opposite effect.

In terms of collective anticrime programs, there are literally hundreds of reports indicating that Neighborhood Watch reduces crime; but a closer look uncovers a curious inverse relationship: the stronger the research design, the weaker the program effects. Although neighborhood studies have underscored the importance of social interaction in developing informal social control, neighborhood crime prevention programs have been unable to stimulate the social interaction, territoriality, surveillance, and other behaviors that are theoretically expected at the block or neighborhood level. Furthermore, the price of attending neighborhood meetings may be an increase in fear of crime.

REFERENCES

Bell, D. and V. Held (1969). "The Community Revolution." *Public Interest*, 19 (Summer):142–177.

Bennett, S. and P. J. Lavrakas (1988). *Evaluation of the Planning and Implementation of the Neighborhood Program*. Final Process Report to the Eisenhower Foundation. Evanston, IL: Northwestern University.

Bennett, S.; B. Fisher; and P. J. Lavrakas (1986). "Awareness and Participation in the Eisenhower Neighborhood Program." Paper presented at the Annual Meeting of the American Society of Criminology.

Bennett, T. (1987). *An Evaluation of Two Neighborhood Watch Schemes in London*. Executive Summary of Final Report to the Home Office Research and Planning Unit. Cambridge, England: University of Cambridge.

Castberg, A. (1980). "Assessing Community Based Citizen Anti-Crime Programs." *U.S.A. Today* (January):33–35.

Curtis, L. (1987). "The Retreat of Folly: Some Modest Replications of Inner-City Success." *The Annals*, 494: 71–89.

DuBow, F. and D. Emmons (1981). "The Community Hypothesis." In D. Lewis (ed.), *Reactions to Crime*. Beverly Hills: Sage.

DuBow, F.; E. McCabe; and G. Kaplan (1979). *Reactions to Crime: A Critical Review of the Literature*. Washington, D.C.: U.S. Government Printing Office.

Erskine, H. (1974). "The Polls: Fear of Violence and Crime." *Public Opinion Quarterly*, 38 (Fall):131–145.

Feins, J. (1983). *Partnerships for Neighborhood Crime Prevention*. Washington, D.C.: National Institute of Justice.

Garofalo, J. and M. McLeod (1986). "Improving the Effectiveness and Utilization of Neighborhood Watch Programs." Draft Final Report to the National Institute of Justice, State University of New York at Albany.

Greenberg, S.; W. Rohe; and J. Williams (1985). *Informal Citizen Action and Crime Prevention at the Neighborhood Level: Synthesis and Assessment of the Research*. Washington, D.C.: U.S. Government Printing Office.

Henig, J. (1984). "Citizens Against Crime: An Assessment of the Neighborhood Watch Program in Washington, D.C." Unpublished manuscript. Washington, D.C.: George Washington University.

Hope, T. (1988). "Support for Neighborhood Watch: A British Crime Survey Analysis." Her Majesty's Stationery Office.

Kohfeld, C.; B. Salert; and S. Schoenberg (1981). "Neighborhood Associations and Urban Crime." *Community Action* (November–December).

Latessa, E. and H. Allen (1980). "Using Citizens to Prevent Crime: An Example of Deterrence and Community Involvement." *Journal of Police Science and Administration*, 8(1):69–74.

Lavrakas, P. (1981). "On Households." In D. Lewis (ed.), *Reactions to Crime*. Beverly Hills: Sage.

———. (1985). "Citizen Self-Help and Neighborhood Crime Prevention Policy." In L. Curtis (ed.), *American Violence and Public Policy*. New Haven: Yale University Press.

Lavrakas, P.; J. Normoyle; W. Skogan; E. Hertz; C. Salem; and D. Lewis (1980). "Factors Related to Citizen Involvement in Personal, Household, and Neighborhood Anti-Crime Measures." Final Report to the National Institute of Justice, Northwestern University, Evanston, IL.

Lewis, D.; J. Grant; and D. Rosenbaum (1988). *The Social Construction of Reform: Community Organizations and Crime Prevention*. New Brunswick, NJ: Transaction.

Lewis, D. and G. Salem (1981). "Community Crime Prevention: An Analysis of a Developing Perspective." *Crime and Delinquency*, 27:405–421.

Lindsay, B. and D. McGillis (1986). "Citywide Community Crime Prevention: An Assessment of the Seattle Program." In D. Rosenbaum (ed.), *Community Crime Prevention: Does It Work?* Beverly Hills: Sage.

McDonald, S. (1986). "Does Gentrification Affect Crime Rates?" In A. Reiss and M. Tonry (ed.), *Communities and Crime*, Vol. 8 of M. Tonry and N. Morris (eds.), *Crime and Justice: A Review of the Research*. Chicago: University of Chicago Press.

McGahey, R. (1986). "Economic Conditions, Neighborhood Organization, and Urban Crime." In A. Reiss and M. Tonry (ed.), *Communities and Crime*, Vol. 8 of M. Tonry and N. Morris (eds.), *Crime and Justice: A Review of the Research*. Chicago: University of Chicago Press.

Marx, G. and D. Archer (1971). "Citizen Involvement in the Law Enforcement

Process: The Case of Community Police Patrols." *American Behavioral Scientist*, 15(September–October):52–72.

National Crime Prevention Council (1987). "The Success of Community Crime Prevention." Topics in Crime Prevention Series. Washington, D.C.: Author.

O'Keefe, G. and H. Mendelsohn (1984). *"Taking a Bite Out of Crime": The Impact of a Mass Media Crime Prevention Campaign*. Washington, D.C.: National Institute of Justice.

Pate, A.; M. Wycoff; W. Skogan; and L. Sherman (1986). *Reducing Fear of Crime in Houston and Newark*. Washington, D.C.: Police Foundation.

Pennell, S.; C. Curtis; and J. Henderson (1985). *Guardian Angels: An Assessment of Citizen Responses to Crime*. Volume 2, Technical Report to the National Institute of Justice. San Diego: San Diego Association of Governments.

Percy, S. (1979). "Citizen Coproduction of Community Safety." In R. Baker and F. Meyer (ed.), *Evaluating Alternative Law Enforcement Policies*. Lexington, MA: D.C Heath and Co.

Podolefsky, A. (1983). *Case Studies in Community Crime Prevention*. Springfield, IL: Charles C. Thomas.

Podolefsky, A. and F. DuBow (1981). *Strategies for Community Crime Prevention: Collective Responses to Crime in Urban America*. Springfield, IL: Charles C. Thomas.

Rich, R.; D. Chavis; P. Florin; D. Perkins; and A. Wandersman (1987). "Block Associations and the Community Development Approach to Crime Control: A Preliminary Analysis." Paper presented at the Annual Meeting of the American Society of Criminology.

Rifai, M. (1976). *Older Americans' Crime Prevention Research Project*. Portland, OR: Multnomah County Division of Public Safety.

Rohe, W. and S. Greenberg (1982). *Participation in Community Crime Prevention Programs*. Chapel Hill, NC: University of North Carolina.

Rosenbaum, D. (1986). *Community Crime Prevention: Does It Work?* Beverly Hills, CA: Sage.

———. (1987). "The Theory and Research Behind Neighborhood Watch: Is It a Sound Fear and Crime Reduction Strategy?" *Crime and Delinquency*, 33:103–134.

———. (1988). "A Critical Eye on Neighborhood Watch: Does It Reduce Crime and Fear?" In T. Hope and M. Shaw (ed.), *Communities and Crime Reduction*. London, England: Her Majesty's Stationery Office.

Rosenbaum, D.; D. Lewis; and J. Grant (1985). *The Impact of Community Crime Prevention Programs in Chicago: Can Neighborhood Organization Make a Difference?* Evanston, IL: Northwestern University.

Rosentraub, M. and K. Harlow (1980). "The Coproduction of Policy Services: A Case Study of Citizens' Inputs in the Production of Personal Safety." Unpublished Manuscript, Institute of Urban Studies, Arlington, TX.

Russell, R. (1982). "Neighborhood Security Patrols Are Working in Anne Arundel County, Maryland." *Police Chief*, May:42–43.

Schneider, A. (1975). "Neighborhood Based Anti-Burglary Strategies: An Analysis of Public and Private Benefits from the Portland Program." In D.

Rosenbaum (ed.), *Community Crime Prevention: Does It Work?* Beverly Hills: Sage.

Schwartz, A. and S. Clarren (1978). *The Cincinnati Team Policing Experiment.* Washington, D.C.: The Police Foundation.

Skogan, W. (1986). "Fear of Crime and Neighborhood Change." In A. Reiss and M. Tonry (eds.), *Communities and Crime*, Vol. 8 of M. Tonry and N. Morris (eds.), *Crime and Justice: A Review of Research.* Chicago: University of Chicago Press.

———. (1987). "Community Organizations and Crime." In M. Tonry and N. Morris (eds.), *Crime and Justice.* Chicago: University of Chicago Press.

Skogan, W. and M. Maxfield (1981). *Coping with Crime: Individual and Neighborhood Reactions.* Beverly Hills: Sage.

Taub, R. (1977). "Urban Voluntary Associations: Locality Based and Externally Induced." *American Journal of Sociology*, 83:425–442.

Titus, R. (1984). "Residential Burglary and the Community Response." In R. Clarke and T. Hope (eds.), *Coping With Burglary.* Boston: Kluwer-Nijhoh.

Trojanowicz, R. (1986). "Evaluating a Neighborhood Foot Patrol Program: The Flint, Michigan Project." In D. Rosenbaum (ed.), *Community Crime Prevention: Does It Work?* Beverly Hills: Sage.

Washnis, G. (1976). *Citizen Involvement in Crime Prevention.* Lexington, MA: D. C. Heath.

Whitaker, C. (1986). "Crime Prevention Measures." Bureau of Justice Statistics Special Report. Washington, D.C.: U.S. Department of Justice.

Yin, R. et al. (1986). "Community Crime Prevention: A Synthesis of Eleven Evaluations." In D. P. Rosenbaum (ed.), *Community Crime Prevention: Does It Work?* Beverly Hills, CA: Sage.

17

Suburban Crime and Citizen Action

Lisa Sliwa

We have become a nation of finger pointers. Misled by the poor example of our politicians, who avoid responsibility at any cost, we are quick to lay blame for our crime problems at someone else's feet. We are slow to accept the fact that we must learn to defend and protect ourselves. The alternative is to become spectators at our own demise.

THE SUBURBAN CRIMINAL

Panicky suburban officials, confronted by the cold facts of suburban crime, attribute it to everyone else except those responsible. They tell us that the people breaking into our homes when we are at work or on vacation come from the city, that the mall rats who prey like vultures on women in the barren shopping center parking lots come from the wrong side of town, that the vandalism of churches, synagogues, and schools is being committed by outsiders—tough, underprivileged youth who are angered by suburban affluence.

The ugly truth is that we do not have to look too far from our front porch to find the suburban criminal. More often than not the thieves breaking into your home are not the inner city drug addicts who hop off a commuter train, but neighborhood punks who know your every move and habit, because they live on your street or around the corner.

From *The Journal of Community Action* 1(5), 1983. Reprinted with permission of the Center for Responsive Governance.

They are most often the sons, and sometimes the daughters, of fine upstanding citizens—laborers, executives, business owners, and doctors—who steal not to put food on the table, but for kicks and a sense of power. Like their friends who hang out in gangs in the mall parking lots and fast-food restaurants, they find satisfaction through intimidation. The only time they stop is when they face someone they cannot push around.

Of course, there is a small group of professional thieves who know the value of things and can disassemble an elaborate security system in 30 seconds. But they live in the suburbs too. Their vital information is supplied not by street corner lookouts or crooked building superintendents, but by a network of service people, like garage mechanics, delivery men, cleaning ladies, hairdressers, and repairmen, who sometimes unwittingly, and more often for a price, relay the vacation plans, work schedules, and personal habits of their employers and customers.

CRIME AND SUBURBAN VALUES

There is no question that the pressure is on to keep the image of crime-free suburbia spick-and-span. After all, what would it do to property values if the town or village developed the reputation as the county crime capital? The bottom line in the suburbs, despite evidence that the crime wave is dramatically increasing, is to protect property values and hold fast to an "it can't happen to me" attitude.

This suburban value system that money can buy you out of any problem is inadequate and even grotesque when tested against the crisis of violent crime. We can take the attitude of "thank heavens it happened to someone else" only until we too find ourselves in the victim's shoes.

With every passing day, people who have lived in the same house for 5, 10, or even 15 years without any problems now find themselves faced with the same violence and ugliness that originally made them flee the city. They find that they cannot go out for a peaceful walk after dinner; they cannot freely use the public parks and recreational facilities they support with their tax dollars; they live with the daily fear that they will return to a ransacked house.

Despite the fact that crime has become the number-one concern for suburban residents, the taboo on publicly dealing with the problem remains. We sweep the dirt under the rug and keep mum about it. This practice works fine until we discover that we cannot sweep away the body of a missing or murdered person.

INADEQUATE POLICE RESPONSE

Some suburban residents, especially the politicians, smugly reassure themselves that if they keep the property taxes high enough to keep the riffraff out of town, and if they appropriate enough money from bonds to pump yearly increases into the police department budget, that crime will remain under control. To think that enough money for police can put suburban crime in check is like thinking you can isolate one tiny part of the human body and save it from a cancer that is ravaging the rest.

And ravaging it is. A recent ABC-TV national crime survey found that suburban crime has increased 67 percent over the past 10 years. That statistic only accounts for the crime that is actually reported to police departments. Today, many people will not even bother to report a crime unless the value of the stolen property is large enough to warrant an insurance claim.

No matter how well-equipped they are with the latest computerized squad cars and other high-tech crime-fighting devices, our suburban police departments face more than they can handle. The idea that police officers should serve as a visible deterrent to crime and public disorderliness was feasible when the center of suburban life was the village square and town hall. It is not practical in today's suburbs where more and more we are replacing the old notion of a town with a sprawling incorporated area.

Where years ago the locally owned business district served as the center of town and residential neighborhoods radiated out from it, with the industrial section on the very outskirts, today's town has become a collection of subdivisions, developments, decentralized shopping plazas, malls, and convenience stores.

All this decentralization and the vast areas now comprising many towns makes it next to impossible for the local police departments to cover their jurisdictions. A police officer in a squad car, who in some cases must cover a 50- to 100-square-mile area, is next to invisible to taxpaying citizens and criminals alike.

The average response time of suburban police departments ranges from 15 to 25 minutes, mainly because of the great distances the police officer must travel to get from one place to another. By the time the police arrive on the scene of an emergency call, the criminal has long since left and is at home in bed.

FUTILITY OF CRIME WATCH

Given the distances and their work overload, suburban police departments, like their counterparts in the big cities, have taken to advocating crime watch programs. Their programs give citizens some training and a lot of crime watch paraphernalia—stickers, signs, buttons, jackets—everything they need to watch crime except the popcorn and soda pop. They give people a feeling of false satisfaction that they are actually doing something constructive to reduce a problem that seems beyond everyone's control.

The number-one proponents of crime watch, the local police departments, instruct the participants in taking accurate descriptions of the criminals they spot through their venetian blinds. But what good is the description of a perpetrator if it matches that of 2,000 other people wanted for crimes in the county and what good is the license plate number if it has been taken off a stolen car or van?

In fact, far from being helpful or even harmless, crime watch programs are an open invitation to criminals to ply their trade in the crime watch neighborhood. For a criminal, seeing the THIS IS A CRIME WATCH NEIGHBORHOOD sign is like giving him carte blanche to take whatever he wants without fear of being stopped. He knows he can go wherever he wants to, that no one will stop him, and that no one will dare to come out into the streets from behind their peepholes. He can load up the truck with the stereo, the video recorder, the silver, the refrigerator, and even the food in it because he knows no one will take a single step to stop him. It's no concern if a neighbor gets the license plate number because the truck was stolen, too.

The suburban criminals have learned that they have more to gain because of the affluence and less to lose because of fear and crime-watching than their counterparts in the city. There are many sections in our cities where there is literally nothing left to steal except the copper pipes from abandoned buildings. But in the suburbs, there is a veritable gold mine of material goods.

What is even better is that no one will even stand in the way of the thief who grabs for them. It is easier and far more lucrative to break into a house, rob a convenience store, or mug someone in the suburbs than in the city because the chance of resistance or being seen is less, and the gain is so much greater. How much different it would be if the thieves, upon leaving a house or apartment, risked being surrounded by angry neighbors who refused to let them leave!

CITIZEN ACTION AGAINST CRIME

As a society, we pride ourselves on our technological developments and great scientific discoveries. But we are living in little better than a barbarian age when we cannot leave our homes for fear of their being ransacked, and when women and children cannot go out without danger of being raped and abused.

The only different between us and the cavemen who had to stand guard at the cave entrance to protect their women, children, and belongings from roving thieves is that the cave has been replaced by a two-story colonial with a two-car garage, and that most modern men are afraid to fight for what they have earned.

The many fights our country has waged for freedom both here and abroad and the rights guaranteed to us by our Constitution are meaningless if we lack the most basic human freedom: the freedom of movement, of unimpaired passage from one point to another. This is different from the freedom to run from crime. The weapon that we need to deal with crime was given to us long ago in the United States Constitution. It is the right to make a citizen's arrest when we see a crime being committed.

Too often today this right is ignored. We are afraid of the personal injury, or even death, that may result if we act as Good Samaritans and intervene to stop a crime. We are reminded constantly by law enforcement officials that if we physically get involved, we could be sued and end up paying someone else's mortgage for the rest of our lives.

Clearly the individual solution is no solution at all. We can only go so far by acting alone. The vigilante revenge mentality portrayed by Charles Bronson in *Death Wish* merely leads to more violence, death, and destruction.

If we are to stem this tidal wave of violence that is rapidly engulfing us, we cannot be afraid to exercise our right to make a citizen's arrest together. We must regard it as a responsibility to apprehend people who are violating the law, and to turn them over to the police. Working in community groups, we minimize the danger to ourselves and enhance the safety of the entire community.

An example of this active community participation is an organization of unarmed citizens called the Guardian Angels. In four years' time, we have made 383 citizen arrests with only one fatality at the hands of a Newark, New Jersey police officer, and no serious injuries to our 4,000 members nationwide.

CONCLUSIONS

With one crime being committed every two seconds in the United States, we cannot afford to waste any more time rationalizing about the causes of crime. Nor can we waste any more energy, not to mention human lives, on window-dressing solutions. There is no place left to run and hide. We must face the fact that our greatest enemy in the war on crime is not the criminal, but our own fear.

We need to stop kidding ourselves, evading our responsibility, and pointing fingers, and accept the commonsense solution to the crime problem. No amount of bars on the windows, locks on the doors, complicated security systems or hungry attack dogs will do what only we can do for ourselves. The only way to stop crime is by organized community action that will stop the criminals physically, so that they know they will not get away with it.

18

The Guardian Angels: The Related Social Issues

Dennis Jay Kenney

The debate concerning the extent to which private citizen groups should become involved in the law enforcement process is currently centered largely around their potential for effectiveness. Although the present research is directed primarily at this issue, we should recognize that effectiveness is but one of several important questions to be considered before decisions about such groups should be made. This point was recently emphasized by one observer of citizen action who, while commenting about the Guardian Angels, declared that "they act far beyond the scope of the ordinary citizen." As a result, he warned, "the concept of the Guardian Angels, what they purport to represent, is a dangerous one. . . . They are as close to vigilantes as we've had in this city [New York]" (Edelman, 1981). In light of the importance of these concerns, as we examine the context and implications of the operations of the Guardian Angels, we must additionally consider the social and organization issues that are so closely related to the debate.

THE ISSUE OF VIGILANTISM

For many observers of the Guardian Angels the question of whether the organization is a vigilante group is foremost. Critics who question their value contend that they are, and warn that they come dangerously

From "The Related Social and Organization Issues," from *Crime, Fear, and the New York City Subways*. New York: Praeger Publishers, 1987. Reprinted with permission.

close to "taking the law into their own hands." Defenders, however, respond that "to call them vigilantes is nonsense" (Edelman, 1981). After declaring that "these are not vigilantes," one lieutenant governor has described them as "the best society has to offer" and has suggested that "we should be encouraging their kind of strength and their kind of courage" (Pileggi, 1980).

The Background

The issue of vigilantism in American law enforcement is hardly new. Its origins can be found in the early efforts of frontiersmen who were determined to leave their colonial security and resettle into new, more promising lands. However, as the colonial expansion moved steadily further from the older settled areas, the pioneers found it increasingly difficult to retain the order and stability that they had once known. Faced with a virtual absence of an effective system of law enforcement and a growing problem of outlaws and "marginal types," many settlers began to seek alternatives to social chaos. Often their solution was vigilantism.

Beginning in 1767 with the formation of the South Carolina Regulators, and lasting until around the 1860s, at least 116 separate occurrences of this traditional vigilantism appeared (Brown, 1983). In each of these instances the primary concern was with horse thieves, counterfeiters, outlaws, and "bad men" who threatened the social stability of the local community. In most cases, a strong community consensus existed in support of the vigilante's actions that permitted the problem of disorder to be dealt with straightforwardly. The movement was usually then disbanded.

By 1856 the tradition of vigilantism in America began to change. Although many of the more than 200 movements that followed would emulate the South Carolina example, the emergence of the San Francisco Vigilance Committee as America's largest and most powerful vigilante effort marked a turning point. Describing the movement as "neo-vigilantism," historian Richard Maxwell Brown has explained that while the San Francisco Committee frequently spoke of a crime problem, an examination of crime in that city fails to find an out-of-control crime rate. In fact, it appears that the regular law enforcement structure had San Francisco well under control. Far from fighting crime, these citizen activists seemed to be motivated more by a desire for local political and fiscal reform (Brown, 1975). By developing their parallel law enforcement structure and using it to drive away their opponents, the vigilantes were successful at organizing a "People's Party" and electing their own candidates to power (Burrows, 1976).

As a result of the considerable attention that was directed at the movement, the San Francisco Committee of 1856 had a tremendous impact on subsequent American vigilantism. While the old movements had been directed primarily against lawlessness and arose to fill a void, the new vigilantism, or neo-vigilantism, was a more complex phenomenon. No longer confined to the rural areas, the new movements were free to focus upon minorities, immigrants, laborers and labor leaders, and even defenders of civil liberties. The earlier concern with frontier disorder was replaced with a search for solutions to America's new urban problems (Brown, 1975).

From an historical perspective, then, it is clear that the concept of vigilantism is sufficiently broad to include a wide range of organizations attempting to accomplish a variety of purposes. Organizations seeking crime-control as well as those attempting social/group-control may properly fall within the boundaries that delineate vigilante action. As such, to refer to an organization simply as a vigilante group explains little, since such a characterization fails to account for the group's motivations, its level of community support, or whether it is socially constructive or socially destructive. Therefore, in examining an organization's vigilante characteristics it is helpful if we recognize these differences and ask if the organization is representative of a specific type of vigilante action. Of course, we should remember that individuals within an organization can have multiple goals that may cause considerable overlap between the different types (Rosenbaum and Sederberg, 1976).

The Guardian Angels as Vigilantes

Although the concept of vigilantism is derived from the Latin word "vigil," which translates as "being aware or observant," as we have already seen, its American usage has always been far more active. In its classic sense, vigilantism refers to "organized extralegal movements that take the law into their own hands." These movements, according to Professor Brown, can be distinguished from spontaneous actions—such as lynch mobs—in that they have an established organization and exist for a definite period of time (Burrows, 1976).

While the concept appears to be quite straightforward, its application to modern organizations, including the Guardian Angels, is usually hotly debated. This is largely the result of differences of opinion over what it means to be an "extralegal" organization, as well as over what types of citizen actions are required for an individual or group to "take the law into their own hands." In responding to a question concerning just this issue, Lisa Sliwa, the organization's National Coordinator, explained why the Angels were not vigilantes:

[Y]ou have to remember, we're not taking any authority unto ourselves that any average citizen doesn't have. All we're doing is going out in organized groups of at least eight or more and exercising what is a constitutional right of everybody here in this room and that is to make a citizen's arrest when you see a felony committed. (Donahue, n.d.)

Curtis Sliwa, on a different occasion, seemed to be making the same point when he assured his audience that the Angels would only become involved with serious crime. He went on to explain that "the Guardian Angels have clearly defined roles, there are no shades of gray in between" (Philadelphia City Council, 1981).

As studies and observations cited below indicate, however, the role of the Guardian Angels may not be so clearly defined as we have been led to believe, and the "shades of gray in between" may be considerable. As such, the line that separates the work of the Guardian Angels from vigilante action is far less distinct than their supporters have cared to admit.

After extensive studies of American vigilantism, Professor Brown and others have defined the term to include many modern citizen protection groups. While explaining that vigilante action often appeared as "a blunt, inexpensive solution" to the problems of inadequate law enforcement and uneven judicial systems, Brown characterizes the neighborhood patrol organizations of the 1960s and 1970s as "being in the authentic vigilante tradition." This is so, he says, since they are "associations in which citizens join together for self-protection under conditions of disorder and lawlessness" (Brown, 1976). As such, the label of vigilante can be applied to these organizations despite the fact that they were often nonviolent and cooperated with the police. When we remember that the Angels justify the existence of their organization as being needed for self-defensive action in the face of a "spiraling crime rate" that the police are helpless to prevent, it is clear that they too are in the vigilante tradition.

Beyond this general characterization, when we consider the full range of Angel activities, their role as extralegal law enforcers becomes even more obvious. While most of us are familiar with their deterrent role performed on subways, what few people realize is that the Guardian Angels have not been content to perform only this highly visible function. As a result, in New York and other cities, the Angels have begun to attempt to do more than just prevent crime and pacify its associated fear.

Guardian Angel undercover operations first came to the attention of this researcher during related research on the Philadelphia chapter. After explaining that the police in that city were both unable to control the rising crime and were often disinterested in the neighborhoods they policed, several of the chapter's supervisors reported that they had been contacted by numerous bars in the gay district of center city Philadelphia.

The owners of these bars were said to be dissatisfied with the quality of the police protection they were receiving and wanted assistance from the Guardian Angels. The Angels responded with undercover operations.

The operations undertaken reportedly consisted of having Angels dress inconspicuously as bums and winos so as to blend into the existing street life. As a group they would wait until a crime occurred, preferably with one of them as the intended victim, and then respond to apprehend the offender. It is difficult to imagine an "arrest" being made under these circumstances without a serious confrontation and the strong possibility of accompanying violence. While no arrests were actually made, the operations were nonetheless considered to be highly successful. To show their "gratitude," the bar owners reportedly donated $200 to the organization.

Nor is this the only report of this nontraditional style of citizen patrol. William Reinecke, a free-lance writer living in Philadelphia, attended a recruitment program conducted by the Philadelphia chapter and then accompanied the elite "Suicide Squad" as they patrolled the same center-city neighborhood. What is particularly striking about Reinecke's report is the constant emphasis that he observed being placed upon the use of violence (Reinecke, 1982).

Although the national leadership espouses the ideal of reducing the level of street violence, the Angel recruiters were certainly concealing this goal from their potential pledges. One recruiter is reported to have explained the excitement and benefits of being an Angel by promising:

And you'll feel so good after training—your mind will be sharp, you'll be smarter and you'll have so much energy—before, I used to drag myself out of bed, but now I pop right up, I take my vitamins and two raw eggs and I'm *bad* all day long—bad.

I've had my life threatened 37 times, shot at twice and been called everything from Apple to Zodiac—but here you'll learn to take a man *out*, that's right, man, take him out—I go for the eyes, but that's a personal preference—you may want to break a wrist, or break a rib, pull out his groin, break a neck, but me, I go for the eyes.

Or bite a nipple off. That's right, man—a guy goes nuts. . . . (Reinecke, 1982)

While the recruiter's description may be little more than talk designed to impress prospective members, the chapter's use of the Suicide Squad indicates that the premium on toughness exists in other parts of the organization as well. Described by Reinecke as "the elite corps of the Guardian Angels . . . who roam the city's streets in search of trouble," the Suicide Squad is unlike the standard Angel patrols. According to Reinecke's report, they are not confined to the subway trains, and while they sometimes patrol on foot, they also frequently worked from a customized Monte Carlo complete with a baseball bat in the back. On the night that Reinecke traveled with the Suicide Squad, they had been sent into the projects where they hoped to encounter and probably fight with gangs responsible for over a dozen attacks upon citizens (Reinecke, 1982).

Lest one get the impression that these methods are restricted to the Philadelphia chapter, it should be noted that similar observations have been reported from other cities. Reporter Michael Cordts, who clandestinely joined the Chicago chapter in 1981, tells of a special group of that city's Angels being assembled for the purpose of challenging the Disciples street gang. "We were told to hope for a rumble," explained Cordts. The coleader's instructions were that "If something happens, you jump on their heads. Be a barbarian" (Cordts, 1981a). And in New York City—Sliwa's own chapter—a special unit of Angels is said to wear red baseball caps and call themselves the SWAT team. This group conducts its operations in the especially tough areas of the city and reportedly "comes perilously close to practicing entrapment by having some of the Angels dress in a vulnerable manner" (Pileggi, 1980).

What is clear from these accounts is that it is quite reasonable to characterize the Guardian Angels as modern vigilantes. They are an unauthorized group that has chosen to exercise police powers through a variety of active operations. However, as was discussed earlier, it is not enough to simply apply the vigilante label. If we are to understand the organization and its impact upon our society, then additional consideration must be given to their purpose, any specific operational problems, and their level of public support.

THE ORGANIZATIONAL ISSUES

If we are to understand an organization such as the Guardian Angels, we must be careful to distinguish among the possible purposes of their actions as well as determine if they represent a socially constructive or destructive force. Is the group a crime control organization in the mold of the South Carolina Regulators, or are they more interested in some social or political impact and, therefore, more closely like the San Francisco Committee of 1856?

The Organization

That the Angels are organized is beyond dispute. While there is apparently considerable fluctuation in the overall design, the organization basically operates on a two-tiered command structure. At the local level, each chapter is free to develop according to the needs of the specific community in which it operates. Because the "local chapters must creatively find their own niche" (Newport, 1982), each is permitted to make its own decisions as to the type of relationship it will establish with the regular law enforcement system, where and when it will patrol, and even what variations to the original uniform it will permit.

Meanwhile, the national leadership—primarily Curtis and Lisa Sliwa—is occupied with the effort to establish new chapters as well as with developing and monitoring overall policy. Although considerable local autonomy is permitted, the extent to which they have remained in command of the organization was demonstrated in 1982 when Curtis Sliwa intervened in both the Chicago and Los Angeles chapters and removed the local leaders of each (see Weinberg, 1982; Reis, 1982). During an interview for this research, the leader of one local chapter advised us to "make no mistake about it, New York still gives the orders."

In providing their service of citizen protection, the national leadership has been quite specific in defining what the accepted procedure for the local chapters is to be. Having declared the Guardian Angel principle to be "the highest form of volunteer service that a person can render to his community," Sliwa has explained that his organization is refusing to accept the defensive philosophy being offered by the police. Instead of adopting what he characterizes as the "don't get involved, call the cops" attitude, Sliwa and his Angels assert that "as citizens of this country we have a right to defend one another . . . and no one should be able to tell you that you don't have the right to do it." Therefore, while patrolling in groups of eight or more, the Angels will become actively involved if a crime is observed. One member notifies the police from the nearest telephone, two stay with the victim to render aid, while five chase and attempt to arrest the suspect or suspects (Newport, 1982).

It would appear, then, that the Guardian Angels are intended to be a crime control organization. Acting upon the "imperative of survival," they are organized and take action as a supplement to the established law enforcement system. Their action is directed against individuals who are believed to be committing criminal acts, and their operations are undertaken in an effort to provide a greater degree of community order. Not surprisingly, they are often encouraged and congratulated by commuters, particularly the elderly ones, who return home late from night-time jobs.

Despite this apparent support, there remain lingering doubts. After changing their name to the Guardian Angels in September 1978, the organization significantly expanded its operations. No longer confined to the subways, Angel patrols now roam throughout parks, public housing, other forms of mass transit, and even neighborhoods and city streets. With the expansion of operations came efforts to widen the range of services, so that the Angels of today have at least the desire to be more than just a citizen protection group. "I see so many ways we could set up programs," was how Lisa Sliwa explained the organization's potential. "There could be self-defense for women. Or tutorial programs. Or work with the senior citizens." Her husband, Curtis, who has never been criticized for small ambitions, speaks of the Angels as being "like Vista or a domestic version of the Peace Corps, but more successful" (Weinberg, 1982).

Predictably, these latter interests have caused considerable concern over the direction in which the Angels are evolving. Citing an incident where the organization attempted to close a movie by protesting outside of theaters, as well as reports that they make a point of embarrassing the families of graffiti artists (Pileggi, 1980) and are providing security services for political candidates and at outdoor events (Reinecke, 1982), several observers have begun to warn of the organization's potential for harm. After one recent encounter in which 24 Angels were arrested for refusing to abandon a "Home for the Homeless" protest, Mayor Koch of New York City went so far as to liken the organization to "the mobs that seemed to rule Iran during the hostage crisis." The incident that provoked the Mayor's attack occurred when numerous Angels assembled and lived in a cluster of cardboard shacks on the sidewalks just south of his official residence. For approximately five weeks the protesting Angels maintained their demonstration to call attention to what they labeled as "the failure of the city to rehabilitate hundreds of city-owned abandoned buildings to be used by thousands of homeless people." In responding to claims that the city was refusing to meet with the Guardian Angels "to sit down and talk about how we could . . . solve the homeless problem," the Mayor accused the Angels of lying and of "using the homeless as a ploy to help them [the Angels] get a building of their own."

Although these are serious charges and concerns, Sliwa's commitment to the goals and actions of his organization remains steadfast. Claiming that the Angels are responsible "for pulling people off that fine line . . . between being decent citizens or not" (Gilman, 1982), he contends that the issue is one of role models. What the Guardian Angels are trying to do is to demonstrate that individuals can make a difference and that communities can attack their problems from a self-help point of view. "What I'm saying," he explains, "is that people have to begin assuming more of the responsibility of their daily lives themselves—as long as it's righteous, lawful, and correct" (Capozzi, 1981). Unfortunately, what he does not say is how easily the meanings of these three concepts can become blurred.

The Recruitment and Training of Angels

It has been recently noted by researchers Gary Marx and Dane Archer that the common problems of recruitment and training with which regular law enforcement agencies so frequently struggle may be particularly severe for organizations such as the Guardian Angels. According to them, "it is intuitively likely that self-defense groups—which often experience manpower shortages, and which have less stringent screening or membership requirements—would stand a far greater chance of recruiting people not emotionally (or, in some cases, morally) suited to policing others" (Marx and Archer, 1971). If this is so, then the manner in which the Angels attract new members and prepare them for their responsibilities is of great importance.

In describing the application process, Curtis Sliwa has explained that all new recruits must come with a personal recommendation from either a current angel or from someone who "understands totally the principle of what it is to be a Guardian Angel." The applicant must then undergo a series of four separate interviews, each conducted by a different person, and an extensive background check. Only after having satisfactorily completed these requirements is the applicant accepted into the organization and permitted to begin training.

The actual training period reportedly lasts for three months. According to Lisa Sliwa, the first month is devoted to the physical training of the recruit and includes conditioning—a three-mile run, stretching exercises for all parts of the body, and basic calisthenics—as well as self-defense. During this phase, the new Angel is taught to block both armed and unarmed attacks and to apply a variety of holds which will subdue a suspect without injury. The new recruit is required to attend at least one of these training sessions a week for a minimum of three hours per session.

Following the physical training program, each Angel must next participate in classroom training. Every member is certified in CPR, taught basic first aid, and must receive instruction about making citizen's arrests. Curtis Sliwa adds that during this phase the recruits are "drilled and drilled in terms of what you can do and what you can't do in terms of the penal code of your particular city or suburban area or rural area. . . . " (Philadelphia City Council, 1981).

In the final month of training, the phase that the Angels consider to be most crucial, the new members are prepared for their duties with situation drills. During this phase they are taken to city parks and subway trains where crimes and situations are reportedly reenacted to allow the recruits to gain actual hands-on experience. At this time they are taught to be able to tell which patrol members will apprehend the suspect, who goes for the police, who provides victim assistance, and how to identify and talk to witnesses.

In summarizing the value of the Guardian Angels' recruitment and training process, Curtis Sliwa emphasizes two basic points. One is that because the requirements to become an Angel are exacting, the public can be reasonably assured that unstable and undesirable persons cannot become, or at least remain, members. Those that do make it into the organization are almost certainly discovered and removed during the phases of the training program that test coolness and calmness under pressure. And second, because the training program is ongoing, a high level of quality control is built into the organization. In making this point, Sliwa notes that even police departments, with their strict entry guidelines, often do not provide veteran members with any continuing training. In comparing the two, Sliwa has noted that "at least the Guardian Angels have gone that far above what the police officers have." Unfortunately, when permission was asked to observe a training session that was reportedly in progress during an interview in one local chapter, the leaders stated that they must, of necessity, remain closed to the public. A few independent observations are, however, available.

As previously mentioned, during July 1981, reporter Michael Cordts of the *Chicago Sun Times* clandestinely joined that city's chapter of the Guardian Angels in an effort to learn more about the organization. Although many of his subsequent reactions to the experience were quite positive, what Cordts discovered about the recruitment and training procedures is, at least, disturbing.

Far from being highly selective so as to prevent the acceptance of unstable or undesirable applicants, Cordts found that the screening process was, in fact, almost nonexistent. In an article that he wrote in November 1981 he explained that:

National rules require that the first 60 members of any chapter must have no criminal record. But coleader Dan deGrazia was quoted as saying many of the Chicago Angels were former gang members and "we don't look that close at a person's past."

In fact, they don't look at all. Beyond elementary questions at the time of application—such as quoting the last four digits of an applicant's social security number—screening is based on gut instinct. . . .

No attempt was made to verify application information, not even criminal records. The Angels went on faith. (Cordts, 1981b)

While screening may have been bad, training seems to have been even worse. Noting that the Angels' Chicago chapter was poorly prepared for anything but the use of force, Cordts learned that the rigorous, ongoing training program described by the Sliwas only vaguely resembled reality. Among the discoveries that he reported were the conclusions that:

• Fewer than half of the recruits who graduated with him underwent legal training. Those who did received their instruction from a "well-meaning but self-described 'burned-out private eye.' "

- Fewer than one-third were trained in CPR. Those who received this training were warned by their instructor, himself an Angel recruit, not to mention that the required three-hour course was completed in only one hour.

- Two of the graduates were viewed by both their leaders and fellow Angels as "powder kegs, prone to breaking heads and not turning the other cheek." They were graduated anyway, for the sake of numbers.

- Patrol tactics, the key to avoiding and handling trouble were virtually ignored.

- Physical training consisted primarily of nightly sessions at a local health spa where an Angel leader who taught the martial arts handed out regular punishment to the recruits while playing the song, "Hit Me with Your Best Shot." (Cordts, 1981b)

When we recall the Philadelphia observations discussed earlier, as well as our own observations during this study of an applicant gaining on-the-spot acceptance into a patrol, the deficiencies found in Chicago are cause for concern. When Clayton Cortes, one of several subsequent leaders of the Chicago chapter, was asked about these problems, his response was that the reports were biased. "It may have seemed insufficient to the undercover reporter who became a Guardian Angel," the interviewer noted, "but the Angels themselves felt it was enough" (Reis, 1982). In light of the historical tendencies of vigilante movements to attract violent types and the estimate by one of the Chicago chapter's original leaders that "I think a majority who joined want to bust heads" (Cordts, 1981a), it is probable that other observers will disagree.

Even were these problems of membership not present, a related problem of nonmembers masquerading as Guardian Angels remains. In an interview in Philadelphia, Curtis Sliwa gave recognition to this concern and indicated that were cities to recognize his organization and supply identification cards that could be worn on the outside of Angels' uniforms, the dangers would be greatly reduced. Beyond that, he noted that many people are also arrested each year for impersonating police officers.

Although the extent of this problem is not known, numerous reports of counterfeit Angels and even offshoot organizations have begun to emerge. Ironically, when Angels interviewed in one local chapter were asked about these other groups, they displayed a great deal of distrust and suspicion for both the groups and their motives. Using terms similar to those directed at themselves by critics, they went so far as to describe one of the groups—the Angel Guardians—as a "street gang with nothing to do." On the wall of their chapter's headquarters they proudly displayed T-shirts which they reported they had "stripped" from these rivals. Despite such efforts, it is probable that Sliwa is correct, and that only a combination of strict controls over uniform use, official identification procedures, and clear criteria for membership offer any real protection.

Incentives for Survival

From their research into citizen involvement in law enforcement, Marx and Archer make the point that a large proportion of self-defense groups fail to develop the requisites for prolonged group survival. Because of this, the existence of many groups seems to depend largely upon charismatic leadership or a sudden felt crisis. Should these conditions disappear, many such groups tend themselves to then disappear.

In addition to the need to deal with a sudden problem—such as crime—many self-defense groups attract members for a variety of reasons unrelated to the group's objectives. These reasons, such as the desire for novelty, excitement, authority, and machismo, will assist in sustaining the group to the degree that they are satisfied or frustrated by the group's actions and operations. This means, of course, that a citizen organization that is not effective in its stated mission is likely to encounter increased pressure to satisfy its membership's peripheral desires. Because these problems relate so directly to this research, they deserve further attention.

There is little dispute that the leadership of the Angels is charismatic. Few who have spent time around Curtis Sliwa have failed to be impressed, both with the image he projects and with his ability to command his organization. He is articulate and seems to be equally at ease wither barking orders to his Angels or providing smooth answers and anecdotes to the myriad of interviewers and reporters with whom he constantly deals. As for his ability to hold his organization together, perhaps Robert Keating, New York City's Coordinator for Criminal Justice, expressed it best when he observed that:

There is no question about Curtis's charismatic power over the Guardian Angels. He's a tough kid and someone the Angels respect. Most of the kids come from such bad areas that Curtis might be the first real leader they have encountered. He is also their conduit to something outside of the ghetto. (Pileggi, 1980)

While it is likely that Sliwa's strong personality is a positive factor for group solidarity, the fear of crime that pervades many communities and the need for escape and excitement that many youths experience are undoubtedly major motivators for membership. The Chicago leaders and Philadelphia recruiters seemed to be showing their awareness of this by constantly emphasizing to recruits and potential Angels the physical dangers and action that might be present on Guardian Angel patrols. Interviews with individual members confirm these motives since everything from the desire to meet women to a wish to protect the elderly from attack have been cited as the reasons for initially becoming an Angel. Although these variables may be helpful in recruiting large numbers of new members, they also pose problems since, by their own admission, Angel patrols are most often routine and uneventful.

"He pretty much runs it all himself—brilliantly, I might add," is how New York City Transit Police Chief James Meehan has described Sliwa's importance to the Angels. If this is so, then we must wonder what might happen should the ambitions of the national leadership cause them to abandon the organization they have created. What might remain is a large, potentially unstable organization composed primarily of ghetto kids lacking in leadership.

Even more likely, however, is the danger that the Angels will discover, as the police have before them, that preventive patrol work is basically boring. As this begins to occur, the organization's turnover of members could increase, placing even greater strains on the already weak screening and training procedures. To counter this problem it may be necessary for Angel leadership to expand the organization's operations and redefine its goals. External challenges, such as conflicts with the police and other authorities, may also relieve some of this pressure. Recent allegations made by former members that the Sliwas faked attacks upon themselves and other Angels, and that they padded membership rolls by including names taken from the telephone book (Esposito and Pearl, 1983), could be evidence that this process may already be occurring.

REFERENCES

Brown, R. (1975). *Historical Studies of American Violence and Vigilantism*. New York: Oxford University Press.

———. (1976). "Vigilantism in America." *Vigilante Politics*, H. Rosenbaum and P. Sederberg, eds., Philadelphia: The University of Pennsylvania Press.

———. (1983). "Vigilante Policing." In *Thinking About Police: Contemporary Readings*, Carl B. Klockars, ed. New York: McGraw-Hill Book Company.

Burrows, W. (1976). *Vigilante!* New York: Harcourt Brace.

Capozzi, R. (1981). "The Guardian Angels: An Interview with Curtis Sliwa." *The Libertarian Review*, August.

Chema, A. (1983). "The Philosophy of an Archangel." *Karate Illustrated*, January.

Cordts, M. (1981a). "I Was a Guardian Angel." *Chicago Sun Times*, November 8.

———. (1981b). "Angels 'Training'—Infighting and Suspicion." *Chicago Sun Times*, November 8.

Donahue, P. (unknown date). "Vigilantes." *Phil Donahue Show*, Donahue Transcript #01072.

Edelman, B. (1981). "Does New York Need the Guardian Angels?" *Police Magazine*, May, p. 52.

Esposito, R. and M. Pearl (1983). "Guardian Angel Chiefs Probed in New York and Jersey." *New York Post*, October 21, p. 1.

Gilman, A. (1982). "Penthouse Interview: Curtis Sliwa." *Penthouse*, August.

Haskins, J. (1983). *The Guardian Angels*. Hillside, New Jersey: Enslow Publishers.

Marx, G. and D. Archer (1971). "Citizen Involvement in the Law Enforcement Process." *American Behavioral Scientist*, September/October.

Newport, J. (1982). "Opinion on Angels: A Devil of a Division." *Fort Worth Star Telegram*, March 21.

Philadelphia City Council (1981). "Testimony of Curtis Sliwa." March 11.

Pileggi, N. (1980). "The Guardian Angels: Help—or Hype?" *New York*, November 24, p. 14.

Reinecke, W. (1982). "Marching with the Avenging Angels." *Today/The Philadelphia Inquirer*, January 31.

Reis, B. (1982). "The Guardian Angels: Safe-Guarding the Subways." *The Circle Alumni News*, The University of Illinois at Chicago Circle.

Rosenbaum, H. J. and P. Sederberg (1976). "Vigilantism: An Analysis of Establishment Violence." In *Vigilante Politics*. Philadelphia: The University of Pennsylvania Press.

Weinberg, D. (1982). "The Guardian Angels Are Watching You." *Mademoiselle*, October.

_____VI

Management Issues in Policing

Police Unions and the Rejuvenation of American Policing

Robert B. Kliesmet

Police, like all workers, organize "out of the necessities of their situation; a single worker was helpless in dealing with an employer" (*NLRB v. Jones & Laughlin Steel Corp.*, 1937). The necessity of worker organization is intensified in the police workplace. The need to have a secure base from which to "resist arbitrary and unfair treatment" is essential for police officers for two reasons: the nature and demands of modern policing, and the history and practice of police management in the United States (for that matter, in most democratic societies). Before I elaborate on this position, however, some history about police unionization is in order.

THE EVOLUTION OF UNIONS IN POLICING

Historically, police unions are a relatively new phenomenon in the United States (see also, Leibig and Kliesmet, 1988). Before 1900, policing in many large cities, especially in the East, was a patronage-based occupation in which fraternal ties and organizations grew quite naturally. As early as 1887, the American Federation of Labor (AFL) considered and rejected the formation of a police council—as much out of dislike of the public police role in handling labor disputes and union-organizing efforts during the late 19th century as for any other reason. In June 1919, the idea of a police council was reconsidered and the AFL reversed its earlier position. The response in the police world was swift: within the next two months 37 police unions were chartered.

It was not as simple as that, however. Although Samuel Gompers, for example, spoke of the importance of collective action for all workers, he reneged when it came to the police. He took the position that despite chartering police unions, they were chartered only with the understanding that they could not strike. The test came early.

Before the end of 1919, the city of Boston and its police commissioner suspended nineteen police officers for union activities (a right now acknowledged to be clearly protected by the United States Constitution). Of 1,544 Boston police officers, 1,134 voted to strike (Kliesmet, 1985).

On September 1919, the Boston police strike started. Major rioting began almost immediately. The striking officers were summarily fired, the act justified by the Massachusetts governor's melodramatic statement: "There is no right to strike against the public safety, anywhere, anytime."

Contrary to popular belief, this was not the first police strike; police had earlier struck both in Cincinnati, Ohio and London, England without major social problems developing. In Boston, however, neither city nor state officials made the prudent preparations that officials had in Cincinnati and London.

Twenty years of litigation followed but none of the officers were ever reinstated to duty. The Boston Police Department, one of the country's finest police departments at the time, was decimated: until then a corruption-free department, the Boston Police Department then suffered the major problems of corruption that had characterized so many other police departments of that era. President Woodrow Wilson labeled the strike a "crime against civilization." The AFL revoked all police charters. The Fraternal Order of Police were no longer able to recruit officers, even into fraternal police groups. As late as 1958, the International Association of Chiefs of Police continued to cite the Boston police strike in its support for condemnation of police unions. Even during the 1980s, so-called "progressive" police chiefs still cite the Boston police strike as evidence of the horrors of police unionization and still consider police unions responsible for most of the current ills of policing in the United States.

The consequences for police officers and organizers of the political and organizational manipulation of the Boston police strike was that police unions faced tough times for the next 50 years. Effectively, the Boston debacle quashed police unions and their national development. However, during the late 1950s, and continuing into the 1980s, local police fraternal and union organizations grew and played important roles on the local level.

Depending upon local conditions and locally generated leadership, police organizations grew across a broad spectrum: from purely local fraternal clubs organized by a single department, often managed and controlled by police management, to vigorous labor unions. By engaging in collective bargaining, political activity, and taking advantage of local arbitration procedures, the more competently managed groups have become some of the most sophisticated, highly organized labor organizations in the country. Currently, nearly every police officer in the country is a member of at least one police organization—a local association, a fraternal lodge, as association of a loosely affiliated police organization, a police benevolent association, a statewide group, a local union affiliated with the AFL-CIO or the organization that I lead, the International Union of Police Association (IUPA), AFL-CIO.

With the above as background, let me return to my two original themes: police unionism is essential in American policing for two reasons—the nature and demands of modern policing, and the history and practice of police management in the United States.

THE NATURE OF MODERN POLICING

It is a sign of the maturation of the police occupation and the public perception of policing that the rhetoric of mid–20th century police chiefs has been largely discredited and abandoned. That rhetoric insisted that police work was largely, if not exclusively, law enforcement. Indeed, one contemporary legacy of this rhetoric is that for many, policing and law enforcement are considered one and the same. It is clear that they are not. Police departments do law enforcement, but it is a small portion of their total responsibility. Moreover, and consistent with the view that policing was merely law enforcement, police work was described as nondiscretionary: police simply enforce the law without exercising professional judgment. This view has not only been discredited; intelligent and skillful use of discretion has come to be seen as of the essence of good policing.

If the view that policing was simply law enforcement and nondiscretionary was merely inaccurate, it may not have been especially troublesome. After all, there are many occupations that thrive on inaccurate depictions of the nature of their work. What was troublesome, indeed disastrous to rank-and-file officers, was that the characterization of police work promulgated during this era demeaned and trivialized the work of police. It demeaned it by ignoring the full-range centrality of problems with which police deal. It trivialized it by denying the extent to which patrol officers use discretion, especially in the handling of disorder.

Let me discuss the problems with the strategy of denying the full range of police functions. First, despite their attempts to narrow police functioning, police administrators have never really succeeded in doing so. Researchers have noted what line patrol officers knew all along: only a small portion of citizens' requests for service or police responses have anything even remotely to do with crime (Wycoff, 1982). Moreover, despite denials, use of discretion continued to characterize all aspects of police work—a fact well-known by police officers and administrators who use it every day.

It can be argued, and with some legitimacy, that portraying police as crime fighters who enforce the law in an evenhanded way without use of discretion served some purposes. It certainly rallied police executives around an image of policing that they found gratifying and were able to sell to the public. Arguably, it may also have been instrumental in reducing corruption.

But the strategy has had negative consequences as well. First, it demeaned the skill of police officers. Rather than portray the police role as it was—a multifaceted role within which complex decision making was required—police were portrayed as simply patrolling in cars looking for "bad guys" and making an occasional arrest. True, because they did spend a preponderance of time dealing with crime, the detective role was enhanced in this strategy. But, it can be argued that the enhancement achieved was largely at the expense of the patrol officers, since research into criminal investigation has suggested that to a large extent detective effectiveness in making arrests can be attributed to information provided them *by* patrol officers (Eck, 1983). Demeaned as the patrol officer role has been, it should not be surprising that pay levels have stayed low. I can recall as a leader in the Milwaukee Police Association trying to educate both city officials and fact finders for years that classifying the complexity of the job of Milwaukee police officers in the same category with bookbinders simply was inappropriate. Not intended as a criticism of bookbinding, the point is that dispensing justice and resolving conflicts day after day on the streets is a far more complex role than that which has been promulgated and accepted by most citizens and public administrators.

But perhaps an even greater problem has been the administrative strategy that has been adopted by most police executives. Even the most cursory overview of police administration with its emphasis on command and control, formal rules, patterns, of supervision, specialization, pyramidlike hierarchy and other features, demonstrates that police organizations remain as testimonies to the pre–1920s organizational theory. And at least two assumptions of that theory of Frederick Taylor, a theory largely abandoned in the private sector, must be remembered: (1) workers find work largely distasteful; and (2) the central problem of management is to maintain strict control of workers to ensure efficiency. What is especially detrimental about organizing police departments around these assumptions is that, even if they were true, the very nature of policing renders futile the administrative practices derived from them. Police officers work alone in the community, they operate without supervision, and the problems they face are not amenable to standardized responses.

I raise these issues at this time because policing is at a watershed. The shape of the demand for police services is changing. The complexity of what police do and can accomplish has been recognized and police departments are beginning to adjust their tactics to these recognitions. Let me explain.

Disorder has created serious problems in many cities. The 1960s orientation of "letting it all hang out," deinstitutionalization of delinquents and the emotionally disturbed, decriminalization of drunkenness, as well as increases in the number of homeless people on the street, have all contributed to increased levels in both the public perception and actual levels of disorder. It is now clear that this disorder has created serious problems of citizen fear (Skogan and Maxfield, 1981). Fear, in turn, has led citizens to restrict their movements, abandon inner-city shopping areas, stay in barricaded apartments and homes, refrain from using public transportation, and take other actions, including the widespread purchase of firearms.

Patrol officers, given the opportunity, have tried to respond to these concerns (Wilson and Kelling, 1982). Note that I write "patrol officers" have tried to respond to these concerns, not, "police departments have tried to respond. . . ." My reason is simple: maintenance of order on city streets, until very recently, has been a relatively low priority for police departments. In fact, when citizens complained about disorder in the past, many police executives simply took the stance that their departments were too busy fighting crime to be bothered with disorder.

But that has changed. Citizen demands for more order, the impact of foot patrol on fear, the recognition by politicians of the seriousness of the problem, and the possibility that disorder can lead to serious crime have led police executives to rethink their positions about how much emphasis police should place on disorder. New policies seem to be forthcoming. My concern is how they will be devised.

As a representative of rank-and-file police officers, I would like to be sure that the development of policy and the implementation of programs will be done correctly. This is important for the sake of citizens, my profession, and my members. What, however, *is* a correct approach?

First, we patrol officers have a good sense of what and where community problems are. Other data sources are important—calls for service, citizen groups, reported crime, and others. But, police executives must find systematic ways to talk to us and learn what we know about the problems in the community.

Second, we have been conducting order maintenance activities continuously, despite attempts to narrow our functioning. We have some sense of what works, where, and when. Talk to us about solutions. If police executives are planning to do research about possible solutions to problems, they should let us in on the research—not just as subjects, but as full partners. We have a real vested interest in finding out the most skillful ways of handling problems. After all, we get the grief when mistakes are made.

Third, we are proud to be police officers and do a good job. We don't find work distasteful. Given the chance to help define problems and create solutions, we believe that we have much to contribute.

Fourth, police executives must view us as partners, not obstinate persons who have to operate under strict control. Strict control in police departments is largely a myth. Administrators must acknowledge this, and devise methods to recognize, obtain, and use us to our greatest potential. We know that there are a few incompetents in all police departments (not just patrol officers, either), but executives can no longer manage police departments on the basis of the least common denominator. Police executives, as well as rank-and-file police officers, are demeaned and stagnate under such a limited vision of our potentials.

In short, policing is entering a new era. Let's do it right this time.

REFERENCES

Eck, J. (1983). *Solving Crime*. Washington, D.C.: Police Executive Research Forum.

Kliesmet, R. (1985). "The Chief and the Union: May the Force Be with You." In Geller, W. (ed.), *Police Leadership in America*. Chicago: American Bar Foundation.

Leibig, M. and R. Kliesmet (1988). *Police Unions and the Law*. Alexandria, VA: Institute for Police Research, (IUPA/AFL-CIO).

NLRB v. Jones and Laughlin Steel Corporation (1937). 301 U.S. 1 at 33.

Skogan, W. and M. Maxfield (1981). *Coping with Crime: Individual Neighborhood Responses*. Beverly Hills: Sage.

Wilson, J. and G. Kelling (1982). "Broken Windows." *The Atlantic Monthly* (February).

Wycoff, M. (1982). *The Role of Municipal Police*. Washington, D.C.: Police Foundation.

20

Police Accreditation

Sheldon Greenberg

The concept of accreditation has existed in the United States since the early history of the nation. In 1887, the State of New York legislated a program requiring Regents to visit and review the work of every college in the state to assess the quality of their work. The Regents then had to prepare reports and submit them to the State Legislature for review. The concept of accreditation then spread to medical schools and, by the 1950s, most major hospitals were actively involved in working to meet accreditation standards. The development of accreditation standards for the field of corrections began in the 1960s and, in 1974, the Commission on Accreditation for Corrections (CAC) was formed. Following nearly a decade of planning and with funding provided by the Law Enforcement Assistance Administration (LEAA), the Commission on Accreditation for Law Enforcement, Inc. (CALEA), was established in 1979 to oversee a voluntary accreditation program for law enforcement agencies.

The basis for accreditation in the field of law enforcement parallels that for hospitals, colleges, and universities. In its text, *Law Enforcement Agency Accreditation to 1985*, CALEA cites the three-part definition of Kenneth E. Young, the first president of the Council on Postmasters Accreditation, as the basis for understanding accreditation. Young points out that: "voluntary accreditation should be defined in terms of a *concept*, a *process*, and a *status*."

[It is] a *concept*...unique to the United States by which...professional associations form voluntary, nongovernmental organizations to encourage and assist institutions in the evaluation and improvement of their... [operational] quality and to publicly acknowledge those institutions... that meet or exceed commonly agreed-to minimum expectations of... [operational] quality.

[It is] a *process* by which an institution... formally evaluates its... activities, in whole or in part, and seeks an independent judgment that it substantially achieves its own objectives and is generally equal in quality to comparable institutions.... Essential elements of the process are: (1) a clear statement of... objectives, (2) a directed self-study focused on these objectives, (3) an on-site evaluation by a selected group of peers, and (4) a decision by an independent commission that the institution or specialized unit is worthy of accreditation.

[It is] a *status* of affiliation given an institution... which has gone through the accrediting process and has been judged to meet or exceed general expectations of... [operational] quality. (Cotter, 1985).

Following this definition, law enforcement accreditation was conceived and developed as a "voluntary, nongovernmental concept, process, and status" (Cotter, 1985).

Establishment of the Standards

Four leading law enforcement organizations participated in the development of accreditation standards. They were the International Association of Chiefs of Police (IACP), Police Executive Research Forum (PERF), National Sheriffs' Association (NSA), and the National Organization of Black Law Enforcement Executives (NOBLE).

Each of the four organizations assumed responsibility for the development of standards within specific subject areas. Their research and development was reviewed by police executives and practitioners. Each standard was reviewed, discussed, revised, and reviewed again. When the process of development was completed, over 900 standards were written and adopted.

Standards were grouped in chapters according to subject area. In the *Standards for Law Enforcement Agencies* (1983), a total of 83 chapters are divided into nine broad categories. The categories are:

- Law Enforcement Role, Responsibility and Relationships
- Organization Management and Administration
- The Personnel Structure
- The Personnel Process
- Law Enforcement Operations
- Operation Support
- Traffic Operations

- Prisoners and Court-related Activities
- Auxiliary and Technical Services

Individual chapters set forth detailed standards. For example, within the broad category of Organization (Chapter 12), standards guide the agency's chief executive officer's responsibility to establish agency policies, address designation of command during absence of the chief, accountability of supervisors for performance of subordinates, and establishment of a written directive system.

Following each standard is a "commentary" that guides the agency in understanding the intent of the item. For example, in Chapter 42 of the *Standards* (1983), Criminal Investigation, standard 42.1.4 reads as follows:

42.1.4 An administrative designation of "open," "suspended," or "closed" is assigned to each case, as appropriate.

COMMENTARY: This designation is an internal administrative procedure to assist in case management and control. The categories are comprehensive in that "open" indicates the case is assigned to an officer and investigative efforts are active; "suspended" indicates all available leads have been exhausted but the case has not been brought to a satisfactory conclusion and investigative efforts may be resumed; and "closed" indicates that case has been satisfactorily concluded.

Once standards were developed and approved by the Commission, they were reviewed by police agencies of varied size and in various regions of the nation. A structured field review was conducted by 300 agencies in all 50 states. The four participating associations (IACP, PERF, NSA, and NOBLE) then considered the results of the field review and made appropriate changes. The revised standards were then reviewed by the Commission a second time and formally adopted. An ongoing process was implemented for adding, deleting, and revising standards as needed to meet changing needs within the profession.

The four associations and the Commission recognized that police agencies in the United States vary in size and the nature of responsibilities they assume. As such, levels of compliance with accreditation standards were established to recognize this diversity. Levels of compliance are determined by the size of the agency, with the smallest component being 1 to 9 employees and the largest being over 1,000.

Standards were also established so that certain ones are mandatory, some are optional ("other than mandatory"), and some "not applicable" to the agency. Once the Commission and the department undergoing accreditation determine which standards are mandatory, the agency must demonstrate compliance with all mandatory standards and meet 80 percent of those in the "other than mandatory" category.

STEPS IN THE ACCREDITATION PROCESS

The process of accreditation is voluntary. The total process, as outlined by the Commission, consists of seven steps: (1) Application; (2) Completion of the Agency Questionnaire; (3) Self-assessment; (4) On-site Assessment; (5) Commission Review; (6) Award Ceremony; and, (7) Reaccreditation.

Following initial application, the Commission requires the department to complete a lengthy questionnaire detailing the agency's size, structure, nature of jurisdiction, duties, relationship to other agencies, budget, and more. This information is used to determine which standards apply to the department.

The agency then undertakes a self-assessment that involves an "in-house" evaluation to determine its ability to meet the standards. This evaluation is also designed to ensure that the agency has compiled the vast amount of documentation required to meet accreditation standards. Data are required on policies, procedures, workload, and resource allocation, personnel practices, community interaction, and more.

The on-site assessment occurs when the department completes the self-assessment process and believes that it has gained compliance with all applicable standards. The department notifies the Commission that it is ready for the on-site team. The Commission then assembles a team of assessors. Assessors are generally law enforcement administrators (chiefs, bureau and division commanders, etc.) who are thoroughly familiar with the accreditation process. They are not necessarily from accredited agencies. The department undergoing the on-site assessment is given the opportunity to review the team selected by the Commission to identify potentials for conflict of interest.

Once the team is selected and approved, the site visit begins. Assessors examine the department's policies, procedures, and the data collected by the agency to support compliance with the standards. Depending on the nature of the department and its documentation, the team may conduct personal interviews with employees, government officials, members of the public, and others. The team will also conduct telephone interviews and review the process by which the department pursued accreditation. Finally, the team of assessors will prepare a report to the Commission.

At the next scheduled meeting of the Commission, the assessment team report is reviewed and accreditation is either granted or denied. If the standards were met, accreditation is granted. If accreditation is deferred, the department is informed of where noncompliance with the standards was identified. Should the department disagree with the findings of the Commission, an appeal process exists, designed to resolve differences and determine reconsideration of the agency's effort.

If all criteria are met, the department is notified that it has achieved accreditation during the Commission meeting. The Commission then works with the department to hold a formal award ceremony within its local jurisdiction. The award ceremony is generally attended by representatives of the Commission. Accreditation is maintained for a five-year period.

The award of accreditation for a finite period of time parallels reaccreditation processes for hospitals, colleges, and universities. The reaccreditation process also places greater emphasis on operational practices and less on written policy and procedure. The aim is to determine if the department, having developed the written data as part of the accreditation process, has put it into practice.

Before the end of the fifth year, the agency must apply for reaccreditation. Data collection, comparison of operational practices to standards, and an on-site assessment are required as part of the reaccreditation process (Pearson, 1983).

THE DEBATE SURROUNDING ACCREDITATION

A national accreditation program for law enforcement agencies has its critics as well as its proponents and there has been opposition to the Commission since its inception. In 1987, the *Washington Post* published an article citing that most law enforcement agencies were receptive to and supportive of the national accreditation program, driven, in part, by the increasing number of lawsuits filed against departments. According to a chief of police in Virginia, the award of accreditation to a police agency parallels in meaning the placement of an Underwriters Laboratory tag on an electric appliance. It lets the public know that the agency has met established standards.

According to a loss prevention director for a state insurance organization, accredited police agencies exhibit better policies and procedures, particularly in "high-risk" areas. To encourage departments to participate in the process, his organization offers to pay one-half of the accreditation fees for any member city. The organization also offers reductions in the cost of liability insurance to accredited agencies.

Critics of the national accreditation program cite cost, the imposition of a national program on state and local agencies of government, the amount of time and resources necessary to complete the process, and standards that do not adequately meet the varied nature of police agencies as major concerns.

The commission's standards often require what Stonehill College sociology Prof. John J. Broderick said may be only "the lowest common denominator" among regulations of widely varying departments. Moreover, the substance of many rules is left up to each department. (McAllister, 1987)

Since the early beginnings of the national accreditation program, the largest number and most vocal critics have been in the states of California and New York, although a small number of agencies in both states have participated in the accreditation process.

The strongest opposition is coming from California, where law enforcement standards are more rigorous than in most states. . . . Although the California Peace Officers Association and the California Chiefs Association opposed national accreditation, the groups are studying the possibility of state standards.

"We don't think that a set of standards trying to embrace the entire nation is an appropriate way to go," said Los Angeles County Sheriff Sherman Block, president of the peace officers association. "The overwhelming sentiment is to do it statewide." (Iwata, 1987)

The cost of accreditation, not including in-kind fees, varies depending upon the size of the police agency. The initial application fee is $100. However, total cost, including application, site visit, and other fees may range from $5,000 to in excess of $20,000. For example, a sheriff's department of 150 deputies noted in its budget that fees to the Commission would be approximately $12,000 from the start of the process to conclusion.

Some critics of the national accreditation program claim that in-kind fees represent the greatest cost in the process. While some agencies assign responsibility for coordination of the accreditation process to their planning units, most assign staff to oversee the effort on a full-time basis. An accreditation manager is generally appointed within the agency to oversee various steps in the process and maintain liaison with the Commission staff.

In most of the agencies that have participated in the process, the accreditation manager has been a sworn officer with at least supervisory rank. Many have held command rank. In addition to the manager, command staff, field officers, and specialists may play a major role in their agency's efforts. Since the accreditation process takes eighteen months or more, critics claim the process pulls the manager and others involved away from routine duties for too long a period of time.

Proponents of the national accreditation process believe that it was developed to help law enforcement agencies accomplish the following:

- increase agency capabilities to prevent and control crime;
- enhance agency effectiveness and efficiency in the delivery of law enforcement services;
- improve cooperation and coordination with other law enforcement agencies and with other components of the criminal justice system; and
- increase citizen and staff confidence in the goals, objectives, policies, and practices of the agency.

According to William K. Stover, former Chief of the Arlington County, Virginia, Police Department, "When an agency can prove it meets standards that were mutually developed by several leading law enforcement associations, courts will be more likely to conclude there is no negligence." Chief William Wiebold of Indian Hill, Ohio, added, "Accreditation is assurance of excellence to our local governing body and the citizens we serve. In addition, we can demonstrate that we adhere to national standards, a testament to our insurability" (Commission on Accreditation, 1984).

One of the primary benefits to accreditation, according to proponents, is that is requires departments to better document and coordinate their policies and practices. Mayors, city managers, and county executives who support accreditation note that this documentation serves their needs well and helps them to better understand and support the needs of their police agencies. According to Don Dernings, Executive Director of the Illinois Association of Chiefs of Police, accreditation "clearly establishes accountability for police performance. You put police performance on the record so that it can be evaluated on the record" (Emstead and Seigel, 1987).

The Commission and agencies supporting national accreditation cite eleven primary benefits to participation:

1. nationwide recognition of professional excellence;
2. continued growth and improvement;
3. community understanding and support;
4. employee confidence; esprit;
5. state and local government officials' confidence;
6. state-of-the-art, impartial guidelines for evaluation, and change, when necessary;
7. proactive management systems; policies and procedures documented;
8. liability insurance costs contained or decreased;
9. liability litigation deterred;
10. coordination with neighboring agencies and other parts of the criminal justice system; and

11. access to the latest law enforcement practices (Commission on Accreditation, 1984).

FOLLOW-UP AND ANNUAL REPORTS

Once accreditation is awarded to an agency, it must file annual reports with the Commission. The reports are detailed and are often completed by the person who served as accreditation manager during the process. These reports provide the Commission staff with information on the progress of the agency and any changes or problems it may experience.

The Commission holds regular meetings at locations throughout the nation. Accredited agencies host most of the meetings. At these meetings, accredited agencies and those going through or considering the process share experiences and observe the final consideration of those agencies who have completed all criteria for accreditation, including the team site visit. Activities of the meetings are published and mailed to agencies.

REACCREDITATION

As stated earlier, an agency must apply for reaccreditation and it must occur prior to the 42nd month following accreditation. The filing of its first annual report following accreditation is actually the first step in the reaccreditation process. Annual reports are an integral part of the reaccreditation process.

Once application is made, the agency files a plan for achieving reaccreditation with the Commission. The plan requires that the agency provide progress reports to the Commission at months 45, 48, and 51. Before month 60, an on-site assessment is planned. The length of time and makeup of the on-site assessment parallels that of the accreditation process.

There are two significant differences between the accreditation and reaccreditation processes. The reaccreditation process focuses more on agency goals and objectives, operational activities, and its relationship to the community and criminal justice system. It asks, "Is the agency putting into practice the policies and procedures refined as part of the initial accreditation process?" There is less emphasis on examining written documentation than occurs in the initial process.

Reaccreditation also requires a higher level of compliance with nonmandatory standards. While initial accreditation requires compliance with 80 percent of the nonmandatory standards, the first reaccreditation process requires compliance with 85 percent. The second reaccreditation process increases compliance to 90 percent and the third and subsequent processes require 95 percent compliance with nonmandatory standards.

As with the initial process, agencies must comply with all mandatory standards in the reaccreditation process. This includes compliance with new standards enacted by the Commission since the award of accreditation or reaccreditation. The award of reaccreditation is approved or denied by the Commission after review of the assessment team report.

Agency Status at Time of Reaccreditation

At the time of reaccreditation, an agency is placed in one of four categories by the Commission. They are:

• Accredited;
• Accredited-with-a-Time-Limit—to remedy deficiencies by pursuing a plan of action filed with the Commission;
• Accreditation Suspended—assigned when the agency has not achieved compliance with applicable standards but could regain accredited status by pursuing a plan of action; and
• Accreditation Revoked—assigned when the agency is regarded as no longer accredited.

At any point in the process, an agency may withdraw from participation or give up its accreditation.

ACCREDITATION IN THE FUTURE

At the beginning of 1989, the Commission and the accreditation process remained strong. In 1988, the Department of Justice awarded a second grant to the Commission to provide additional support and expand its activities. According to the Commission, approximately 700 law enforcement agencies have become involved in the accreditation process. Over 70 agencies achieved full accreditation and more than a dozen agencies began looking toward reaccreditation. Meetings were held to refine and review the reaccreditation process in order to meet the needs of these agencies.

While opposition to the national accreditation program continues, a far greater number of agencies tend to support the process than oppose it. The four law enforcement associations continue to provide support to the Commission and maintain active involvement. Insurers of cities, counties, and agencies continue to support accreditation for its role in reducing potential liability and defending against liability suits.

Most significantly, the Commission meetings have evolved from attendance by only a handful of interested agencies to attendance by more than 500 people. Accreditation was summed up by Mayor W. L. Dobbs of Covington, Georgia, who stated, "The need for law enforcement standards that are consistent throughout our nation is very real. It is understood that there will always be situations that address themselves to particular locations or areas of our country but, by and large, a set of standards such as those sought by this certification will definitely prove to be an asset to us all" (Commission on Accreditation, 1984).

REFERENCES

Commission on Accreditation for Law Enforcement (1984). *Accreditation Program Overview.* Fairfax, VA.

———. (1986). *Background on the Accreditation Process.* Fairfax, VA.

Cotter, J. (1985). *Law Enforcement Agency Accreditation to 1985.* Fairfax, VA: Commission of Accreditation for Law Enforcement Agencies, Inc.

Emstead, R. and J. Seigel (1987). "Accreditation Opens Police Books to Public." *Chicago Tribune*, July 12.

Iwata, E. (1987). "A Move to Set Standards for Police Forces." *San Francisco Chronicle*, July 25.

McAllister, B. (1987). "Spurred by Dramatic Rise in Lawsuits, Police Agencies Warm to Accreditation." *Washington Post*, March 17.

Pearson, J. (1983). "National Accreditation: A Valuable Management Tool." *Western City Magazine.* League of California Cities, July.

21

Managing Police Information

Robert Taylor

Computers impact upon nearly every aspect of our daily lives. We have computerized cars, automated teller machines, digital watches, electronic headphones—the list is endless. Indeed, the computer age is here. In the field of law enforcement, there has also been a tremendous increase in computer automation processes. This technological trend has brought about dramatic changes in police personnel, roles, and services and, for the most part, these changes have resulted in increased police efficiency and effectiveness.

Unlike years past, computers are no longer expensive first-time investments requiring outside subsidies or matching federal grants for their purchase. Today's computers provide even the smallest departments with the capability of becoming automated at a cost they can afford. Further, the networking or "tying together" of small computers can surpass the memory capacity that was previously available to only large and expensive mainframe computers.

The information society so accurately predicted by futurists of the 1960s is now an American reality in which "individual and organizational survival is dependent on the ability to access information" (Archambeault and Archambeault, 1984:4). Law enforcement agencies are vast information-processing organizations. All too often, managers and the general public think of police work in terms of physical security, patrol cars, weaponry, crime control, and traffic enforcement. In fact, most police work involves the collection, manipulation, structuring, collating, and assimilating of information, so much so that an automated records and communication system is no longer viewed as a luxury but a necessity (Swanson, Territo and Taylor, 1988:365–366).

The purpose of this chapter is not to evaluate the impact of computer technology and information systems, but rather to identify and discuss a number of organizational and social issues arising from this technological change. For the most part, computerization has offered police organizations a powerful tool for resource utilization in such areas as workloads, scheduling, performance, budgeting, and program evaluation (Sykes, 1986). Computers enable police agencies to do what they have traditionally done—collect and process enormous amounts of information—but in increasingly faster and more efficient ways. As it was an inevitable fact fifteen years ago that the public sector, like the private sector, must embrace technological change or face certain extinction, so it is with today's police managers. The presence of computers in an organization generates an "institutional demand" for changes to maintain and also to upgrade existing systems. This "affective demand" arises because computing offers the possibility of not only improving productivity of current activities but also of adding new ones that were previously unavailable (King and Kraemer, 1985:178).

INFORMATION TECHNOLOGY IN LAW ENFORCEMENT

Information technology is the combination of automated data processing, storage, and retrieval with the distance transmission capabilities of telecommunications. Information technology resources include the hardware, software, and personnel used in supporting electronically based information systems. This necessarily includes data, text, voice, and image forms of information.

A review of some of the applications of information technology in policing provides state-of-the-art end user systems. For instance, in St. Louis, Missouri, an automated data base is enhanced by an integrated report writing system. In this manner, information does not have to be "reentered" into a data base. Officers simply write the original report which interfaces with a software package that actually gleans important data points for inclusion in the automated records system. This type of data manipulation significantly reduces the duplication of work and effort.

One of the more innovative and interesting projects that is directly related to improving automated records systems is "live reporting" (George and Kleinknecht, 1985). Police officers produce reports by telephoning a records specialist who directly enters the information into the computer. This system produces professionally typed reports and serves as the primary source of management information that is accessible instantaneously from remote locations.

Additionally, with the advent of more powerful, programmable, battery-powered, notebook-sized computers that weigh less than four pounds, with a full-sized keyboard, a built-in telephone modem, and preprogrammed word processing communications, some police departments, such as those in St. Petersburg and Ocala, Florida, are pioneering the use of portable computers for writing formatted police reports in the field. Officers in these cities take the portable computer to the actual crime scene where they write their reports to either disks or tapes, which are later transported to a central receiving station.

Regarding advanced visual data applications in law enforcement, some agencies (such as the Houston P.D.; Prince George County, Maryland S.O.; and the California Department of Justice) have enjoyed the benefits of AFIS—Automated Fingerprint Identification System. This revolutionary automated system allows the computer to scan and digitize fingerprints. The data base consists of spatially digitized maps of prints which are routinely compared against latent prints at crime scenes or identification prints at jails/prisons. Making incredibly fine distinctions among literally thousands or millions of prints, an AFIS computer can compare a new fingerprint with massive collections of file prints in a matter of minutes and can make identifications that previously were possible only through a time-consuming and error-prone process of manual comparison (Wilson, 1988:23).

These new techniques greatly enhance existing automated record systems by (1) reducing time spent by uniformed police officers in preparing reports, thus increasing officer and supervisor "street time"; (2) providing instant on-line management information and instant retrieval of data from any remote location, such as the precinct or detective office; (3) reducing office space used to maintain "hard copies" in filing cabinets or vaults by storing reports in computer memory; (4) improving the quality, accuracy, and timeliness of crime analysis, management reports, and uniform crime reports (UCR) by electronically processing, aggregating, distributing, and filing of these documents; and (5) improving the quality, legibility, and accuracy of police reports (George and Kleinknecht, 1985 and Swanson, Territo and Taylor, 1988:370–371).

Finally, one of the newest techniques involving automation is directly associated with one of the oldest applications of information technology in law enforcement. Computer-assisted or computer-aided dispatch (CAD) plans were designed originally to improve the allocation of uniformed officers in a given patrol district and thereby reduce response time and improve criminal apprehension rates. CAD systems now utilize enhanced graphics for increased officer safety and case information. In Phoenix, Arizona, a CAD system utilizing mobile digital terminals (MDTs) in patrol vehicles provides both a written description and visual map/diagram of neighborhoods, buildings, and houses queried.

MOVING TO THE NEXT GENERATION

While the above examples are only a few of the current applications of information technology in policing, one can see that the emphasis is on increasing the use of such technology in the way police officers do their jobs. Historically, information technology in law enforcement has focused on the "demand side" of the police function and mission. That is, information technology has been offered as a way to enhance the productivity of the organization by:

• increasing numbers of arrests and cases cleared;

• measuring efficiency and effectiveness of individual officers;

• counting numbers of crimes committed and tickets written;

• improving patrol car response time.

Rarely has information technology been offered to increase the performance of police managers. To no surprise, the same is true in the private sector. Much attention in automation has been given to increasing the efficiency of the individual worker, but very little to improving the quality of management. It is only recently that advances in decision support systems and "knowledge management" systems have been addressed. Caudle (1987) points out that such emphasis holds great benefits for law enforcement managers to include increased analytic capabilities, integration of extensive data sources, early warning and preventive systems, and ongoing tactical, operational, and strategic planning support. Indeed, these types of advanced information technology systems, dubbed "Information Resource Management Systems," represent the next evolutionary step in the information management function. Basically, the concept behind Information Resource Management centers on information as a resource, which includes information systems, data processing, telecommunications, information management, and all of the hardware, software, and data communication technologies that support information exchange (Corbin, 1988:12).

Integral to the development of an information resource management system is the classic set of functions originally described by Henri Fayol (1916). An adaptation of this work was later elaborated on by Luther Gulick (1937) who coined one of the most familiar and enduring acronyms of administration, POSDCORB: *P*lanning, *O*rganizing, *S*taffing, *D*irecting, *Co*ordinating, *R*eporting, and *B*udgeting.

Integrated Resource Management (IRM) enhances these classic managerial functions by providing the hard data on which to make plans and decisions. However, the overall impact of IRM goes well beyond just providing numbers; its main focus is to force managers to recognize organizational opportunities for using information technology, and to develop strategies that exploit these opportunities at the most advanced level. Inherent in these objectives is an increased awareness of analysis, problem solving, dispute resolution, and decision making—the heart of management.

ARTIFICIAL INTELLIGENCE AND EXPERT SYSTEMS

The advent of artificial intelligence (AI) systems offers hope to police managers seeking answers to next-generation questions. Basically, artificial intelligence can be defined as a shift from mere data processing to an intelligent processing of knowledge (Awad, 1988:355). Artificial intelligence involves four major areas of research:

- Natural languages—systems that translate ordinary human commands into language that computer programs can understand and execute.
- Robotics—machines that move and relate to objects as humans do.
- Visualization systems—machines that can relate visually to their environments as humans do.
- Expert systems—programs that mimic the decision-making logic of human experts (Horwitt, 1985:49).

It is this last area of expert systems that police managers find most promising. Basically, expert systems attempt to supplant rather than supplement human efforts in arriving at solutions to complex problems. In the area of policing, expert systems can assist managers with complex planning and task scheduling. However, their greatest benefit may be in changing the way organizations behave by promoting a different way of looking at problem solving. In law enforcement, this necessitates a creative and innovative police executive, one who challenges traditional assumptions concerning the police function and mission. Indeed, with the development of expert systems that attempt to combine textbook knowledge with rules of thumb or "heuristics" to make informed guesses about a specific problem, executives need no longer rely on their own intuition or inspiration. What may have worked well in the past may appear foolish when contrasted to solutions based on expert systems.

IMPLEMENTING NEW TECHNOLOGIES

The continued spread of computer literacy and the increasing user-friendliness of computers within police organizations will play a significant role in the future diffusion of expert systems throughout the police organization. For law enforcement managers, it is important to remember that the assimilation of new technologies into an organization goes through certain distinct phases. This diffusion process can be an inhibiting factor to the overall impact of information resource management if specific awareness of barriers to success are not realized (Raho, Belohlav, and Fielder, 1987).

According to Toffler (1985), "new technologies abruptly destroy the present while simultaneously creating the future." Viewing this from the perspective of organizational culture—that is, the set of key values, beliefs, and understandings that are shared by members of a police organization—and correlating it to the traditional police organizational structure and hierarchy, leads one to assume that the implementation of IRM will face specific challenges. Many of these challenges will directly affect personnel. One common problem arises from the simple misunderstanding of new technological advances, commonly expressed by fear on the part of staff members. Another well-documented problem is resistance to change, be it administrative or technical (Taylor, 1985). Pressman and Wildavsky's (1973) classic study of implementation suggests that there are no guaranteed guides or plans to successful program implementation; only that a number of issues must be recognized in order to avoid "the seamless web" of failure. To this end, three problematic areas in implementing information resource systems are addressed: Controlling Technological Growth, Dealing with Information Elites, and Confronting Loss of Privacy and Computer Crime Liability.

CONTROLLING TECHNOLOGICAL GROWTH

Police information systems of the past all have one thing in common— they are host systems. These hosts are always central processing in nature and normally require point to point connection to user workstations. A typical data processing design for a large police department focuses on a mainframe computer with either tape or disk storage devices and end user terminals cabled directly to the mainframe via controllers. However, in the past two years, law enforcement (and the rest of the world) has witnessed the virtual explosion in the development of local area networks (LANS). These systems represent a new and advanced scheme for the processing and transference of police information such as text, data, and graphics operating *within* a building or site. Basically, a local area network connects terminals and computers (usually referred to as nodes), as well as other devices (such as printers), in a cost-effective fashion. This allows users to access the data and peripheral devices of their own choice. Phone lines may be used to tie the systems together, but more often than not the physical interconnections are made by locally installing various kinds of cable. Coaxial, multicore, twisted pair and even fiber optic cables may be employed by various local area networks.

The operating speed of LANS varies greatly, however many rival even the fastest and largest mainframe. At one time, office communications were limited to about 16Kbps (kilo bits per second) over the phone lines. Today, networks typically operate at about 80Kbps, and as newer high-speed digital devices become available the operating speeds should increase to as high as 10 million bits per second (10Mbps) or even faster. These speeds are not needed or intended for the connection of terminals alone. They are intended, however, for computer-to-computer data transfer or for allowing computers scattered around a specific site to share expensive common resources such as data storage devices, a high-speed printer, a plotter, or an electronic map as used in many computer-aided dispatch centers. High speeds are also needed to handle speech in digitized form, as often expressed in an investigative tool such as the psychological stress evaluator. Unfortunately, such new developments have caused great concern for executive level control.

Along with these new LAN developments has come the newer, faster, and most important, cheaper PC "clone." A clone is a non-IBM brand personal computer usually selling for much less than leading market models. Managers argue that their respective divisions can operate more efficiently using a closed LAN with clones without the expense of IBM standard equipment. In this manner, managers emphasize the security and the reliability of such systems in comparison to host mainframe designs. In a host system, when the processor "goes down," the entire system is dead. However, in a local are network (LAN) the same is not true. Even though managers may be correct in their assumption of a cleaner, more efficient, and effective computerized system as designed by local area networks, there are still a number of ensuing problems which must be remedied.

First, one can easily predict what occurs. With a number of different divisions come a number of different clones and local area networks. Without proper supervision, these systems proliferate throughout an organization causing separate and nonconnected capabilities. Most clones have difficulties in a network environment as their specifications do not meet those demanded by the network configuration. Further, different clone networks are rarely compatible with each other or with mainframe operations.

Second, there are a number of hidden costs in maintenance and training associated with the development of a local area network. If such systems are decentralized, various existing maintenance contracts may be voided, thereby requiring additional training of personnel and/or vendor acquisition.

Corbin (1988:13) reenforces the advantages of an information resource management plan. One of the side objectives of an IRM concentrates on managing distributive information resources—that is, controlling the capability of non-mainframe resources. Crucial to the implementation of such a plan is the idea of synergism, or the power of cooperative effort. Information resource management attempts to provide integrated and compatible information systems as well as improve information exchange through the use of new and varied technology. This cannot be a haphazard experiment, it must be a well thought out plan implemented through a series of phases on a timely basis. Without such objectives in mind, existing resources often flounder and noncompatible systems proliferate.

DEALING WITH INFORMATION ELITES

Police executives must also be aware of a growing managerial problem existing within information system personnel. Most police chiefs are not highly computer-literate and, therefore, must rely on the technical advice and expertise of subordinates. This situation makes the executive vulnerable to the "information elite." Kraemer and Danziger (1984) identify the information elite as a person who:

combines a high level of technical expertise in their organizational domain with some sophistication in the use of computer and/or computer based information. ... The information elite gains control over others (influence) and resists control by others (supervision) by a combination of persuading others through the force of their data and information based arguments and of serving others as an effective information broker whose competencies are essential.

In some cases, executives are almost held "hostage" by those who have the technical knowledge to operate an automated system. Information is critically important to an organization such as the police. Individual officers must have immediate and instantaneous information (such as warrant information) for their own safety as well as the accomplishment of the police mission and function. This demand places a high value on those who know how to operate the computer-based information system.

Unfortunately, some organizations have attempted to remedy this problem by promoting the highly skilled and technical individual to ranks of executive management. All too often, the "Peter Principle" applies: Managers are promoted to the level of their own incompetency (Peter and Hall, 1969). Individuals who are competent technically are suddenly thrust into management positions without the necessary training and/or expertise that accompanies that position. Managers must have strong leadership capabilities, interpersonal skills, and decision-making qualities. These are attributes that highly technical individuals rarely receive on the job, since they are often cloistered in cubicles and assigned specific programming or design tasks. This is not to say that technically skilled people cannot become managers; only that significant preparation and training is often required.

Once again, the move toward an information resource management (IRM) format will assist executives in controlling personnel. It must be remembered that IRM focuses on all aspects of the information gathering, processing, and assimilating function. Therefore, expertise at various levels and in various areas is required, which often mandates the transferring of a number of people throughout an organization to gain knowledge on specific systems necessary to accomplish a specific task. In this manner, no one person knows everything about the information processing system. Of course, this has a side advantage in that not only do more people gain a stronger technical knowledge of the inner workings of a system; but also a diffusion of computer awareness permeates the entire organization at each and every level.

This side benefit is very important in addressing the implementation problems often observed with the advent of new technologies in an organizational structure. Sankar (1988) accurately points out that new technologies in any organization will impact on all elements of corporate culture, such as "observed behavior patterns, norms, dominant values, organizational ideology, rules of the game, and the climate of the organization." These elements of organizational culture have the potential to inhibit the effective management of advanced technologies. It is for this reason that even the most ambitious writer advocating technological change warns the astute manager to "go slow." Technological implementation necessitates incremental steps for adoption by existing personnel. Particularly is this true in police organizations, where the level of advancement and sophistication in computerization has not kept pace with the private sector. All too often, police executives are in a "hurry" to automate their department. The manager must be aware that computerization is a continuing and ongoing process; a process that may never be fully "completed."

CONFRONTING LOSS OF PRIVACY AND COMPUTER CRIME LIABILITY

The very nature of police information dictates the need for a secure and confidential system. Considerable private information about suspects, victims, and witnesses exists in computerized data bases housed in police agencies—the most famous being the National Crime Information Center (NCIC) operated by the Federal Bureau of Investigation. This data base consists of criminal records on more than twenty million people. Most recently, fear has been voiced concerning the possible abuse of such police systems. Civil libertarians argue that political pressures, voluntary policies, and inaccurate data plague the entire system (*Business Week*, 1988). These fears have traditionally been warranted as police agencies have been successfully sued in a number of cases wherein inaccurate or "intelligence" information was collected and inappropriately disseminated without cause.

To make matters worse, these issues come on the heels of highly publicized computer crime cases wherein "supposedly" the most secure of systems have been defeated by outside "hackers" (Schmemann, 1987). The worry, of course, is how secure are local police information systems if sophisticated national computer centers (such as NASA) have been compromised? The answer is quite spurious when one considers the various types of policies and laws designed by each police department and jurisdiction in an attempt to control access to an automated system and to insure the accuracy of the data placed in that system. To be quite frank, information security must be a top priority for the executive manager or police chief.

We live in an information society and, undoubtedly, abuses in information security resulting in computer crime and release of sensitive data will only grow in the future. Unfortunately, the losses suffered directly from computer crimes or compromised sensitive data may be only a part of the overall economic devastation potentially facing government agencies (like the police) and private corporations. Indeed, the civil litigation resulting from loss of privacy and the ensuing fiduciary responsibilities of executives may compose a much more lasting and severe economic loss to victims of information security breaches (Taylor, 1988).

LOOKING INTO THE FUTURE

The socioeconomic impact of the computer revolution has received considerable attention from futuristic writers. Most noteworthy are the observations of Naisbitt (1982), who asserts that power is directly related to "information control." Those individuals who have information knowledge can create an economic value and reality. One can support Naisbitt's argument by observing the well-documented increase in white-collar and service jobs as manufacturing jobs have declined. Fundamental shifts in an industrial society will occur, but not necessarily along the lines that economists, planners, political scientists, and bureaucrats usually monitor. Toffler (1980) suggests that civilization has grossly fragmented or "de-massified" into a number of idiosyncratic and socially diverse institutions. He argues that the more mass society fractures and the more the economy becomes differentiated, then the more information must be exchanged to maintain integration in the system. This has brought about the evolution of the "Third Wave" or the dependence on technology and information sharing. Toffler (1980), as well as many others, has dedicated considerable time and effort to attempting to assess the impact of this change on society and world civilization in general.

Paradoxically, there is little empirical research focusing on the impact of automation on the police, an institution that often reflects society attitudes and perspectives. Sykes (1985), however, pointed out that the reform movement toward professionalism during the last twenty years required the use of computerization of records and reports. Further, the increased demand for information for criminal justice agencies and police management needs may alter the existing role of individual police officers. Bittner (1971) has provided a colorful and dramatic image of the soldier-bureaucrat "as an individual totally controlled by administrative tasks, unable to perform rudimentary duties, and make discretionary judgments." Sykes (1986) suggests an even darker scenario as the "line officer, metaphorically speaking, could become an appendage of the machine."

In any event, there are a number of projections that can be made regarding continued issues in managing police information. First, an important issue for the future is the need to develop some standardization among law enforcement agencies, especially in the areas of software (program) design and the manner in which data files are collected. Police departments, courts, prosecutors, jails, probation, and other criminal justice components need to be able to share information and communicate efficiently with each other. There is much redundancy that could be eliminated by agencies agreeing on a standardized format that would reduce duplication of paperwork and repetition of effort. The ability of related criminal justice agencies to combine and share their data is cost-effective. Currently, we see some advances in this area through the implementation of Wide Area Networks (WANS). These systems allow agencies to provide an integrated, single data entry system. Considering the information resource management concept, wide area networking becomes a very cost-effective and beneficial linkage. Through such networks, small agencies can achieve the benefits of a large system.

This type of plan distributes computers throughout criminal justice agencies to points where computer power is needed. It then links these computers together, allowing them to exchange information. This type of approach has more flexibility than purchasing one large computer system and then linking other agencies to that system (Masland, 1987:20). Electronic mail, for example, is a relatively simple application that provides for point-to-point communications. Electronic mail (E-Mail) can typically streamline an organization by limiting "telephone tag" and the number of employee meetings required, as well as increasing the efficiency of information and data distribution.

Second, in 1992, the Western European nations will culminate a five-

year plan to standardize currencies, certifications, and economic manufacturing techniques, thereby providing a more competitive "block" of
power against other countries in the global arena. One of the side benefits of this project is shared criminal justice communications between
countries in Western Europe focused on criminal apprehension. The
hope is that the future will provide data interface capabilities between
existing mainframe operations in both Western Europe and the United
States. International (digital) transmissions relating to criminal justice
matters could become as commonplace as long-distance telephone conversations, especially concerning the current advances in satellite communications.

Third, the proliferation of private electronic data bases (as held by
large corporations on employees) will demand some type of federal
policy and legislation. Currently, there exists a Senate subcommittee
studying alternative restraints on employer monitoring of computer
work and telephone conversations (*Business Week*:1988). A natural extension of this work will be to provide guidelines or indicate restrictions
for data base information centers as to *what* type of information can and
cannot be collected and maintained on individuals. The AIDS crisis has
already provided new areas of discussion regarding electronic data base
systems that report positive test results. Notwithstanding this issue,
more advanced technological and automated systems (such as AFIS) will
be highlighted in the next century. Police automated records systems of
the future will essentially be advanced identification monitors. Records
will routinely include not only digitized fingerprint information, but also
retina patterns and DNA encoding. Further, advanced interface capabilities will allow one police data base to communicate to others instantaneously. Messages will be transmitted electronically upon inquiry of
a person's record and a documented printout will be mandatorily
checked to insure the security of the system.

Finally, with such advanced automated systems, the privacy and security issues of today will remain in the forefront of discussion. Considerable efforts will be made severely to limit the use of such information
data bases; however, the "fear of crime" will outweigh these types of
arguments. Considering the political ideology of the current Supreme
Court and the recent decisions eroding previous search-and-seizure protections, it can be safely assumed that reasonable technological advances
directly aimed at apprehending criminals will be both socially and ju-
dicially supported.

REFERENCES

Archambeault, W. and B. Archambeault (1984). *Computers in Criminal Justice Administration and Management*. Cincinnati, OH: Anderson Publishing.

Awad, E. (1988). *Management Information Systems: Concepts, Structure, and Applications*. Menlo Park, CA: Benjamin Cummings Publishing.

Bittner, E. (1971). *The Functions of Police in Modern Society*. Washington, D.C.: U.S. Government Printing Office.

Business Week (1988). "Privacy." (March 28), 61–68.

Caudle, S. (1987). "High Tech to Better Effect." *The Bureaucrat* (Spring), 47–52.

Corbin, D. (1988). "Strategic IRM Plan: User Involvement Spells Success." *Journal of Systems Management* (May), 12–16.

Danziger, J. and K. Kraemer (1985). "Computerized Data-Base Systems and Productivity Among Professional Workers: The Case of Detectives." *Public Administration Review* (January/February), 196–209.

Fayol, H. (1949). *General and Industrial Management*, translated by Constance Storrs. London: Sir Isaac Pittman.

George, D. and G. Kleinknecht (1985). "Computer Assisted Report Entry—CARE." *FBI Law Enforcement Bulletin* (May).

Gulick, L. (1937). "Notes on the Theory of Organization." *Papers on the Science of Administration*, eds. L. Gulick and L. Urwick. New York: August M. Kelley Press.

Horwitt, E. (1985). "Exploring Expert Systems." *Business Computer Systems* (March), 48–49.

King, J. and K. Kraemer (1985). *The Dynamics of Computing*. New York: Columbia University Press.

Kraemer, J. and K. Danziger (1984). "Computers and Control in the Work Environment." *Public Administration Review* (January/February), 32–42.

Masland, A. (1987). "Networks Restructure Law Enforcement." *American City and County* (October).

Naisbitt, J. (1982). *Megatrends: Ten New Directions Changing Our Lives*. New York: Warner Books.

Peter, L. and R. Hall (1969). *The Peter Principle*. New York: Bantam Books.

Pressman, J. and A. Wildavasky (1973). *Implementation*. Berkeley, CA: University of California Press.

Raho, L.; J. Belohlav; and K. Fielder (1987). "Assimilating New Technology in the Organization: An Assessment of McFarland and McKenney's Model." *MIS Quarterly* (March).

Sankar, Y. (1988). "Organizational Culture and New Technologies." *Journal of Systems Management* (April).

Schmemann, S. (1987). "West German Computer Hobbyists Rummaged NASA's Files for Three Months." *New York Times* (September 16).

Swanson, C.; L. Territo; and R. Taylor (1988). *Police Administration: Structure, Processes, and Behavior*. New York: Macmillan Publishing.

Sykes, G. (1985). "The Functional Nature of Police Reform: The 'Myth' of Controlling the Police." *Justice Quarterly* (March), 53–65.

———. (1986). "Automation Management and the Police Role: The New Reformers?" *Journal of Police Science and Administration* (March).

Taylor, R. (1985). "Computer Applications in Law Enforcement: Considerations in Planning." *Police Chief* (March), 56–60.

———. (1988). "Computer Crime and Information Security: Assessing Problem." *Information Security Yearbook*. London: IBC Services.

Toffler, A. (1980). *The Third Wave*. New York: William Morrow.
————. (1985). *The Adaptive Corporation*. New York: McGraw-Hill.
Wilson, T. (1988). "Law Officers Scoring More Hits: Automated Fingerprint Identification Systems." *Government Technology* (July/August), 1.

Conclusion: Paths to Police Reform—Reflections on 25 Years of Change

Sam Walker

A retired command officer in the New York City police department recalled the end of the team policing experiment: "No one knows when it ended. There was no memo, no announcement. It just faded away." His remark dramatizes a melancholy truth about police reform. Many bold and exciting experiments end in quiet failure. They just fade away and are forgotten. The shame of it is that we often do not learn from these failures. Yesterday's exciting new idea is quickly forgotten as we rush to embrace the latest fad. There is little reflection on what went wrong with a particular reform. Were the basic assumptions flawed, or was it simply implemented poorly?

The past 25 years have been an extraordinarily innovative period in American policing. Despite their reputation for being resistant to change, the American police have been surprisingly open. In 1975, James Q. Wilson wrote that "A few police departments . . . have shown themselves to be remarkably innovative, experimental and open to evaluative research. There are not as yet many prosecutors or courts about which one can say the same thing" (Wilson, 1975:97). Events over the intervening thirteen years have sustained that judgment.

This chapter reviews some of the major police reform efforts during this period in an attempt to determine what "lessons," if any, can be drawn from the experience. What have we learned? What works? What has failed? What can we recommend about future reform? These questions are raised in the context of a prevalent notion that "nothing works." Several observers argue that well-intentioned criminal justice reforms fail, or worse, backfire and produce counterproductive results (see Do-leschal, 1982 and Martinson, 1974). This argument, drawn largely from rehabilitation-oriented programs in corrections, does not apply to all police reforms. While many have indeed failed, some have succeeded. Some things do work.

THE CONTEXT OF CHANGE: FROM THE 1960s TO THE 1980s

The Forces of Change

The past 25 years have been a period of enormous change in American policing (Walker, 1980). We can only briefly summarize the major elements of change here. The Supreme Court issued a number of landmark decisions creating a new body of law governing police procedures. While liberals and civil libertarians hailed these decisions, police officials claimed they were being "handcuffed" in their efforts to fight crime. Conservative politicians accused the Court of being too sympathetic to criminal suspects and of disregarding the interest of law-abiding citizens.

Meanwhile, the civil rights movement mounted a concerted attack on police misconduct. This represented a demand for justice on the part of the principal "clients" of police services: racial minorities and the poor (see Cox, 1968). The vast majority of the riots of the 1964–1968 period were precipitated by an incident involving the police (*National Advisory Commission on Civil Disorders*, 1968 and Waskow, 1967).

The combination of the Supreme Court's landmark decisions, the escalating police-community relations crisis, and a real rise in serious crime thrust the crime issue to the forefront of national politics. It emerged as an issue in presidential politics for the first time in 1964 and remained a volatile issue through the 1988 campaign (Caplan, 1973). As a result of this public concern, the federal government launched the first serious effort to provide financial and technical assistance to criminal justice. This, in turn, fostered a "research revolution" that enormously expanded our knowledge base about policing. Finally, the speed of collective bargaining completely transformed the managerial environment of police departments.

The Search for Better Policing

Each of these developments, overlapping and interacting with each other, stimulated a broad-based movement for police reform. It was not a unified movement, however. Reform efforts proceeded in many different directions, addressing particular problems and often embracing conflicting assumptions. A few examples will suffice. Some reformers argued that police professionalism should be modeled after the professions of law, medicine, and education. With improved education and training, officers should be given broad latitude to exercise their professional judgment in the exercise of law enforcement powers (Bittner, 1970). Other reformers sought to subject police discretion to tighter bureaucratic controls (Walker, 1986). Many wanted the police to require college degrees of all recruits, while others argued that this would disadvantage black applicants victimized by unequal educational opportunities.

The various reform efforts can be divided into three general categories based on their primary focus. They include efforts to: (1) change the officers; (2) change the organization; and (3) change the environment of policing.

REFORM STRATEGY #1: CHANGE THE OFFICERS

In the early 1960s there was a near unanimous feeling that police personnel standards needed major improvement. In the heat of the police-community relations crisis, critics attacked police officers as uneducated, racist, lower middle-class white males who flouted the law and opposed all social change. This stereotype was overdrawn, but did receive some academic support from early studies of the "police subculture." William Westley emphasized the solidarity of the police in the face of external criticism and their willingness to lie to cover up misconduct (Westley, 1970). Arthur Niederhoffer, meanwhile, emphasized the authoritarian aspects of the "police personality" (Niederhoffer, 1969). Because of low pay and inadequate benefits, police departments could not attract and retain qualified officers. The President's Crime Commission concluded that "The Nation's police departments are encountering serious difficulty in maintaining their forces at authorized strength" (President's Commission on Law Enforcement and Administration of Justice, 1967). On top of this, both the Crime Commission and the Kerner Commission found that blacks were seriously underrepresented in big-city police departments—a factor that aggravated police-community tensions.

The goal of improving policing by changing the police officers took two approaches. One called for better training and improved supervision. The second called for recruiting different kinds of people into police work.

Improved Training and Supervision

The campaign to raise police personnel standards achieved considerable success. Preservice training of recruits has improved in terms of both length and content. On average, training programs are more than twice as long as they were in the mid–1960s, rising from an average of about 200 hours to more than 400 hours (U.S. Department of Justice, 1987). Perhaps even more significant, most states now require preservice training of all recruits and have developed state training programs for recruits in small departments that cannot maintain their own academies. Finally, a few states have begun to license police officers, which means that individuals fired from one department cannot be employed by another in the state (Goldman and Puro, 1987).

The additional hours of training are filled with new subjects—such as the history and culture of racial minorities and the nature of domestic violence. The federal Law Enforcement Educational Assistance Program (LEEP) spent over $40 million a year through the 1970s to support nearly 100,000 students either currently working for criminal justice agencies or planning careers in the field. As a result, the educational attainment level of police officers has steadily risen (U.S. Department of Justice, 1975). This, in turn, helped foster the growth of criminal justice as an academic discipline.

Supervision also improved. Several critical areas of law enforcement have been subjected to increasingly tighter control through written policies, required reports, and automatic review of incidents (Walker, 1988). The best example is the use of deadly force where the relatively permissive "fleeing felon" standard has been replaced by the more restrictive "defense of life" standard. The result has been a significant reduction in police shootings and, at the same time, a reduction in the racial disparity in persons being shot and killed (Fyfe, 1979; Sherman and Cohn, 1986). In most departments the policies include a mandatory report of every firearms incident and an automatic review of the reports by top command officials.

Several departments achieved notable success in controlling corruption through a similar combination of clearly stated agency policy, often in writing, and effective monitoring of officer conduct (Sherman, 1978a). Other aspects of police work have been covered by written policies and, in many cases, required reports. Policies are codified in departmental standard operating procedure (SOP) manuals. These manuals are now typically several hundred pages in length and have become the central tool of management and supervision (Krantz, 1979). There is some debate over the wisdom of this approach to controlling on-the-street police conduct. Advocates of the administrative rule-making approach to policing applaud the development. Skeptics, however, argue that police work involves inherent uncertainties that are beyond the control of formal rules (Brown, 1981).

All of the improvements in personnel standards are generally regarded as positive developments. Many were long overdue and represent minimal standards. It can be argued, however, that most of these reforms are only one part of a general effort to improve police conduct. In other words, no single improvement can stand alone. Improved education and training would be meaningless in the face of inadequate supervision. Better supervision, meanwhile, can achieve only so much if officers are inadequately trained to begin with.

Recruiting Different Kinds of People

A different strategy for changing police officers involved recruiting different kinds of people into police work. This was based on the assumption that college-educated officers would perform better than less educated ones (i.e., would better understand legal principles, would be more tolerant of cultural diversity, etc.), that black officers would relate to the black community better, and that women officers would be less aggressive and better able to resolve conflicts through mediation. The effort to recruit different kinds of people into policing has reshaped the composition of police forces (Walker, 1985).

Although few departments have adopted the recommendation that a college degree be required of all recruits, many select officers who have more than the minimum.

There has also been a significant improvement in racial minority employment. Litigation and voluntary affirmative action programs have brought most departments closer to a theoretical "ideal" level of minority employment, based on the composition of the community (Walker, 1983, 1988). The percentage of women police officers doubled to 3.6 percent of the total in 1983, although the largest departments report having at least twice that figure (International City Management Association, 1983). Equally significant, police departments have abandoned the practice of segregating women officers into certain limited assignments and now assign them to routine patrol.

While recruiting officers of more diverse social backgrounds is valuable—indeed, important and required from an equal employment opportunity standpoint—there is no evidence that these different kinds of people behave differently as police officers. The college-educated officer does not appear to act any differently than the officer with less education (see Sherman, 1978b). Black officers appear to behave the same as white officers (Fyfe, 1981; Black, 1980). The absence or presence of minority officers may affect community perceptions of a department but that is different from on-the-street police behavior. There is no evidence that female officers act differently from their male counterparts (Bloch and Anderson, 1974; Sichel, 1978).

The evidence suggests that the proposal to recruit different kinds of officers was based on faulty assumptions. The critical variable is not the background characteristics of the officer but the working environment of policing. This consists of two components: the nature of the job itself and the supervisory environment of the department. We now turn our attention to efforts to alter each of those factors.

REFORM STRATEGY #2: CHANGE THE ORGANIZATION

Another element of police reform focused on the formal structure of law enforcement organizations. Critics identified the bureaucracy itself as the problem. Departments were stagnant, unresponsive, self-serving, isolated from the public, and reflexively defensive in the face of criticism (Angell, 1971). Moreover, they failed to make good use of their personnel and undermined the morale of low-ranking officers. Despite the fact that they were in direct contact with the community, patrol officers were expected to follow orders with no opportunity to contribute to policy-making. Opportunities for advancement or meaningful recognition were limited because of the rigid civil procedures and the prevailing quasi-military organizational structure—both of which have been reinforced by union contract provisions (Guyot, 1977). Finally, the quasi-military atmosphere of police departments was deemed incompatible with the demands of policing a democratic society (Bittner, 1970).

This critique spawned several proposals to decentralize law enforcement organizations. The most extreme were John Angell's "democratic model" of policing (Angell, 1971) and a proposal placed on the ballot in Berkeley, California to divide the police department into three neighborhood-controlled units (Skolnick, 1975).

Team Policing

Team policing was the label applied to the practical experiments in decentralization. From the late 1960s to the early 1970s, team policing was one of the most exciting police reforms. It seemed to promise all things to all people: more efficient and effective policing, improved police-community relations, and enhanced police officer morale. The neighborhood focus would make policing more responsive to community needs. Presumably it would result in more effective crime fighting. It would also help improve police-community relations. Decentralized decision making would enhance the morale of lower-ranking officers and enhance professional development. Several departments attempted it, although not all embraced all of the key elements of the concept (Sherman, Milton, and Kelly, 1973).

After a few years of experimentation, the enthusiasm for team policing faded. Radically restructuring a large bureaucracy proved to be far more difficult than anyone had imagined. Many experiments were launched with little or no planning. The experiments also exposed a number of unresolved problems in the basic team-policing concept. There was an inherent tension between the goal of flexibility and the demands of accountability. How far from basic departmental policies could a team deviate? The idea of community input also had not been thought through. What if community residents wanted tough crime-fighting measures (i.e., street sweeps) that violated existing standards of due process? Evaluations of team-policing experiments failed to find significant improvements in crime reduction, public attitudes, or enhanced police morale (Schwartz and Clarren, 1977).

Although team policing was generally regarded a failure, the experience left one valuable and enduring lesson. There was a much better recognition of the difficulty of making sweeping changes in a police organization. Subsequent reform efforts have thought in terms of working within the existing organizational structure of departments. Some of the elements of team policing resurfaced in the 1980s under the rubric of "community-oriented policing" (Greene and Mastrofski, 1988; Sherman and Cohn, 1986). The attempt to restructure the organization was abandoned, but the goal of bringing police officers into closer touch with community needs gained new life.

Restructuring Decision Making

One element of team policing—enhancing the decision-making authority of officers in the lower ranks—was embodied in the concept of using departmental task forces. This approach would simply bypass the formal decision-making structure rather than attempt to change it. The task force idea achieved an early success in the planning process that led to the Kansas City Preventive Patrol Experiment (Kelling et al., 1974). Several experts suggested expanding it into a general approach to police policy-making. Hans Toch, for example, incorporated it into an experiment in reducing officer misconduct (Weisbord et al., 1974; Toch, 1975).

It is difficult to render a verdict on the task force concept. In the absence of systematic research, we do not have a good idea of how extensively it is currently being used, much less how effective it might be. Herman Goldstein remains optimistic about its potential, despite a somewhat disappointing experience in the Madison, Wisconsin police department (Goldstein, 1982). A reform-oriented chief in Omaha, Nebraska instituted a number of task forces, but most faded away within a year. This experience resembles the fate of many police reforms: they are launched amid great expectations and much publicity but, without a sustained commitment from top management, fade away under the pressure of day-to-day policing.

REFORM STRATEGY #3: CHANGE THE ENVIRONMENT OF POLICING

A third line of reform thinking focused on changing the broader environment of policing.

Rethinking the Police Role

Recognition of the complexity of the police role was one of the major findings of the American Bar Foundation (ABF) Survey of the Administration of Criminal Justice in the late 1950s (Newman, 1966). The first systematic field observation of police work heightened recognition of the fact that the police performed many different tasks and were subjected to often-conflicting legal, social, political, and administrative pressures. The police did far more than "fight crime" and the arrest power itself was often used for purposes other than prosecution (LeFave, 1965).

Improved policing would result, some experts argued, from a clearer understanding of the police role. The police could more effectively plan and utilize their resources, while the public would have a more realistic understanding of what the police can and cannot do. Herman Goldstein, a member of the ABF field research staff, proposed redefining the police as a general service agency of government (Goldstein, 1979). Recognition on this broader role would facilitate development of dispositional alternatives other than arrest. Although the ensuing debate was intellectually rich and contributed greatly to a better understanding of contemporary policing, it produced little in the way of practical results. By influencing understanding about the police, however, it did have a subtle but pervasive effect on virtually all subsequent discussions of policing and police reform.

A more traditional school of thought argued for focusing the police role more narrowly on crime fighting. To a great extent, reform efforts along this line involved applying the management principles long advocated by O. W. Wilson. These emphasized greater efficiency in the deployment of personnel and maximizing patrol "coverage" to increase its deterrent effect. One important by-product of this effort was a series of major research projects evaluating traditional police operations. The Kansas City Preventive Patrol Experiment was the first attempt to test scientifically the deterrent effect of patrol (Kelling et al., 1974). The Rand Corporation study of the Criminal Investigative Process cast the first critical eye on detective work (Greenwood, 1975; Eck, 1983). The Newark Foot Patrol Study examined the impact of foot patrol.

Ironically, the experiments had the effect of undermining the goal of enhancing police crime fighting. They only seemed to prove that there was little hope of increasing the deterrent effect of patrol or of increasing the apprehension rates of detectives. This research inspired James Q. Wilson and George Kelling's highly influential "broken windows" article (Wilson and Kelling, 1982). The lesson, they argued, was that we should redirect our thinking toward improving police handling of "little" problems. The police neglect of small order maintenance problems contributed to citizen fear and neighborhood deterioration. Police could not reduce crime more than they already did; but they could enhance public feelings of safety.

The "broken windows" thesis stimulated the new interest in community-oriented policing. One initial experiment that grew directly out of the Newark Foot Patrol Experiment was a series of fear-reduction experiments in Newark and Houston. Most of those specific projects, however, did not achieve their objectives (Pate et al., 1986). The jury is still out on community policing generally, however.

Herman Goldstein's thinking led to his concept of "problem-oriented policing" (Goldstein, 1979). Rather than attempt to change the tasks that befall the police, Goldstein argued that the police could and should alter their priorities about which ones they respond to and, equally important, how they respond. Instead of reacting to isolated incidents, the police should proactively identify discrete community problems and develop programs to deal with them. In short, the police need to free themselves from the telephone calls for service and determine their own priorities. Goldstein's proposal attracted considerable interest and resulted in one major experimental application. An evaluation of the Newport News program deemed it a success (Eck and Spelman, 1987). Some skepticism remains, however, about the claims of significant crime reduction (35 percent reduction in burglaries; 45 percent reduction in robberies). Such claims are frequently made in defense of police innovations and there is a long history of exaggeration and ignoring the long-term return to normal patterns of behavior.

The Legal Environment

Arguably, the most significant development in policing over the past three decades has been the due-process revolution. The consequences, both intended and unintended, have been far-reaching and have produced major changes (Walker, 1988). The core of the due-process revolution is a series of Supreme Court decisions on police procedures. The two most famous, *Mapp* and *Miranda*, continue to be matters of great controversy. These decisions were, in turn, part of a broader legal change that affected every criminal justice agency. Even though the Court has subsequently narrowed the scope of both the exclusionary rule and the *Miranda* doctrine, the principles underlying the original decisions continue to reverberate through American policing.

At the simplest level, the Court's initiatives represented a new set of rules governing the police. Despite the complaints of some police officers and conservative politicians, there is no evidence to support the charge that the Court handcuffed police crime-fighting efforts (Walker, 1989). Instead, there have been a number of positive long term consequences. The decisions introduced legal norms into policing and, in the process, significantly altered the working environment. A recent study of Chicago narcotics detectives, for example, found considerable support for the exclusionary rule among the officers most heavily affected by it (Orfield, 1987). With each passing year, a new cadre of officers is socialized into an environment where accountability to legal norms is a fact of life. While they may complain about the rules, and try to evade them in certain circumstances, the principle of accountability has gained an important, and some would argue, a permanent foothold.

The impact of the Court on the working environment has implications for several of the reform efforts discussed earlier. As we indicated, there is a general consensus that the background characteristics of individual officers is not a critical variable. Instead, individuals from diverse backgrounds seem to adapt to the working environment. By changing an important element of that environment, the revolution in the law has affected officer behavior in a positive direction. It appears that officers will conform to the legal and bureaucratic pressures applied to them. Sherman's research on police corruption and Fyfe's deadly-force research are the strongest evidence in support of this interpretation.

The Court also stimulated police professionalization. Most of the improvements cited earlier in recruitment standards, training, and supervision are a direct consequence of the Court's decisions. One could argue that the Court was the principal catalyst for reform during the period (Walker, 1980). There is good reason to believe that preservice classroom training is quickly eroded by the initial on-the-street experience (McNamara, 1967). The more training focuses on specific policies and procedures, and is followed up with meaningful supervision, the more it is likely to shape behavior. Education becomes important insofar as it enhances an individual's capacity to cope with an increasingly rule-bound working environment. In short, particular reforms, in isolation, are likely to have only a marginal effect. By changing the working environment, however, the law revolution reinforces the positive aspects of other kinds of reforms.

Much has been written about the police subculture and peer pressure in policing. They are generally regarded as critical variables, for example, in determining the level of corruption in an agency. A change in the working environment, in the direction of respect for the rule of law, represents a change in the prevailing norms in the subculture.

The due-process revolution also stimulated the accreditation movement. In corrections as well as law enforcement, it emerged in part as a way of avoiding litigation and externally imposed constraints. Accreditation has many pros and cons, but as the first serious effort at self-regulation it is a significant development in the direction of professionalism. It is still too early to render a verdict on the impact of accreditation on policing.

At the same time, the very controversy over the Court's decisions served to educate the public about both the Bill of Rights and police procedures. Greater public awareness can be seen as an important element of reform in that it serves to constrain officers in particular situations (when suspects claim their "rights") and by creating a political constituency for other reform efforts.

WHAT HAVE WE LEARNED? PATHS TO THE FUTURE

Looking back over the past 25 years of police reform, we are struck by the accuracy of James Q. Wilson's comment about the climate of innovation. The police have been remarkably open and receptive to experimentation. Given the ferment stimulated by Goldstein's problem-oriented policing concept and Wilson and Kelling's "broken windows" article—together they sparked a new period of innovation. It is probably safe to say that the spirit of innovation will continue.

But what have we learned from this experience? The major gain, it must be said, has been in wisdom rather than improved policing. We have a much better idea of what policing is all about. We have a much stronger appreciation for what we cannot accomplish. The heady optimism of the President's Crime Commission was shattered long ago. A lot of money and some education will not solve our criminal justice woes. At the same time, however, we should not lapse into easy cynicism or accept sweeping statements that "nothing works." Some things, it seems, *do* work. The challenge is to identify *which* ones do—and why.

Our review of different reform efforts leads to the following conclusions:

1. Improved training, while important, is likely to be effective only in the context of improved management and supervision.

2. Recruiting different kinds of people into policing does not, in and of itself, alter police behavior. Affirmative action in the recruitment of women and racial minorities is important in terms of equal employment opportunity and should be vigorously pursued where necessary. Other things being equal, college-educated recruits are preferable to recruits with less education; but education itself is not a critical variable in shaping officer behavior.

3. Effective supervision can make a significant improvement in police performance. Based on the evidence, the ingredients of effective supervision include written policies guiding the exercise of discretion, mandatory reports in cases of critical incidents, and automatic review of reports and critical incidents.

4. Attempts to make sweeping changes in the structure of police organizations are probably doomed to failure. Relatively small changes, however, offer some possibilities. The ingredients of success include modest expectations, specific goals, and careful planning and implementation.

5. Altering the police role offers some exciting possibilities for improved policing. Past experience, however, suggests that success requires modest expectations. Vague rhetoric, extravagant promises, and nonspecific programmatic objectives are likely to be counterproductive. It remains to be seen whether current experiments in problem-oriented policing and community policing will avoid the pitfalls that beset so many earlier reform efforts.

6. Legal change has proven to have a significant positive effect on policing. The ramifications of the due-process revolution have been multifaceted. It has stimulated a broad range of changes that fall under the rubric of professionalization. Whether there are further opportunities for improved policing along these lines is a matter requiring more exhaustive discussion. The danger of legal formalism—the proliferation of rules without meaningful impact—is ever present.

7. The reform process is a product of a complex interaction between internal and external forces. There are many external forces that neither the police nor police reformers can control. At the same time, external forces can impinge upon the police to produce significant changes. There is no "magic bullet," no single reform that will transform policing. There are many paths to police reform. Some we have learned are not worth taking. Others offer significant possibilities. We are much wiser than we were 25 years ago. The most important things we have learned are that good intentions are not sufficient, that we should entertain modest expectations, and that we should always be alert for the unintended consequence.

REFERENCES

Angell, J. (1971). "Toward an Alternative to the Classic Police Organizational Arrangements: A Democratic Model." *Criminology, 9.*

Bayley, D. and Mendelsohn, H. (1969). *Minorities and the Police.* New York: The Free Press.

Bittner, E. (1970). *The Functions of the Police in Modern Society.* Washington, D.C.: National Institute of Mental Health.

Black, D. (1980). *The Manners and Customs of the Police*. New York: Academic Press.

Bloch, P. and Anderson, D. (1974). *Policewomen on Patrol: Final Report*. Washington, D.C.: Police Foundation.

Brown, M. (1981). *Working the Street: Police Discretion and the Dilemmas of Reform*. New York: Russell Sage Foundation.

Caplan, G. (1973). "Reflections on the Nationalization of Crime, 1964–1968." *Law and the Social Order*, 5.

Cox, A. (1968). *The Warren Court*. Cambridge, MA: Harvard University Press.

Doleschal, E. (1982). "The Dangers of Criminal Justice Reform." *Criminal Justice Abstracts*, (March).

Eck, J. (1983). *Solving Crimes: The Investigation of Burglary and Robbery*. Washington, D.C.: Government Printing Office.

Eck, J. and Spelman, J. (1987). *Problem Solving: Problem Oriented Policing in Newport News*. Washington, D.C.: U.S. Government Printing Office.

Fyfe, J. (1979). "Administrative Interventions on Police Shooting Discretion: An Empirical Examination." *Journal of Criminal Justice*, 7.

———. (1981). "Who Shoots? A Look at Officer Race and Police Shooting." *Journal of Police Science and Administration*, 9.

Goldman, R. and S. Puro (1987). "Decertification of Police: An Alternative to Traditional Remedies for Police Misconduct." *Hastings Constitutional Law Quarterly*, 15.

Goldstein, H. (1975). *Policing a Free Society*. Cambridge, MA: Ballinger Press.

———. (1979). "Improving Policing: A Problem Oriented Approach." *Crime and Delinquency*, 25.

———. (1982). *Experimenting with the Problem Oriented Approach to Improving Police Service*. Madison, WI: University of Wisconsin Press.

Greene, J. and S. Mastrofski (1988). *Community Policing: Rhetoric or Reality?* New York: Praeger.

Greenwood, P. (1975). *The Criminal Investigation Process*. Santa Monica, CA: Rand Corporation.

Guyot, D. (1977). "Bending Granite: Attempts to Change the Rank Structure of American Police Departments." *Journal of Police Science and Administration*, 7(3).

Kelling, G. et al. (1974). *The Kansas Preventive Patrol Experiment*. Washington, D.C.: Police Foundation.

Krantz, S. (1979). *Police Policy-making*. Lexington, MA: Lexington Books.

LaFave, W. (1965). *Arrest*. Boston: Little, Brown.

McNamara, J. (1967). "Uncertainties in Police Work: The Relevance of Police Recruits' Backgrounds and Training." *The Police: Six Sociological Essays*. New York: John Wiley.

Martinson, R. (1974). "What Works? Questions and Answers About Prison Reform." *Public Interest* (Spring).

National Advisory Commission on Civil Disorders (1968). *Report of the National Advisory Commission on Civil Disorders*. New York: Bantam Books.

Newman, D. (1966). "Sociologists and the Administration of Criminal Justice." *Sociology in Action*, ed. A. Shostak. Homewood, IL: The Dorsey Press.

Niederhoffer, A. (1969). *Behind the Shield*. Garden City, NY: Anchor Books.

Orfield, M. (1987). "The Exclusionary Rule and Deterrence: An Empirical Study of Chicago Narcotics Officers." *University of Chicago Law Review*, 54.

Pate, A.; M. A. Wycoff; W. Skogan; and L. Sherman (1976). *Reducing Fear of Crime in Houston and Newark*. Washington, D.C.: Police Foundation.

President's Commission on Law Enforcement (1967). *Task Force Report: The Police*. Washington, D.C.: U.S. Government Printing Office.

Schwartz, A. and S. Clarren (1977). *The Cincinnati Team Policing Experiment: A Summary Report*. Washington, D.C.: Police Foundation.

Sherman, L. (1978a). *Scandal and Reform*. Berkeley, CA: University of California Press.

———. (1978b). *The Quality of Police Education*. San Francisco: Jossey-Bass.

Sherman, L. and E. Cohn (1986). *Citizens Killed by Big City Police, 1970–1984*. Washington, D.C.: Crime Control Institute.

Sherman, L.; C. Milton; and T. Kelly (1973). *Team Policing: Seven Cases Studies*. Washington, D.C.: Police Foundation.

Sichel, J. (1978). *Women on Patrol: A Pilot Study of Police Performance in New York City*. Washington, D.C.: Police Foundation.

Skolnick, J. (1975). "Neighborhood Police." *The Police in America*, ed. Skolnick and Gray. Boston: Little, Brown.

Toch, H. (1975). *Agents of Change: A Study in Police Reform*. Cambridge, MA: Schenckman.

Twentieth Century Fund (1976). *Law Enforcement: The Federal Role*. New York: McGraw-Hill.

U.S. Department of Justice (1987). *Sourcebook of Criminal Justice Statistics—1986*. Washington, D.C.: U.S. Government Printing Office.

Walker, S. (1980). *Popular Justice: A History of American Criminal Justice*. New York: Oxford University Press.

———. (1983). "Employment of Black and Hispanic Police Officers." *Review of Applied Urban Research*, 11.

———. (1985). "Racial Minority and Female Employment in Policing: The Implications of 'Glacial' Change." *Crime and Delinquency*, 31.

———. (1986). "Controlling the Cops: A Legislative Approach to Police Rulemaking." *University of Detroit Law Review*, 63 (Spring).

———. (1988). *The Rule Revolution*. Madison, WI: Institute for Legal Studies.

———. (1989). *Sense and Nonsense About Crime*. Pacific Grove, CA: Brooks/Cole.

Waskow, A. (1967). *From Race Riot to Sit-In: 1919 and the 1960s*. Garden City, NY: Anchor Books.

Weisbord, M., et al. (1974). *Improving Police Department Management Through Problem-Solving Task Forces*. Reading, MA: Addison-Wesley.

Westley, W. (1970). *Violence and the Police*. Cambridge, MA: MIT Press.

Wilson, J. (1975). *Thinking About Crime*. New York: Basic Books.

Wilson, J. and G. Kelling (1982). "Broken Windows." *Atlantic Monthly*, (March).

Selected Bibliography

Archambeault, W. and B. Archambeault (1984). *Computers in Criminal Justice Administration and Management*. Cincinnati, OH: Anderson Publishing.

Awad, E. (1988). *Management Information Systems: Concepts, Structure, and Applications*. Menlo Park, CA: Benjamin Cummings Publishing.

Barker, T. (1986). "An Empirical Study of Police Deviance Other than Corruption." *Police Deviance*, ed. T. Barker and D. Carter. Cincinnati, OH: Anderson Publishing.

Bayley, D. and H. Mendelsohn (1969). *Minorities and the Police*. New York: The Free Press.

Bercal, T. (1970). "Calls for Police Assistance." *American Behavioral Scientist*, 13:267–277.

Bittner, E. (1980). *The Functions of the Police in Modern Society*. Cambridge, MA: Oegelschlager, Gunn and Hain.

Black, D. (1980). *The Manners and Customs of the Police*. New York: Academic Press.

Bloch, P. and D. Anderson (1974). *Policewomen on Patrol: Final Report*. Washington, D.C.: Police Foundation.

Boydstun, J.; M. Sherry; and N. Moelter (1977). *Patrol Staffing in San Diego*. Washington, D.C.: Police Foundation.

Brown, R. (1975). *Historical Studies of American Violence and Vigilantism*. New York: Oxford University Press.

Burrows, J. and R. Tarling (1982). *Clearing-up Crime*. Home Office Research Study No. 73. London: HMSO.

Burrows, W. (1976). *Vigilante!* New York: Harcourt Brace.

Carte, G. and E. Carte (1975). *Police Reform in the United States: The Era of August Vollmer*. Berkeley, CA: University of California Press.

Cascio, W. (1977). "Formal Education and Police Officer Performance." *Journal of Police Science and Administration*, May: 89–96.

Cawley, D. and J. Miron (1977). *Managing Patrol Operations: Manual*. Washington, D.C.: U.S. Government Printing Office.

Chaiken, J. and M. Chaiken (1982). *Varieties of Criminal Behavior*. Santa Monica: The Rand Corporation.

Cohen, R. and J. Chaiken (1972). *Police Background Characteristics and Performance: A Summary Report*. New York: Rand.

Cordner, G. (1982). "While on Routine Patrol: What the Police Do When They're Not Doing Anything." *American Journal of Police*, 1(2):94–112.

Eck, J. (1983). *Solving Crimes: The Investigation of Burglary and Robbery*. Washington, D.C.: U.S. Government Printing Office.

Farmer, M., ed. (1981). *Differential Police Response Strategies*. Washington, D.C.: Police Executive Research Forum.

Fogelson, R. (1977). *Big City Police*. Cambridge, MA: Harvard University Press.

Goldman, R. and S. Puro (1987). "Decertification of Police: An Alternative to Traditional Remedies for Police Misconduct." *Hastings Constitutional Law Quarterly*, 15.

Goldstein, H. (1977). *Policing a Free Society*. Cambridge, MA: Ballinger.

———. (1979). "Improving Policing: A Problem-Oriented Approach." *Crime and Delinquency*, 25:236–258.

———. (1987). "Toward Community-Oriented Policing: Potential, Basic Requirements, and Threshold Questions." *Crime and Delinquency*, 33(1):6–30.

Greene, J. and S. Mastrofski (1988). *Community Policing: Rhetoric or Reality?* New York: Praeger.

Greenwood, P. and J. Petersilia (1975). *The Criminal Investigation Process—Volume 1: Survey and Policy Implications*. Santa Monica, CA: Rand Corporation.

Guyot, D. (1977). "Bending Granite: Attempts to Change the Rank Structure of American Police Departments." *Journal of Police Science and Administration*, 7(3).

Hoare, M.; G. Stewart; and C. M. Purcell (1984). *The Problem Oriented Approach: Four Pilot Studies*. U.K.: Metropolitan Police, Management Services Department.

Inwald, R. (1985). "Administrative, Legal, and Ethical Practices in the Psychological Testing of Law Enforcement Officers." *Journal of Criminal Justice*, 13:367–372.

———. (1987). "Use of Psychologists for Selecting and Training Police." *Police Managerial Use of Psychology and Psychologists*, ed. H. More and P. Unsinger. Springfield, IL: Charles Thomas Publishers.

Kansas City Police Department (1980). *Response Time Analysis: Volume II—Part 1, Crime Analysis*. Washington, D.C.: U.S. Government Printing Office.

Kelling, G.; T. Pate; D. Dieckman; and C. Brown (1974). *The Kansas City Preventive Patrol Experiment: A Technical Report*. Washington, D.C.: Police Foundation.

Lavrakas, P.; J. Normoyle; W. Skogan; E. Hertz; C. Salem; and D. Lewis (1980). *Factors Related to Citizen Involvement in Personal, Household, and Neighborhood*

Anti-Crime Measures. Final Report to the National Institute of Justice. Evanston, IL: Northwestern University Press.

Lewis, D. and G. Salem (1981). "Community Crime Prevention: An Analysis of a Developing Perspective." *Crime and Delinquency*, 27:405–421.

Martin, S. (1980). *Breaking and Entering: Policewomen on Patrol*. Berkeley: University of California Press.

Martin, S. and L. Sherman (1986). "Selective Apprehension: A Police Strategy for Repeat Offenders." *Criminology*, 24(1).

Marx, G. and D. Archer (1971). "Citizen Involvement in the Law Enforcement Process: The Case of Community Police Patrols." *American Behavioral Scientist*, 15 (September–October): 52–72.

McEwen, T.; E. Connors III; and M. Cohen (1986). *Evaluation of the Differential Police Response Field Test*. Washington, D.C.: U.S. Government Printing Office.

Pate, A.; M. Wycoff; W. Skogan; and L. Sherman (1986). *Reducing Fear of Crime in Houston and Newark*. Washington, D.C.: Police Foundation.

Reinecke, W. (1982). "Marching With the Avenging Angels." *Today/The Philadelphia Inquirer*, January 31.

Reiss, A. (1985). "Policing a City's Central District: The Oakland Story." Washington, D.C.: National Institute of Justice.

Rosenbaum, D. P. (1987). "The Theory and Research Behind Neighborhood Watch: Is It a Sound Fear and Crime Reduction Strategy?" *Crime and Delinquency*, 33:103–134.

Sherman, L. (1978). *The Quality of Police Education*. San Francisco: Jossey-Bass.

Sherman, L.; Milton, C.; and Kelly, T. (1973). *Team Policing: Seven Cases Studies*. Washington, D.C.: Police Foundation.

Skogan, W. and M. Maxfield (1981). *Coping with Crime: Individual Neighborhood Responses*. Beverly Hills: Sage Publishers.

Spelman, W. and D. Brown (1984). *Calling the Police: Citizen Reporting of Serious Crime*. Washington, D.C.: U.S. Government Printing Office.

Tien, J.; J. Simon; and R. Larson (1978). *An Alternative Approach in Police Patrol: The Wilmington Split Force Experiment*. Washington, D.C.: U.S. Government Printing Office.

Trojanowicz, R. (1983). *An Evaluation of the Neighborhood Foot Patrol Program in Flint, Michigan*. East Lansing: Michigan State University Press.

Walker, S. (1989). *Sense and Nonsense About Crime*. Pacific Grove, CA: Brooks/Cole.

Wilson, J. (1968). *Varieties of Police Behavior: The Management of Law and Order in Eight Communities*. Cambridge, MA: Harvard University Press.

———. (1975). *Thinking About Crime*. New York: Basic Books.

Wilson, J. and Kelling, G. (1982). "Broken Windows." *Atlantic Monthly*, (March).

Index

About the Contributors

DENNIS JAY KENNEY has over 17 years of experience in varied aspects of criminal justice—as a police officer in Bartow, Florida; as a director of research and planning in Savannah, Georgia; and as a university professor at both the Western Connecticut State University and the University of Nebraska at Omaha. He is currently on leave from the faculty at Nebraska while he directs projects for the Police Foundation. Most recently, he authored *Crime, Fear, and the New York City Subways* by Praeger Publishers.

ROBERT BING is a member of the faculty in the Administration of Justice Department at the University of Missouri at St. Louis. He received his Ph.D. in Criminology at Florida State. His areas of research interest vary widely and include juvenile justice, private security, organizational politics in the courtroom, and personnel issues involving law enforcement.

ROBERT BLECKER, a professor of criminal law and Constitutional history at the New York Law School since 1975, was formerly Special Assistant Attorney General of New York State (Office of the Anti-Corruption Prosecutor). He is the author of several articles including "Beyond 1984: Undercover in America" and "Haven or Hell?: Justifications of Punishment Experienced—Inside Lorton Prison." His anti-federalist dramatic monologue, "Vote NO!" premiered at the Kennedy

Center in Washington, D.C. in 1987 and has since been performed in ten different states. He is a graduate of Harvard Law School and was a Harvard Fellow in Law and Humanities.

CHARLES E. BROWN was on leave from the Kansas City Police Department while working as a member of the Police Foundation's evaluation staff in Kansas City during the preventive patrol experiment. Since that project, he has left Kansas City and now conducts research and planning as a member of the Metro-Dade (Miami) Police Department. He received his education at the Central Missouri State University.

GARY W. CORDNER is an Associate Professor in the Department of Police Studies at Eastern Kentucky University. Prior to joining the Eastern Kentucky Faculty, he spent three years as the Chief of Police in St. Michaels, Maryland. He has also served on the faculties of Washington State University and the University of Baltimore. Dr. Cordner has conducted evaluation research on a number of police interventions, including the Baltimore County Citizen Oriented Police Enforcement Project, the Baltimore County Repeat Offender Experiment, and the Pontiac, Michigan Integrated Criminal Apprehension Project. He has coauthored two textbooks, *Planning in Criminal Justice Organizations and Systems* (1983) and *Introduction to Police Administration* (1988, 2nd ed.) and is currently the editor of the *American Journal of Police*.

DUANE DIECKMAN was a member of the Midwest Research Institute staff during the Kansas City Preventive Patrol Experiment. Prior to joining MRI, he held supervisory positions in computer systems groups and manufacturing sections for Western Electric. Mr. Dieckman has been involved in a broad range of research projects, most of which has been involved in a broad range of research projects, most of which include systems analysis, simulation and modeling, and evaluation. More recently, he has provided management consulting on matters of labor relations.

JOHN ECK is the Associate Director for Research at the Police Executive Research Forum (PERF), a professional organization of heads of large police agencies. He led the research team studying the implementation of problem-oriented policing in Newport News, Virginia. Since 1986 he has coordinated a five city effort to apply problem-solving techniques to drug problems. He has been a consultant to the London Metropolitan Police and has taught research methods at the Canadian Police College. John Eck holds a Master of Public Policy degree from the University of Michigan and has conducted research on policing for PERF since 1977.

CHRIS ESKRIDGE has been a member of the faculty of the Department of Criminal Justice at the University of Nebraska at Omaha since 1978.

He earned his Ph.D. from the Ohio State University and has augmented his academic work by serving as an investigator in the Utah County Attorney's Office in Provo, Utah. He is the coauthor of *Probation and Parole in America* and the author of *Pre-Trial Release: Issues and Trends*.

SHELDON GREENBERG has been the Associate Director of Management Services for the Police Executive Research Forum (PERF) since 1986. Prior to joining PERF, he served as a police officer, Director of Research and Planning, Executive Assistant to the Chief, and Commander of Administrative Services for the Howard County Police Department in Maryland. He has authored or coauthored numerous articles and books on police planning, officer fitness, stress management, and the prevention of physical and mental disabilities.

PATRICIA HARDYMAN is a Senior Research Associate at the National Council on Crime and Delinquency research center at Rutgers University. She received her Ph.D. in criminal justice from Rutgers for a dissertation examining probation processing and decision-making in New Jersey. She has also conducted research at the Federal Probation Commission, the University of Louisville, and Fordham University.

ROBIN INWALD, the founder and director of Hilson Research, Inc., is a well-known expert in the psychological testing field—particularly in the area of pre-employment screening for high risk occupations. She is the author of the Inwald Personality Inventory (IPI), a test used to screen thousands of law enforcement and security officers nationwide each year. She is a diplomate of the American Psychological Association's American Board of Professional Psychology and the American Board of Forensic Psychology and has written over 40 articles and book chapters on the subject of psychological screening.

GEORGE L. KELLING was director of evaluations for the Police Foundation at the time of the Kansas City Preventive Patrol Experiment. He is a social worker whose research and publications deal principally with issues in law enforcement and corrections. Now a professor at Northeastern University, he holds a Ph.D. from the University of Wisconsin—Madison.

ROBERT B. KLIESMET was elected President of the International Union of Police Associations, AFL-CIO in 1983 and re-elected for a second term in 1988. His numerous police labor-related accomplishments include lectures at universities; at the FBI Academy; for the International Association of Chiefs of Police; and at symposiums, seminars, and workshops dealing with police-labor relations. He was recently appointed to the National Institute of Justice Technical Assessment Board and is also serving as the Police Labor representative to the Executive Sessions on Community Policing jointly sponsored by the National Institute of Justice, the Mott Foundations, and the Kennedy School of Government at Harvard University. During his distinguished career as a Milwaukee police officer, he was twice cited for heroism.

JACK KUYKENDALL is currently Professor of Criminal Justice Administration at the San Jose State University where his primary research interests include policing, police administration, and police operations. During the past 20 years at San Jose State, Professor Kuykendall's writings—3 books, 15 chapters, and at least 30 articles—have appeared in many of the profession's most prestigious journals. His most recent book, *Police Organization and Management: Behavior, Theory, and Processes*, became available in 1989.

ROBERT LEUCI is a noted author and lecturer in the fields of law enforcement and criminal justice. He retired from the New York City Police Department in 1981 after 20 years of service, the majority of which was spent in the areas of organized crime and narcotics enforcement. A portion of his career with the NYPD was the subject of the book and motion picture entitled *Prince of the City*. Since retiring from active law enforcement, he has authored three novels: *Doyle's Disciples*, *Odessa Beach*, and *Captain Butterfly*. He is a member of the Writer's Guild, PEN America, and Mystery Writers of America.

SUSAN E. MARTIN has been a project director at the Police Foundation since 1983. Among her recent studies are "Catching Career Criminals" and an experimental effort to reduce felony case attrition by improving police-prosecutor communication. Prior to joining the Foundation, she was a senior staff officer for the Committee on Research on Law Enforcement where her work for the Panel on Sentencing Research resulted in the publication *Research on Sentencing: the Search for Reform*. Currently she is working on two additional projects: one to explore law enforcement handling of child abuse and the other examining the status of women in policing. This latter project is a continuation of her earlier research published in 1980 as *"Breaking and Entering": Policewomen on Patrol*.

JEROME McELROY is Executive Director of the New York City Criminal Justice Agency. He also served as Associate Director of the Vera Institute of Justice, with management responsibilities for the Institute's research department. He has directed major studies on police civilian complaint review procedures; on the effects upon dispositional outcomes of a case preparation process used by detectives in preparing felony arrests for presentation to prosecutors; on the relationships between employment status and experience and criminal behavior; and on the comparative effects of alternative detoxification treatments for public inebriates.

VANCE McLAUGHLIN is currently Director of Training for the Savannah (Georgia) Police Department. He received his M.S. in Criminology at Florida State and his Ph.D. at Penn State. Before joining the Savannah Police Department, he was a faculty member at the University of North Carolina at Charlotte, coordinating their undergraduate and graduate programs in law enforcement. He has published primarily in the areas of police selection, training, and use of force.

ANTONY MICHAEL PATE has been a member of the evaluation staff of the Police Foundation since 1972. During his lengthy tenure, he was coauthor of the Foundation's research on fear reduction and preventive patrol. Additionally, he has directed studies on response time, apprehension techniques, peer review panels, police stress, foot patrol, community crime prevention, and the police cadet corps. He became the Foundation's director of research in 1989.

DENNIS P. ROSENBAUM is the Director of the Center for Research in Law and Justice and Associate Professor of Criminal Justice at the University of Illinois at Chicago. As a social psychologist and criminologist, he has authored many books and articles on community crime prevention and has evaluated a wide range of social interventions in this area.

LAWRENCE W. SHERMAN is both professor of Criminology at the University of Maryland and the founder and president of the Crime Control Institute. Previously, he was director of research at the Police Foundation from 1979–85. He is an internationally known scholar whose research interests and publications include police corruption, officer education, team policing, domestic violence, the use of force, and innovative deployment strategies—including ROP and RECAP.

LISA SLIWA has been National Coordinator of the New York based Guardian Angels since 1983. Having first come to the organization as a recruit, she continues to patrol high crime areas in addition to her management and supervisory duties. A popular speaker at civic groups and on college campuses, she also works as a fashion model in New York. Lisa and Curtis Sliwa, the Guardian Angel's founder, were married in 1985.

WILLIAM SPELMAN is an Assistant Professor of Public Policy at the Lyndon Johnson School of Public Affairs at the University of Texas, Austin. Before joining the University of Texas faculty, he was a Research Associate at the Police Executive Research Forum, where he was assistant director of the Newport News problem-oriented policing study. He has conducted research on citizen crime reporting behavior and the investigation and control of repeat offenders. He earned his doctorate in Public Policy from the John F. Kennedy School of Government at Harvard.

ROBERT TAYLOR is an active consultant to both public and private organizations in the area of Management Information Systems. Currently an Associate Professor at the University of Texas at Tyler in both criminal justice and MIS, he writes frequently on both fields. Most recently he coauthored *Police Administration*.

SAM WALKER has been a member of the criminal justice faculty at the University of Nebraska at Omaha since 1974. A widely published historian, he is the author of *In Defense of American Liberties; History of the A.C.L.U.; Sense and Nonsense About Crime;* and *The Police in America.* His current research interests are focused on administrative rule-making in policing.

DAVID WEISBURD teaches in the graduate program of the School of Criminal Justice at Rutgers University. He received his Ph.D. from Yale University, where he also served as Research Associate for a major study of white collar crime. The research described in this volume develops from his work while at the Vera Institute of Justice, where he directed research on the New York City pilot program in community policing. He is presently the principal investigator for a major effort to replicate the Kansas City Preventive Patrol Experiment in Minneapolis. Among his most recent publications is *Jewish Settler Violence*.